Repression, Re-Invention, and Rugelach

Repression, Re-Invention, and Rugelach
A HISTORY OF JEWS AT COLGATE

Amy Balmuth
Emily Kahn
Cameron Pauly
Kim Ravold
Marit Vangrow
Dominic Wilkins

Edited by Alice Nakhimovsky

Colgate University Press | Hamilton, New York 13346

Cover illustration: Students lighting Shabbat candles in the kosher kitchen in the Student Union. *From left to right:* Sydney Scheinman, Howard Liebman, unknown, unknown, Neal Rosenberg, Howard Sayetta, unknown, Ken Grossman. *Colgate Salmagundi, 1974.*

First Edition 2018
18 19 20 21 22 23 5 4 3 2 1

The paper used in this publication meets the minimum requirements of American National Standard for Information Sciences—Permanence of Paper for Printed Library Materials, ANSI Z39.48-1984.∞™

Library of Congress Control Number: 2018938129

ISBN 978-0-912568-27-0

Manufactured in the United States of America

In memory of

Professor Jerry Balmuth (1924–2017),
lover of Plato, preeminent citizen of Colgate
and the world

&

Gilbert Geis '47,
a model of civic courage

In honor of

President Neil Grabois,
who saw, understood, and acted for good

Contents

Illustrations

Foreword

| A Pioneer |

Noel Rubinton, Jr.

When my father, Noel Rubinton, arrived in Hamilton in September of 1939 for his freshman year at Colgate, he was 16 years old and farther away from his home in Brooklyn than he'd ever been. He had never seen the school before.

Joining the Class of 1943 on campus, he stood out in a hugely significant way besides his young age (he'd skipped a grade) and bright red hair. My father was one of a tiny handful of Jews in his class, and there were few others in the entire school. He was unaware how lucky he was to have been admitted at all—Colgate and many other universities at the time severely limited how many Jewish students they accepted.

My father didn't come from an intensely religious family. He had a bar mitzvah, though he didn't recall going too often to synagogue. His family, however, in its second generation in the United States and with its patriarch born in Eastern Europe still presiding at the crowded Friday night Shabbat dinner table, was strongly connected with Judaism in a cultural way. Extended family, including my father with his parents and brother, lived together in a striking pagoda-style house in Flatbush. Memories of Friday night meals and holiday celebrations, full of Jewish-connected food and tea drunk in Russian-style with sugar held in the teeth, stayed with my father for the rest of his life.

Like other students, my father couldn't have known what awaited him in college. There were many fascinating surprises, academically and otherwise—such as being in Washington for the Colgate Study Group and happening to be standing on the U.S. State Department steps on the December 1941 day that the Japanese ambassador was scrambling up them to be rebuked over Pearl Harbor.

Sadly, however, he also had the intensely frustrating experiences of being a Jewish student of his time, rife with slights and downright humiliations. Among the worst, as he reluctantly related years later, was the refusal of any fraternity to accept him. Though they didn't say it explicitly, it was clearly because of his religion. Perhaps even more painful was when several fellow students refused to share a dorm room with him because he was Jewish.

Some students might have been crushed by such episodes and left. Others might have let it ruin their spirit and faith, and scrape through college. My father, with quiet determination already a key part of his personality, reacted his own way: he buckled down and excelled.

Testing early on at Colgate predicted he would be a C student. Instead, he graduated Phi Beta Kappa. He became a leader in the Commons Club, a group for those not in fraternities. And, in an accomplishment that always brought a smile to his face, he won the campus ping pong championship.

After finishing months early with his whole class in the famous "White Commencement" in snowy Hamilton because of World War II's urgency, he taught classes for military recruits at Colgate and went into the Army, serving as a weather observer for a bomber group in southern Italy. After the war, he graduated from Harvard Law School and went on to a distinguished legal career, including 25 years as the general counsel for Bloomingdale's. He enjoyed his family and Colgate for many years until his death in 2016 at age 93.

It's not possible that my father could have had the perspective in his Colgate undergraduate years that he was part of a great tide of history at the school. It's hard to step back and see ourselves as a part of larger forces and times, especially when you are young. He was on the leading edge of Colgate's Jewish history. Jewish students, and faculty, would go from being a small, isolated group to being a far larger, influential one that has had much to do with Colgate's modern successes.

Judaism was a significant part of my father's life, not so much inside synagogues, but in personal and community service. He made it possible for his children—me and my sister, Sarah—to receive a Jewish education. For all his adult life, he volunteered for various Jewish charities, eventually becoming the lay head of the Jewish Child Care Association, serving needy and vulnerable children in New York City.

My father stayed close to Colgate always (with my mother, Phyllis, a Wellesley grad), at his side until she died in 1985. He took tremendous pride when my sister went on a pioneering journey of her own, joining the first class of Colgate women, graduating in 1974. It was still further happiness for him when Sarah married Jim Laditka, Colgate class of 1973. I didn't go to Colgate but feel like an honorary alumnus, having been to Hamilton so many times—in recent years with my wife, Amy, and daughter, Bella, who have come to love Colgate too—and having gone with my father to dozens and dozens of Colgate football games (another passion of his) over the years.

So it wasn't surprising that my father closely followed matters at Colgate concerning Jewish students and faculty. He was ecstatic in the 1990s when the Saperstein Center and an endowed chair in Jewish Studies came into being, and he derived fulfillment from doing what he could to help those causes.

His pride was great when Neil Grabois became the first Jewish president of Colgate in 1988. It was nearly unbelievable to him when he heard that Grabois had lit the outdoor menorah in downtown Hamilton one night during Hanukkah. Given what he'd lived through, it was astonishing for there to be a menorah on prominent display in Hamilton and have Colgate's president, a Jew, illuminate it.

Many happy moments awaited him in his later years with his class of 1943. He was devoted to his class for decades, hosting gatherings at his vacation house in Hamilton and serving as reunion chair, helping the class endow a scholarship, and other projects. About 15 years ago, he was elected president of his class, quite a reversal from how he was once shunned on campus. More incredibly, several classmates, like him late in their lives, wrote and apologized to him for how they'd treated him as a Jew decades early. My father got satisfaction from this affirmation.

When he went to the Sap in recent years for services and Shabbat dinners, he glowed. Just a few years ago, he introduced himself in a go-around at services, of course mentioning his class year. A few minutes later when students talked about their highlight of the week, one young woman said it was meeting my father and making a connection to a Jewish Colgate of long ago.

In 2008, a gathering was held in New York City celebrating 60 years of Jewish life at Colgate, marking the time since the Colgate Jewish Union was started. It was a warm gathering, led by President Rebecca Chopp and many of those alumni who were instrumental to Jewish growth at Colgate. The irony wasn't lost on my father that the celebration put a start date on Jewish life of 1948, five years after he graduated, and the first Rosh Hashanah services on campus weren't until 1950. He had lived through the prelude to that, and it hadn't been a smooth time. Yet by the turn of the twenty-first century, Jewish life was well established and supported on the Colgate campus. My father was immensely grateful.

How my father would have loved this book project, which his bequest to Colgate has helped to fund. He was a perpetual student of history and a big believer in its power and importance, and he would have loved Colgate getting to its bicentennial and using it for meaningful reflection. On this book, he would have been thrilled that so much of the work was done by such creative students under the inspired leadership of Professor Alice Nakhimovsky and Rabbi Dena Bodian. He was an advocate of the enormous potential of higher education, and Colgate in particular—and this project demonstrates it well.

We cannot know the future, but we certainly are able to learn from the past and salute its importance. This project is a vital example of that. To the Jews of Colgate, past, present, and future: L'Chaim!

Acknowledgments

Thanks are due to far more people than we can include here and not rival the length of our actual text.

Without Jason Petrulis, Colgate's Bicentennial Fellow 2014 to 2016, we would not have known where to start: it was through his work that we began to uncover the history of discrimination that so shaped Colgate in the middle of the twentieth century. Professor Susan Cerasano, the director of Colgate University Press, was a perpetual font of wisdom and information: without her enthusiasm, our papers would have no readers. Rabbi Dena Bodian came up with the idea of honoring the memory and bequest of Noel Rubinton '43 with a book. Following that, she sent out a request for interviews to all Jewish alumni, coordinated the interviews as they happened, researched permissions, did the indexing, and responded to any cry of help that came her way. Noel Rubinton, Jr., whose graceful introduction you have just seen, was with us at every step. We are grateful for the talent and over-the-top dedication of our designer Mary Moore and the pre-press services of Sheryl Rowe.

As we edged our way, unofficially, into the bicentennial year, Colgate people were enormously responsive. Constance Harsh, one of the best Deans of the Faculty ever, scrounged her back pockets for supplemental funding. Professor Jill Harsin, co-chair of the Bicentennial Committee, and Bicentennial Fellow Jennifer Hull were unstinting with good advice—up to the last minute, when they connected us with Carl Petersen, now retired as director of Colgate Archives and Special Collections, who turned out to possess not only invaluable information but also ready-made analysis. Margaret Maurer and her former student Megan Snell '12 were essential companions in our excursion into the intersection of Louis Zukofsky and Colgate.

President Brian Casey came to our class and shared his unusual perspective as both practitioner and historian of higher education (hopefully, we will not ever need to tap his legal advice as well). He encouraged us to keep our own archives, write an afterword, and pointed out that all marginal groups at Colgate begin their public lives in basements. Director of Admissions Gary Ross was with us for a genial and informative hour and left with a copy of a Cutten-era application form. We were relieved that it startled him, too. Vanessa Ochs, now Rabbi and Professor at the University of Virginia, stepped out of our chapters where she is a recurring character, and gave the class wonderful, wide-ranging advice.

We are deeply grateful to everyone who conducted interviews. In no particular order, thanks to Dena Bodian, Chelsea Mohr, Rachel Cohen, Anat Guez, Rich April, Jessica Friedberg, Abe Benghiat, Rob Sobelsohn, and our own Emily Kahn. The entire Jewish Studies department has been a crucial factor in the completion of this book: thank you Lesleigh Cushing, Noah Dauber, Anat Guez, and Steven Kepnes. Steven Kepnes and Professor of Religion Chris Vecsey turned out—who knew?—to possess meticulous private archives, which they generously shared. Ace librarian Liz Bodian came through on multiple unanticipated occasions (future researchers on that perennial topic, Colgate connections, should take note). Sarah Keen and Michelle Smith of Colgate Special Collections unearthed not one but two tapes of the Kwame Ture lecture, allowing one to be digitized in time for us to work with it. The content of this lecture is available nowhere else, and without the library's swift processing, we would be relegated to hearsay.

We are above all indebted to the interviewees themselves: these are your stories, your experiences, and this book would not exist without you. Singling out particular people is a little unfair, but special thanks nonetheless to Tom and Jim Parry for a double interview that should have been videotaped for broad distribution (and also for sending their father's memoirs). Our gratitude to everyone else who was so generous, and so important: Carly Ackerman, Sean Altman, Richard April, Carol April, Thomas Baker, Jerry Balmuth, Henry Bamberger, Adam Basciano, Jessica Benman, Matt Berkowitz, Jerry Berkson, Rebecca Blake, Dena Bodian, Suzanne Brock, Evan Chartier, Bernie Cohen, Richard Cohen, Margie Cohen, Lauren Braun Costello, Lesleigh Cushing, Noah Dauber, Katie David, Alex Djaha, Jessica Dodge, Melanie Dunbar, Bob Emmett, A.J. Farkas, Caryn Fields, Diane Munzer Fisher, Marvin Forland, Marc Frankel, Jessica Friedberg, Rebecca Friedland, Joan Friedman, Harvey Geller, Greg Gilbert, John Glynn, Neil Grabois, Stephen Greenleigh, Peter Greenwald, Moshe Gresser, Nancy Grossman, Frannie Kahan, Jason Kammerdiener, Allie Kashkash, Steven Kepnes, Mark Krinsky, Dana Laxer, Dan Levin, David Levy, Rachel Lutwick-Deaner, Stephen Mendelsohn, Peter Ochs, Vanessa Ochs, Jim Oestreich, Tom Parks, Beth Parks, Jim Parry, Tom Parry, Alfred Pasternak, Alan Posner, Dylan Pulver, Jake Pulver, Neal Rosenberg, John Rubinstein, Noel Rubinton, Jr., Samantha Safran, Susan Schnur, Jennifer Schwartz, Jason Sebell, Ross Secler, Adam Settle, Eric Settle, Jordan Sheiner, Peter Shelsky, Ceci Sibony, Bernie Siegel, Gilbert Simon, Lindsey Skerker, Jordie Slutsky Kattan, Richard Sobelsohn, Sammi Steinfeld, Hillary Stiss, Susan Stone, Joshua Strom, Benjamin Suarato, Chris Vecsey, Don Waldman, Lynn Waldman, Clifford Weinberger, David Werner, Alex Willick, and Charles Winetsky. And we are grateful to some non-Colgate people too: thank you Mary Moore, Sheryl Rowe, Lynn Levy, and John Stone.

And finally, thanks are due to those Jewish students, faculty, and staff we could not reach—to those who felt pressure to hide their Judaism and thus are unknown to us, to those whose contributions to Jewish life have been lost to history, to those who are long since gone from this earth. This is your story as well, and Colgate's Jewish life would not be where it is without you.

Amy Balmuth, Emily Kahn, Cameron Pauly, Kim Ravold,
Marit Vangrow, Dominic Wilkins, and Alice Nakhimovsky

Introduction

But for an unusual confluence of events, this book would not have been written and the history it tells would be known only in fragments. Even in the bicentennial year, the history of Jews is—to most people—marginal to the history of Colgate. Other stories take precedence. Yet for those of us who became involved, and the gratifying number of enthusiasts at Colgate and beyond who helped us, the Jewish story was compelling both in its own right and as a microcosm of Colgate history writ large.

The impetus to search out the Jewish strain of Colgate's story began with a bequest from the estate of Noel Rubinton '43. His son, Noel Rubinton, Jr., contacted Rabbi Dena Bodian and they talked about what to do with the money. A lecture series? Too fleeting. Rabbi Bodian suggested a book. She contacted me, and I thought, *but why should I do it? How about a seminar, in which students do it?* And that, amazingly, is what happened.

The six student authors whose work you will read all applied to join the class. Two of them did outstanding work in an earlier class with me, two came to my office and blew me away with their knowledge and skills, and two simply had amazing applications. That I was originally thinking of five students tells you all you need to know. The class had a striking variety of disciplinary perspectives. Dominic Wilkins '17 studied religion and geography, and his chapter turns often to the spatial dimensions of Judaism on campus. Amy Balmuth '17 concentrated in history and was an editor of the *Maroon*; Marit Vangrow '18 studies religion and was a member of Professor Lesleigh Cushing's sophomore seminar, which took her to Jerusalem. Cameron Pauly '19 is an anthropology major, Jewish Studies minor, and somehow also premed. Kim Ravold '19 studies English and creative writing, and was on home territory with the many writers and identity-seekers who populate her chapter. Emily Kahn '19 majors in history, minors in museum studies, and haunts archives. She also conducted many of the alumni interviews.

The class began with a crash introduction to American Jewish history and culture, with a particular focus on education and social class (Hasia Diner, Ruth Gay, Stephen Birmingham, Philip Roth); admission policies in higher education (Jerome Karabel), and Colgate history (Howard Williams, Maurice Hindus, and a collection of archival materials about discrimination during the Cutten years, put together for us by Jason Petrulis, who was Colgate's Bicentennial Fellow before joining the faculty at Cal Poly Pomona). Following that reading (in fact, considerably more), we discussed what the book would cover. The decision to go thematic was made early. And so, while each chapter is chronological within itself, you will not find here a decade-by-decade overview, and still less a replica of alumni news, though we are enormously grateful to all the alumni whose experiences and perspectives are the underlying fabric of our text.

In the second half of the semester, we wrote and discussed. The degree of collaboration was beyond my expectations, as was the cheerful acceptance of sometimes slash-and-burn editing. Suggestions for further work and, indeed, how to understand what we were seeing came from everyone in the class. I never knew, as I walked into a class, exactly what was going to happen. That is a cliché that professors often use, but in this case I mean it literally: as I walked into a class, I knew whose work we would likely talk about, but had no idea what direction that discussion would take. I cannot remember a class that was not illuminating.

It goes without saying that the book does not, and cannot, represent the entirety of the Jewish experience at Colgate. We miss alumni at both ends: at the beginning, because they can no longer tell their stories, and most recently, because we didn't want to end in a triumphalist way. Yet it is worth noting the ultimate normalization of Jewish life at Colgate. John Golden '66 served on the Board of Trustees from 1994 to 2007 (and was its chair from 2001 to 2007); Jeffrey Herbst was Colgate's sixteenth president (2010–2015). An outcome like this makes sense in the broad context of American history, but it is antithetical to the vision that held sway for so much of Colgate's past.

While there were many possible stories, the ones that we do tell are linked by a few overarching themes. We have tried to reflect them in the title.

"Repression" is perhaps the most obvious: the earliest Jews at Colgate concealed the Jewish aspect of their pre-Colgate lives, and would likely be horrified to see themselves memorialized in this book. Maurice Hindus, class of 1915, and Albert Parry, on the faculty from 1947 to 1969, presented themselves as Russian emigres who were vaguely but suitably Christian. For Hindus, whose pre-Colgate stint in Madison County made him a sentimental if not official Baptist, this was not far from the truth. Parry, who was an atheist, adopted a Christian veneer to blend socially. Hiding his Jewish past was, as the reader will see, just one part of his clandestine life. It also kept him from the fate of a colleague of his who, according to rumor, was denied tenure because he was thought to be Jewish. We have no way of knowing whether or not rumor was true: then, as now, the archives do not preserve tenure deliberations. But rumors take on a validity of their own, and in this case, we ran into that same information repeatedly, with specifics of department and name.

The word "reinvention" is another good descriptor of Parry and Hindus, who were active in crafting what the world saw of them (and in both cases, the world did see them). With respect to later generations of students and faculty, we understand the word in a somewhat different way, as shorthand for the serial re-creation of Jewish community on campus. This reinvention of the wheel is endemic at universities, where institutional memory doesn't last long and activities outside the local mainstream are not sustainable without strong leadership. At Colgate, whose bucolic isolation does not square with a viable Jewish life, leadership has always been crucial. It was under the charmed leadership of Peter Ochs, the first counselor to Jewish Students, that public Judaism burst onto the scene in the late 1970s. But when Peter left, and his successor left, there was an eclipse so profound that, though it lasted only a few years, our respondents from the next generation of leaders (Counselor to Jewish Students Moshe Gresser, Matt Berkowitz '93) both saw themselves as the facilitators of something unprecedented. What they accomplished was powerful and great, but it was not unprecedented. They had no way of knowing.

Rugelach, the Jewish pastry, slipped into the title by way of Shelsky's of Brooklyn (and the irresistible pull of alliteration). Shelsky's of Brooklyn is a classic New York "appetizing store," specializing in smoked fish and arguably the best rugelach on the planet. Peter Shelsky '01 seamlessly combines his love for Colgate with the art and business of Jewish food. In this combination—merely in this possibility—we see something that was unpredictable from the past our class unearthed, and a cause for hope and celebration.

We have dedicated the book to three people. When we completed the manuscript, Jerry Balmuth, Professor of Philosophy at Colgate from 1954 to 2010, was still asking the first question at any lecture. We thought he would live forever, and were devastated by his death. Jerry's thoughts on Jewish life, particularly his notion of "non-Semitism," form part of the analytical backbone of this book. The era of non-Semitism, which succeeded the discreetly anti-Semitic activities of President Everett Case, came to a quiet and positive end with the inauguration of Neil Grabois in 1988. Did the trustees who chose him ever ask him what kind of Jew he was? They did not. He might have been expected to maintain their policy of quiet indifference. But everywhere we looked, as we studied the impressive changes that brought Colgate Jews an academic and a physical home, there was Neil—creating conditions for Jewish Studies, tugging at donors to bring about the Saperstein Center. We are in awe of what he was able to bring about.

Less known to the readers of this book is Gilbert Geis '47: look for him in Chapter 3. Geis was part of a wave of veterans who came to Colgate on the G.I. bill. We do not think that he was Jewish. But he was paying attention to the activities of the state legislature as it sought to end discrimination in admissions (Chapter 1), and correctly suspected that Colgate was part of the problem. The pointed letter that he wrote to President Case on behalf of the *Maroon* presages his distinguished career as a lawyer. In its cool restraint and moral clarity, it is startling even today.

Those of us who worked on the book came away with deep respect for the people who lived it. They were not invariably happy, particularly in the early years. But they persevered, resisted, and built.

Alice Nakhimovsky
Distinguished Professor of Jewish Studies
and Professor of Russian and Eurasian Studies

Timeline

1819	Colgate Founded
1911–1915	Maurice Hindus at Colgate
1922–1942	George Barton Cutten, President of Colgate
1927	Colgate becomes non-sectarian
1927–1959	Colgate Commons Club
1947–1969	Albert Parry, Professor of Russian at Colgate
1948	Austin-Mahoney Bill
1948	Colgate Hillel Foundation founded
1954–2010	Jerry Balmuth, Professor of Philosophy and Religion
1968	Phi Delta Theta Sit-In
1970	Colgate admits women
1970	Colgate Hillel Foundation renamed Colgate Jewish Union
1973	Israel Study Group overlaps with Yom Kippur War
1979–1986	Peter Ochs, Counselor to Jewish Students at Colgate
1988–1999	Neil Grabois, first Jewish President of Colgate
1993	Saperstein Center Dedication
1993	Jewish Studies Program founded
2005	Blue Diamond Society founded
2017	Cutten Complex renamed 113 Broad Street

Repression, Re-Invention, and Rugelach

1

A Hidden Barrier

| The Quota System that Inhibited Jewish Life at Colgate |

Marit Vangrow

Cutten's Theology and Ideology of Discrimination

> Manhood suffrage has been our greatest and most popular failure, and now we double it by granting universal adult suffrage. . . . Of course it was the height of folly to permit people of mental subnormality to vote simply because they were males, or to deny highly intelligent people the privilege simply because they were females. . . . We cannot conceive of any worse form of chaos than a real democracy in a population of an average intelligence of a little over thirteen years.[1]

What appears to be a rallying speech for a radical social or political movement, reminiscent of something we would find in Sinclair Lewis's *It Can't Happen Here*, is Colgate President George Barton Cutten's inaugural address. A college president's inaugural address is intended to inform the faculty, students, and staff of his or her intentions as a leader and educator. Cutten's inaugural address calls for an aristocracy of the most intelligent and well-trained members of American society, implying that Colgate graduates would contribute heavily to this elite ruling class—an idea that, in its embrace of inequality, seems incompatible with everything that Colgate stands for today. Cutten's view of human nature and American society fostered a culture of ethnic and religious discrimination at Colgate that lasted through his presidency and that of his successor, Edward Needham Case, with Jews as a primary target.

James C. Colgate, the President of the Board of Trustees, also spoke at Cutten's inauguration. He highlighted Colgate's heritage as a religious institution and reaffirmed the university's commitment to religious (Christian) ideals.

> Our institution is a small one, but it has a vitality which insists on expansion and growth. Founded by religious men, moved by a religious purpose, its underlying spirit has always been religious. It has sought to discover and teach the truth, not for the purpose of satisfying the scientific curiosity, but to feed and strengthen the craving for that which is true and right, which the Creator has implanted in every heart.[2]

Cutten's vision for Colgate marks a stark departure from the institution's original purpose, as prescribed by Colgate's founders. In the early nineteenth century, Colgate's thirteen founders sought to create an institution that would facilitate the "spread of Christian faith and ideals."[3] The men receiving a Colgate education would ideally become Baptist ministers who would carry the Baptist word of Christ to the Far East and the American West. At this time Colgate was not an elite academic institution: it was an institution meant to educate Baptist ministers. A student's background didn't matter (the assumption was that he was white and Baptist, although the college also educated some American Indians). If his preparation was insufficient, he could begin his studies at the Colgate Academy.[4]

By 1922, more than one hundred years after its inception, Colgate's mission and purpose had fundamentally changed. The institution's purpose was no longer to produce pastors for the local community and missionaries for Burma and India; instead, Cutten hoped Colgate would produce an intellectual aristocracy, suitable to govern the rest of American society. Of course, religion would play a key role in Cutten's

The plaque on Cutten Hall, now renamed. Courtesy of Kim Ravold.

vision of Colgate, as he believed education, religion, and morality were inextricably intertwined. Cutten's inaugural address not only set the tone for his productive and problematic twenty-year tenure at Colgate, but also demonstrates how Christian theology can be transformed into an ideology used to discriminate against individuals who were not deemed, by Cutten and his admissions team, as worthy of a Colgate education.

But who exactly was George Cutten?

Born in Nova Scotia in 1874, George Barton Cutten proved to be an impressive young man. Cutten achieved "exceptionally brilliant record as a student and a leader of men" during his undergraduate years at Acadia University.[5] A well-rounded individual, he distinguished himself both in his academic studies as a PhD candidate and in his athletic pursuits as a center on Yale's beloved football team. After graduation, Cutten held pastorates in Connecticut, New York, and Ohio—

experiences that surely made him an ideal presidential candidate to the Colgate community. Prior to his transition to Colgate, Cutten served as President of his alma mater Acadia University for twelve years. Before his inauguration the *Colgate Maroon* painted him as an exemplary role model for the Colgate student: intelligent yet athletic, accomplished yet pious.

In 1928, Cutten was faced with a decision that would inevitably impact the future of Colgate University. He could either maintain Colgate's Baptist affiliation or transfer the seminary to Rochester and receive a hefty state subsidy. Cutten was a pragmatic man; he knew that Colgate was not a wealthy institution and understood that the institution's survival and expansion were contingent on his ability to secure capital from outside sources. Presumably, he knew that any campus projects or expansion undertaken during his time at Colgate would be his greatest and most enduring legacy. Eventually, he made the decision to abandon Colgate's religious affiliation in order to obtain funds from New York State, funding that would enable the addition of Huntington gymnasium, two new dormitories (Andrews and Stillman), and new academic buildings (Lawrence and McGregory) all during his tenure.[6] Despite expansive and commendable accomplishments under Cutten's presidency, opening Colgate admissions to non-Baptists would have unforeseen consequences for Cutten—most notably the appearance of the "Jewish problem."

Cutten adopted an admissions policy that stressed the fungible qualities of "character" and "morality"—characteristics he believed were the product of a Christian upbringing.[7] Of course, Cutten could not publicly bar an entire group of potential students because of religious beliefs or background. By implementing a rigid quota system, he would prevent Colgate from becoming too "Jewy," while still securing funds from New York State. However, such behavior did not go unnoticed. In 1946, a state-funded study named Colgate as the second most discriminatory (against Jews) nonsectarian liberal arts college in upstate New York.[8] In 1938, Cutten admitted pursuing "certain admissions processes." His successor Everett Case was more cautious, passively denying Colgate's Jewish quota system throughout his tenure and often ignoring inquiries about the institution's admissions process.

Although we might want to believe that only one university turned bigoted racial and ethnic theories into university policy, Cutten was not alone. His contemporaries at Harvard, Yale, Columbia, and other elite institutions held similar views and integrated similar approaches to the "Jewish problem."[9] In truth, Cutten's views are representative of an expansive pattern of anti-Semitism, racism, and xenophobia that extended across the United States during the early twentieth century. President Cutten's views were consistent with three major ideas that proliferated elite society at the time.[10] First, like many, President Cutten feared the decline of American civilization, viewing immigrants and the intellectually inferior as America's greatest threat. Second, Cutten insisted that inequality was natural and inescapable—a premise that he used to justify his embrace of Social Darwinism, eugenics, and his suspicion of American democracy. Cutten also believed that education was incomplete without moral and religious instruction. This view in particular would directly influence Colgate's admissions policies and campus.

Cutten's unwillingness to have Jews at Colgate fits in with his views on immigration more broadly. A critic of the idea of the "melting pot," Cutten stood vehemently against immigration from Southern and Eastern Europe (which meant, in religious and ethnic terms, Catholics and Jews). He believed that immigrants would corrupt American society and render the race weaker by—as he wrote in no less a venue than the *New York Times*—"breeding our brains and obtaining our population from the lowest strains."[11]

Cutten's article, entitled "Nature's Inexorable Law–Inequality," unites Darwin, Christianity, and the foundational documents of American democracy. In Cutten's understanding, Jesus would agree that "not all people are created equal," while the Founding Fathers, when drafting the Declaration of Independence, had only white

American men in mind when they wrote "all men are created equal."[12] According to Cutten, America has always been ruled by the few and only a small segment of society is mentally competent enough to participate in government. From this, Cutten justifies his belief that America's intellectual elite have the duty to govern the mentally inferior.

More relevant to Cutten's role as president of Colgate was his view that a proper education required moral and religious training. Cutten's *New York Times* article "Shall We Abandon Religion?" espouses his belief that religion can help mitigate the effects of modern society; in fact, religion is needed to aid in the solution now "more than any previous age."[13] Cutten stresses the relationship between morality and religion, "Morality is a definite and indispensable part of religion, but religion seems necessary in order to bring morality to its highest fruition."[14] Without morality, Cutten feared that his "intellectual aristocracy" would be unable to govern fairly and justly.

Cutten's views on American society were not kept private: Cutten wrote many articles, gave public speeches, and published scholarly books during his tenure at Colgate. In each instance, Cutten highlights his elitist view of American democracy, drawing support from his problematic strain of Christianity. As Colgate's president, Cutten was an extension of the university: his views were seen as representative of the university as a whole, regardless of whether or not his statements were truly representative of the campus. Cutten's ideology remained constant over the course of his Colgate tenure, an idea maintained by the various works he wrote during those years. According to *Time Magazine*, "In any poll to name the most reactionary U.S. college president, Colgate's burly George Barton Cutten would be likely to win hands down."[15] Although it seems impressive that the president of a small university in upstate New York was recognized in *Time Magazine*, "reactionary" is not an ideal quality for a college president.

Because the "intellectual aristocracy" would ideally rule over the mentally inferior, the teaching of morality was of vital importance for institutions like Colgate:

> In the moral training demanded for an intellectual aristocracy, there must be instilled the great ideas and ideals of responsibility. . . . The object of a college or university is not to develop a self-centered culture, but to use the acquired culture, knowledge and discipline, in the service of one's fellow men. . . . It is thus supremely important,—yes, imperative,—that our intellectual aristocracy should have the highest and best moral training.[16]

By instilling Christian values in Colgate students, Cutten believed that a graduate would be intellectually and morally prepared to govern his fellow citizens, therefore providing for the country's advancement. Cutten assumes that Christianity is morally superior to other religions, declaring that "we are, let us hope, past the day, if indeed it has ever been, when one should make any apologies for the teaching of Christian ideals in connection with a college or university," because "they are of the most benefit."[17] Cutten's statement also claims that the morals taught through Christianity are superior to those taught by any other religion, justifying his discriminatory admissions policy toward Jews.

Cutten's conception of Jesus as a supremely masculine man, a man who courageously challenged the corrupt Jews, inspired his vision for the ideal Colgate man. In a speech to about four hundred members of Colgate's student body and faculty he explained:

> I know no man in history who should appeal to us as much as Jesus. He is often pictured from the pulpit as an effeminate character, one whom real men could not admire. The Jesus of the New Testament is not so. Jesus was a man of great physical power. . . . Single handed he took a stand against the Jewish money changers and drove them from the Temple . . . Jesus is calling upon us to help him. . . . There is need for men who are red-blooded, who are courageous, who are strong.[18]

Cutten vehemently opposed those who preached the idea of Jesus as a man of "passive resistance."[19] In his view, Jesus was able to prevail over the deceptive Jews solely because of his immense physical strength. Because Colgate men should "follow Christ,"[20] Cutten saw the development of each Colgate man's physical strength as of the utmost importance.

The admissions policies implemented under Cutten's tenure reinforced traditional gender hierarchies and were widely influenced by the Nativist movement. Cutten, like many of America's elite, feared the end of white Protestant male dominance.[21] As a result, admissions applications were manipulated to weed out certain people with "disagreeable personal qualities"—a euphemism for Jews.[22] The idea that Jewish men were somehow less masculine than their Christian counterparts was not a new phenomenon. In order to discredit the "effeminate" (though presumably academically worthy) Jew, Cutten and his contemporaries devised admissions applications that prioritized men of "character" over those of academic merit;[23] character implied a high-class Protestant upbringing, an upbringing that produced a man of pride and strength, the perfect embodiment of Cutten's Christ. Because, as the *Colgate Maroon* explained, "Colgate has always been known as a college of virile men, not an aggregation of effeminate creatures."[24]

According to Cutten's reasoning, Christianity is the best moral choice and those not following Christianity are obviously not of the same moral, physical, and intellectual quality or ability, rendering Jews incapable of joining Cutten's intellectual aristocracy. Why would Colgate, if its purpose was to create a moral and intellectual elite, admit students who did not ascribe to Christianity?

The Colgate Man

For President Cutten, a Colgate education meant more than academic proficiency, or even mastery; a Colgate education would transform a boy into a man fit to govern American society. In order to achieve such an arduous task, Cutten implemented a revolutionary academic scheme— the Colgate Plan. Retooled according to his specifications

> . . . a degree from a college or university shall in the future mean not simply the fact that certain courses in Latin or Greek or mathematics or physics have been completed, but it should say in no uncertain way, "Here is a man, physically fit, mentally sound, scholastically competent and morally clean."[25]

Described as the "most advanced educational experiment in all of America," the Colgate Plan outlined five survey courses, designed to give freshmen and sophomores the opportunity to explore a "panorama of knowledge" before choosing a specific field.[26] With the plan, Cutten aimed for the "greater development of individual students."[27]

Coupled with the Colgate Plan, Cutten implemented a mandatory gym requirement—a requirement still in place today. Cutten fiercely argued that too much leisure could destroy a man's life, a danger he took so seriously that he dedicated an entire book to it.[28] By requiring *all* Colgate students to partake in athletic activities, Cutten hoped that Colgate graduates would embody the "muscular Christianity" that he held so dear. Cutten's emphasis on athletics, coupled with his revolutionary academic plan, set the university apart from its peer institutions. As products of Cutten's plan, Colgate students were armed with a distinct "spirit" so that:

> when . . . you meet a man who fights like a man, plays like a man, talks like a man, laughs like a man, lives like a man, and who, being all this, meets your glance with the quiet, honest, level look of a man, then you may know that he is a real Colgate man.[29]

Due to Colgate's emphasis on sports and masculinity, Jews were considered incompatible with and unworthy of a Colgate education. This view was not unique to Colgate; elite institutions like Dartmouth, Yale,

Princeton, and Harvard emphasized physical fitness in order to weed out Jewish applicants and maintain their Puritan character. Despite this stereotype of Jews as inferior men, both physically and morally, a small number of Jewish students participated and thrived in Colgate's sports scene. Most notable is Harold Weinberger class of 1949 whose picture appeared in the 1947 issue of the *Colgate Banter*. Weinberger was a World War II veteran, a highly touted athlete, and a New York State football star—the very antithesis of what Jewish applicants to Colgate and other elite institutions were expected to be.[30]

Though it advanced Colgate's school pride, Cutten's focus on athletics perpetuated a hyper-masculine vision of Colgate that would prove problematic beyond his tenure. Even before Cutten's presidency, Colgate had been considered a jock school. As the *Colgate Maroon* put it, "Colgate has always been known as a college of virile men, not an aggregation of effeminate creatures."[31] Cutten's efforts to expand athletics only reinforced Colgate's image as a university designed for WASP-y jocks that alienated everyone else.

In 1938 the Rockefeller Foundation sent a representative to Colgate to determine whether the university should receive the foundation's funds. The Rockefeller was established in 1913 with the mission of "promoting the wellbeing of humanity throughout the world." The Foundation shared a strong relationship with Colgate, providing generous grants for the university's endeavors. An informant notified the Rockefeller employee—identified below by his initials, KWB—that:

> Colgate has recently declined to associate itself with the prospective fifteen liberal college study of objectives and evaluation of outcomes. KWB's informant on this point advised him to remember that Colgate was committed to a plan for which its president was mainly responsible, that it was also committed to a big football team and "certain racial policies" (there are 7 Jews at Colgate, out of a total student body of 1,000) and that it could be expected to pursue its own program single mindedly for the next 25 years.[32]

In the spirit of President Cutten, Colgate chose an individualistic approach to its education and future. By committing to the Colgate Plan, the university was free to continue both its athletic pursuits and its discriminatory admissions processes without having to conform to the policies and practices of other liberal arts institutions.

Considering Cutten's background as a star football player, his high regard for football and athletics broadly is not surprising. In the 1930s Colgate was noted for its "athletic enthusiasm" so much so that it often "overshadowed its genuine non-athletic accomplishment."[33] Cutten viewed athletics as a worthy enterprise because it brought in generous donations that the small university desperately needed. According to Cutten's logic, the development of manliness and character would foster athletic success and, subsequently, academic success. Under Cutten's tenure, sports became a dominant aspect of Colgate's campus culture. Even decades later, this legacy remains. Colgate continues to be one of few liberal arts colleges with an NCAA Division I Athletics Program; this made Colgate unique during Cutten's time, and continues to make Colgate unique today.

While Colgate's campus expanded and its academic offerings diversified under Cutten's tenure, its student body remained overwhelmingly homogenous. Although Cutten and his administrative staff would *publicly* claim otherwise, Colgate implemented one of the most rigid quota systems in New York State, actively preventing Jewish and African American applicants from gaining admission. Cutten's views on college admissions were strongly influenced by the idea of "survival of the fittest." By attending Colgate, the university's students, in Cutten's opinion, were already the "fittest" that the country had to offer. And Colgate should not dilute itself by admitting the unfit—Jews, African Americans, and other "undesirable" minorities. Cutten envisioned and sought to create a Colgate, and subsequently an America, dominated by masculine, Christian men.

Colgate was not alone in realizing that the "wrong" students were passing the entrance examinations that were then required for admissions. Faced with the arrival of unwanted Jews who were scoring well despite their obvious social and religious unfitness, Harvard, Yale, and Princeton elected to replace their admissions application with more "subjective criteria" to ensure that the Christian character of each institution remained.[34] Colgate and other Northeast universities would soon follow suit. Harvard University, for example, asked an applicant to fill out his: "Race and Color," "Religious Preference," "Maiden Name of Mother," "Birthplace of Father," and "What change, if any, has been made since birth in your own name or that of their father."[35] To ensure that an applicant did not lie about his religion, Harvard also asked the high school principal or private school headmaster to record the religion of student in question.[36]

At first glance, Colgate's admissions application does not seem much different than one we might see today: it asks for an applicant's address, high school, activities, prizes and honors. Yet upon examination, its discriminatory nature becomes more apparent. Colgate's application gave clear preference toward prospective students who have connections to Colgate. It asked an applicant to "give names of any relatives who have attended Colgate," implying that relatives of alumni would receive an edge in the admissions process (as is still the case). It also required applicants to give the names and addresses of two Colgate men "who can give information concerning you."[37] This aspect of the application puts Jews and other minorities at a substantial disadvantage, considering that a Jewish applicant attending a public school in New York City was much less likely to know two Colgate men compared to an applicant attending Deerfield Academy in Massachusetts.

On the admissions application, Colgate asks students to indicate subjects that have been completed or that will be completed by graduation. Listed are English, History (Ancient, Medieval & Modern, English, and American), Civics, Latin, Greek, French, Spanish, German, Elementary Algebra, Intermediate Algebra, Plane Geometry, Solid Geometry, Trigonometry, Physics, Chemistry, Biology, and General Science. To an untrained eye, these appear to be standard subjects expected of a high school student; however, asking the student to indicate

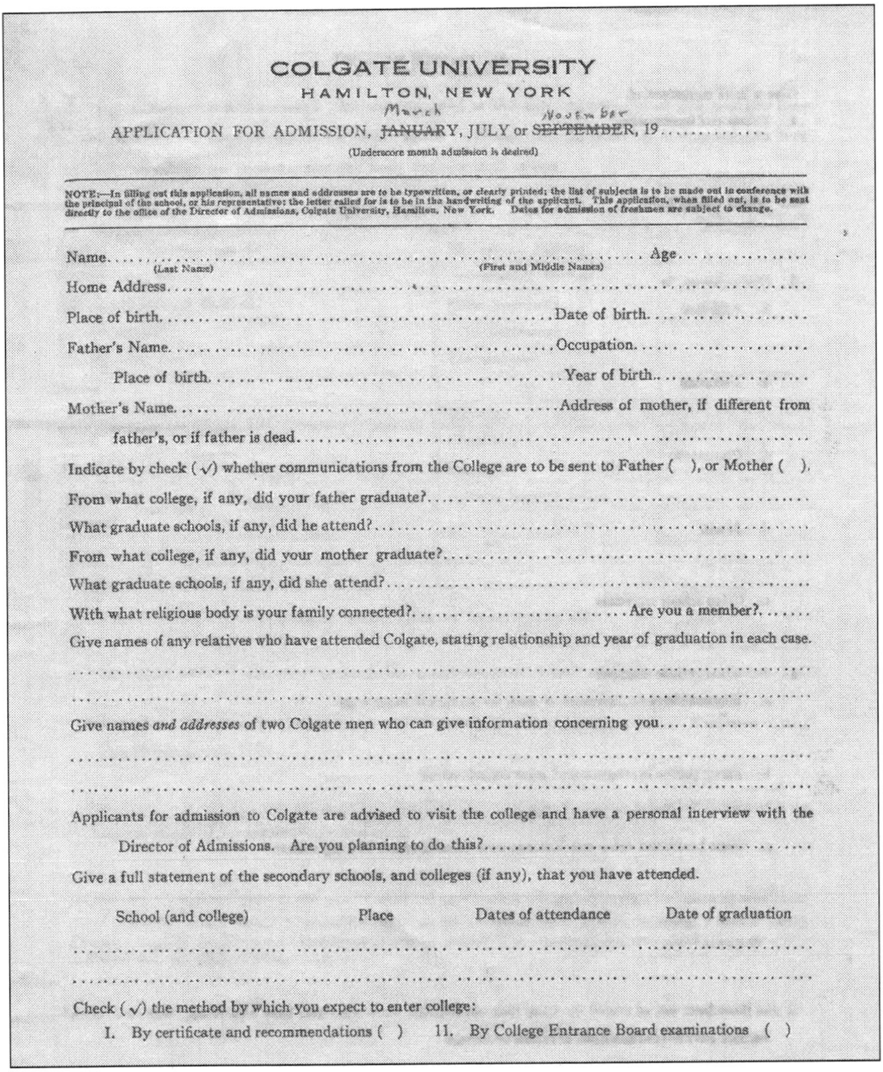

COLGATE UNIVERSITY

HAMILTON, NEW YORK

APPLICATION FOR ADMISSION, ~~JANUARY~~ March, JULY or ~~SEPTEMBER~~ November, 19............

(Underscore month admission is desired)

NOTE:—In filling out this application, all names and addresses are to be typewritten, or clearly printed; the list of subjects is to be made out in conference with the principal of the school, or his representative; the letter called for is to be in the handwriting of the applicant. This application, when filled out, is to be sent directly to the office of the Director of Admissions, Colgate University, Hamilton, New York. Dates for admission of freshmen are subject to change.

Name.......(Last Name).......(First and Middle Names)....... Age.......

Home Address.......

Place of birth....... Date of birth.......

Father's Name....... Occupation.......

Place of birth....... Year of birth.......

Mother's Name....... Address of mother, if different from father's, or if father is dead.......

Indicate by check (✓) whether communications from the College are to be sent to Father ( ), or Mother ( ).

From what college, if any, did your father graduate?.......

What graduate schools, if any, did he attend?.......

From what college, if any, did your mother graduate?.......

What graduate schools, if any, did she attend?.......

With what religious body is your family connected?....... Are you a member?.......

Give names of any relatives who have attended Colgate, stating relationship and year of graduation in each case.

....

....

Give names *and addresses* of two Colgate men who can give information concerning you.......

....

....

Applicants for admission to Colgate are advised to visit the college and have a personal interview with the Director of Admissions. Are you planning to do this?.......

Give a full statement of the secondary schools, and colleges (if any), that you have attended.

School (and college)	Place	Dates of attendance	Date of graduation
....	....	....	....
....	....	....	....

Check (✓) the method by which you expect to enter college:

I. By certificate and recommendations ( ) II. By College Entrance Board examinations ( )

Colgate University Application for Admission. There is a final page for an essay, called a "personal letter (in your own handwriting)." The applicant is told to describe "(a) why you wish to go to college, (b) why you selected Colgate, and (c) what you expect to make your chief interest while attending college." Courtesy of Office of the Provost and Dean of the Faculty, Colgate University Special Collections and University Archives, and Colgate University Libraries.

ACTIVITIES RECORD

Give a brief statement of

1. Prizes and honors won

2. School offices held

3. Participation in
   a. Athletics
   b. Debating
   c. Dramatics
   d. Music
   e. Other school activities

4. Activities outside of school:
   a. Remunerative employment or work for parents without wage
   b. Participation in religious and other organizations
   c. Some books and other publications read, outside of school assignments

If you have been out of school for more than six months, state what you have been doing meantime, including any part time attendance at school or college.

Colgate University Application for Admission (continued)

whether or not he had taken Latin and Greek was a simple way for an admissions team to determine if a student was Jewish, within a small margin of error. Students from public schools in predominantly Jewish areas, such as New York City, were not obligated to take Latin or Greek and most usually could not, as their schools didn't offer those subjects.

LIST OF SUBJECTS

Fill in, below, the subjects which you have completed or will have completed when you graduate from school, entering additional subjects in the vacant spaces. Indicate, also, the years (½, 1, or more) you have studied each subject, the number of periods a week, and your mark to date.

SUBJECTS	YEARS	PERIODS A WEEK	MARK TO DATE	SUBJECTS	YEARS	PERIODS A WEEK	MARK TO DATE
English (College requirements)				Elementary Algebra			
History (Ancient)				Intermediate Algebra			
History (Medieval & Modern)				Plane Geometry			
History (English)				Solid Geometry			
History (American)				Trigonometry			
Civics							
Latin				Physics			
Greek				Chemistry			
French				Biology			
Spanish				General Science			
German							

If some of your marks are low, what in your own view are the reasons for this?

What do you plan to do (if you have a plan) after graduation from college?

Will you have to earn any part of your expenses while attending college?................ If so, what is your plan for doing this?

You should send with this application a small (size 2½x2) photograph of yourself, which will be placed in the college records, if you are enrolled as a student.

On account of the limited number that can be admitted applicants are requested to sign the following statement:

I have given careful thought to my college needs and am convinced that Colgate is the college I wish to attend. I promise to advise the Director of Admissions as soon as possible if any circumstance over which I have no control interferes with my plans to attend Colgate.

....

(Signature)

Colgate University Application for Admission (continued)

But private schools and boarding schools almost all required students to learn both classical languages.[38]

Colgate's application required an applicant to enclose a photograph of himself that would be "placed in the college records" upon enrollment. However, the photograph requirement was another method used by college admissions teams in order to determine whether not a student would be a desirable addition to the campus community; basically, the photograph gave strong evidence to pinpoint a student as being of Eastern or Southern European descent or African American. The Jewish nose was a useful discriminatory marker for the gatekeepers of college admissions. But since the shape of an applicant's nose was not infallible, Colgate and other institutions had more comprehensive measures in place to ensure that no Jew was unaccounted for.

According to the application, prospective students were "advised to visit the college and have a personal interview with the Director of Admissions." Although an interview seems like an extra opportunity for an applicant to prove his worth, it functioned as another discriminatory measure used against Jews to prevent their acceptance. Recommending, but not requiring, an on-campus interview helped weed out Jews and other minorities who did not have the means to travel to rural, upstate New York on a whim. Even those who secured an interview could be labeled Jewish because of their distinctive vocal tics.[39] The Yiddish-accented language of the Jew was not seen as compatible with the high culture that Colgate and other elite institutions embraced, making the fear of sounding different and sounding "too Jewish" a legitimate concern of Jewish applicants.[40] In sum, the college interview functioned as a "second line of discrimination" against Jewish applicants.[41]

Of course, Cutten claimed that the moral component was "the most important" aspect of the admissions application.[42] Yet, this form of evaluation is inherently subjective and biased toward the admissions team's interpretation of morality, an interpretation that could easily be skewed toward preventing certain groups of people (Jews) from obtaining admission. The application's question about religion was quite precise: "With what religious body is your family connected? Are you a member?" What appears to be a highly invasive question was the norm for elite academic institutions like Colgate. Requiring a candidate to list his religion enabled Colgate's admissions team to tally how many

Jews applied in total and then calculate how many should be accepted in order to maintain Colgate's desired ratio of Jews to non-Jews. Although an applicant could decide against disclosing his religious affiliation, an incident preserved in Colgate's archives shows that this would not necessarily help.

A Rejection, a Complaint, an Excuse

The story is an interesting one. In 1931, a prominent Jewish businessman, wrote to his friend and Colgate trustee Orrin R. Judd, notifying him of Colgate's unfair admissions policies. In the letter, the businessman explained that his son had "carelessly omitted" entering his faith on his Colgate admissions application.[43] Colgate contacted the applicant, inquiring why the omission was made, to which the young man responded that it was merely an oversight. On June 1st, he received a "short, curt, and rude" letter from Colgate Dean James D. Howlett that, the father said, was "no doubt directed at [the young man] due to his unfortunate error, or possibly due to the fact that he is of Jewish persuasion."[44]

Mr. Judd, the trustee, directly expressed his concern over what had transpired in a letter to President Cutten, confessing "I wonder whether the rejection of [the young man] was really based on his character and scholarship record or other reasons. It does seem to me that Dean Howlett's letter is subject to [the father's] criticism . . . I know that occasionally Jewish boys have been admitted."[45] He then mentions the father's wealth and prominence: except for his religious "persuasion," the applicant was exactly the kind of scion Colgate sought. As a trustee, it was Judd's responsibility to preserve and protect Colgate's prestige; Judd realized that an incident like of this kind had the potential to tarnish Colgate's reputation.

Cutten had no other choice than to reply to the father, admitting that "there is no doubt in the world but that the matter looks bad but it is entirely the result of a concatenation of circumstances, the interpretation which you made being the most natural one."[46] However, Cutten assures him that Colgate cannot possibly have prejudice against Jewish students:

> We always have a number in college. The president of the Pan-Hellenic Council, which is one of the most important officers in the student body, was a Jewish student this year, and one of the six honorary degrees conferred at Commencement was conferred upon a Jew who is also one of our alumni. Three years ago two of the recipients of honorary degrees were Jews and we have a number of Jews among our most illustrious alumni.[47]

Cutten denies any accusation of unfair treatment of Jews by stressing the achievement of Colgate's (few) Jewish students and alumni; however, the fact that Cutten can only recall four Jewish students, current or past, is disconcerting. Because Colgate had a few token Jewish students, Cutten contended that the young man's religion could not have prevented his admission to the university. Instead, Cutten insisted that he had failed to meet Colgate's academic standards, explaining that "every mark that he [the applicant] presents is below that required for certification."[48] However, it seems unlikely that academics played a role, as the father pointed out, considering that Colgate's faculty had not received his son's school record when his admissions decision was made.

In 1931, a representative from Colgate, in a *public* meeting, quoted his dean as saying "there never would be more than six Jews in the university at once" and "if the charge of anti-Semitism should be raised, the six would be an adequate exhibit to disprove it."[49] Although this testimony could be dismissed as hearsay, data directly from the Colgate Board of Trustees proves otherwise. Admissions information collected from January 1929–January 1942 demonstrates a steady number of Jewish students at Colgate; over the 13-year period there were consistently one to two Jewish students per class, meaning that there were only six or seven Jews on campus in total. Colgate's strategy, like many of its peer institutions, was to admit an adequate number of Jews so that no one could accuse the administration of a discriminatory admissions process. In effect, the claim that there would never be more than six Jews on campus at a time proved to be quite accurate.

Maintaining the Status Quo

After twenty years of service, George Barton Cutten officially retired from Colgate in 1942. A young Baptist with an Ivy-League education, grand athletic achievements, and extensive experience with monetary policy, Everett Needham Case was widely considered Cutten's ideal successor.[50] Although President Case guided Colgate through uncertain times in both the country's and the institution's history, he was not as successful in his attempts to secure Colgate's reputation as a white, Protestant institution. Like Cutten, Case admitted a small number of Jews in order to guard against any accusations of discrimination. However, his efforts were not as successful as Cutten's; eventually, Colgate's dearth of Jewish students attracted the attention of students, alumni, journalists, and ultimately, the New York State legislature.

Unlike Cutten, Case did not publish major works during his tenure at Colgate that demonstrated anti-Semitic, racist, or classist views. Still, a look at his private correspondence reveals a June 1945 letter to his brother Jim, in which he says that he and his wife cancelled their vacation reservations at Plymouth because of reports that "they were opening their doors to a large number of Jews."[51] Presumably, this social anti-Semitism made Cutten's system of discrimination congenial to him and influenced his decision to uphold it.

In the midst of World War II and continuing into the postwar years, valiant efforts were made domestically to challenge existing admissions processes and make a college education, public or private, more accessible to all Americans. The draft was not discriminatory: any

American man of good health and proper age was viewed as vital to the war effort, regardless of education, race, ethnicity, class, or religion. As millions of men were drafted in the 1940s to support the war effort, the Roosevelt administration prepared the "G.I. Bill of Rights," a piece of legislation that helped young veterans secure a proper education and prevented high unemployment in the postwar years.[52] The G.I. Bill enabled veterans who could not otherwise afford a college education the opportunity to study and move on to a professional career.[53] Colgate University was one of many institutions of higher education that would experience an influx of veterans far more diverse than the students they were used to seeing in the decade following WWII.

In 1945, President Case received a letter from Mr. Meier Steinbrink, the chairman of the Anti-Defamation League of B'nai B'rith, an organization founded in response to growing anti-Semitism in the United States during the early twentieth century.[54] The ADL capitalized on post-Holocaust goodwill toward surviving Jews; the organization pressed Colgate and other colleges in the Northeast to change their admissions policies to enable Jews who had been marginalized before the war a greater opportunity to achieve an elite education. Mr. Steinbrink's letter openly accused Colgate of discriminatory admissions policies and urged President Case to change "such an undemocratic practice" before the end of the war.[55] Because the returning soldiers would come from varied national origins, Steinbrink advised Case to remove "any inference of discrimination" that would "provoke resentment on the part of our returning veterans."[56]

President Case responded to Mr. Steinbrink a full month later in an attempt to explain Colgate's admissions process and dismiss his accusations of religious and racial discrimination. Case wrote,

> Our admission form, I find, asks no questions concerning an applicant's race but does seek information concerning his religious affiliation, if any. It includes no complicit request for

> information on national origin but asks the place of birth, both of the applicant and of his parents.[57]

Case failed to acknowledge that Colgate's application (as we have seen) asked each applicant for his photograph, the goal of which was almost certainly—unless attractiveness was an issue—to determine his race or ethnicity. However, even Case could not deny that requiring an applicant to disclose his religion and nation of origin is somewhat troubling when exposed to the public. He conceded "such information, I agree, is susceptible of abuse, or at least the suspicion of abuse," but assured Steinbrink that Colgate asked these questions solely for "constructive use by counselors and others concerned about the successful adjustment of the individuals who make up a student body." The letter concludes by rejecting Steinbrink's suggestions and informing him that Colgate did not plan to make changes to its admissions application anytime soon.

Around the same time as he was responding to Mr. Steinbrink, Case received a request from Lawrence E. Spivak, a publisher at *The American Mercury*. Spivak, an accomplished journalist and proud Jew, wrote to Case and asked him to answer questions on an enclosed questionnaire that would help "throw light on the general practices used in admitting students" to institutions like Colgate.[58] Case obliged, but in his answers to *The American Mercury*'s "College Study Questionnaire," Case claimed that Colgate did not have a quota system against African Americans, Jews, or any other minority group. However, he disclosed that Colgate did not have any African American students and that an applicant's religion was taken into account during the admissions process. According to Case, Colgate required a personal interview to account for the fact that Colgate had "far more applicants than we have facilities to care for."[59]

This issue of discrimination in Colgate's application process invoked concern not only among journalists and civil rights advocates, but also with multiple alumni and a student on the *Colgate Maroon* staff. In 1946, Edward Van Dyke '40 wrote to President Case and provided him with various newspaper clippings mentioning Colgate in discussions of discrimination in college admissions. Van Dyke admits that he noticed the "obvious scarcity of the more pronounced minorities: Negroes and those of the Jewish religion" during his time at Colgate.[60] He ends his letter with a powerful statement, "Believing sincerely that any form of discrimination is contrary to our true American heritage, I would welcome any thoughts you may have on the subject and how it affects Colgate."[61] Hubert Reynolds '36 also wrote Case, arguing that, in light of World War II, a change in the university's racial policies was needed "now more than ever."[62] On both accounts, Case did not respond due to yet another "absence from the office."[63] Yet Case sent out correspondence from his office those same days, suggesting that he was absent only for those minutes when the complaints were received.

It is important to note that the Cutten-Case admissions policies also drastically impacted African American applicants. In a concise letter to President Case, notable alumnus Congressman Adam Clayton Powell, Jr., inquired about the absence of African Americans on Colgate's campus.[64] In his response, President Case dodged Congressman Powell's accusations and denied any responsibility for Colgate's policies before his presidency in September 1942.[65] Yet African Americans were barred from the fall of 1926 until the fall of 1948, when, against Case's will, a law barring discrimination in college admissions passed the state legislature and was signed by Governor Nelson Rockefeller.

Case claimed that Colgate's rural location rendered it less desirable to African Americans and other minorities who were from the "cosmopolitan centers of population."[66] Like Cutten responding to the angry Jewish father, Case claimed that "the caliber of the relatively few who have applied has, generally speaking, afforded no assurance that the candidate would, if admitted, do successful college work or be as representative of his people as you and we would want him to be."[67] In other words, Case believed that a minority would want only the best representatives of his race at Colgate and, at that point, none of Colgate's African American applicants were up to that standard.

One of the most compelling letters in Case's archives was written by a *Colgate Maroon* student contributor named Gilbert Geis. In a concise and direct letter, Geis invited President Case to clarify the university's official position on discrimination and quotas, including seven questions posed by a *New York Times* correspondent and Colgate's own student body for Case to answer. However, President Case never answered the enclosed questions, nor did he ever acknowledge that he had received the letter.

In 1946, almost a year after Lawrence E. Spivak's letter to President Case, *The American Mercury* published an article addressing religious and racial discrimination in colleges. The article's author Dan W. Dodson points to Colgate as one of the worst offenders when it came to discrimination against Jewish applicants,

> The evidence leaves little doubt that the traditional, well-known colleges reject many thousands of students each year on the primary ground of race and religion. For example, Colgate University admits about four or five Jewish boys each year. Yet Colgate receives anywhere from 200 to 300 applications from Jewish students.[68]

Dodson used the survey information gathered by Mr. Spivak in order to illuminate Colgate's admissions process. Despite Case's claim that Colgate did not have a quota against Jews or any other minority, Dodson saw through this facade and used Case's own answers to corroborate the data against him.

Dodson's article sparked the interest of Robert D. Leigh, a consultant for the Temporary Commission on the Need for a State University. In a letter to President Case, Mr. Leigh implored Case to comment on the validity of Dodson's insidious claims about Colgate's quota system.[69] Case responded and conceded "Dodson's accuracy was roughly 50 per cent."[70] However, Case belittled Dodson's work as an investigative journalist, accusing him of "extreme carelessness. . . in checking his facts."[71] He defended Colgate's past as a Baptist institution and claimed "a more liberal policy has prevailed" and has done much "to mitigate, as we hope it will one day eliminate, those prejudices of which discriminatory practices in any field are the visible symptoms."

Although it might be tempting to assume that discrimination stopped once a Jewish student gained admission to Colgate, it is clear that anti-Semitic rhetoric permeated the institution for decades after. In a letter to President Case, Colgate's director of public relations Mr. Emerson Reck voiced his distaste for "certain" Jewish students,

> We can say truthfully today that faculty members and students at Colgate don't know that a boy is Jewish unless he makes the fact known himself (barring, of course, the possibility that his appearance reveals his race). I know that I had two Jewish boys in a class of eight a few semesters back. One of them stamped himself as Jewish in a prejudicial sense from the first day by his acts and attitude. The other boy, one of the nicest chaps I have ever had, revealed his race during a conversation one date late in the spring. I am positive that no one ever held his race against him.[72]

Mr. Reck makes it clear that the ordinary Jew—an unacceptable candidate for Colgate—reveals himself by how he looks and how he acts. Requiring applicants to provide a personal photograph was supposed to prevent unwanted Jews, like the first student mentioned, from gaining admission to Colgate. In the eyes of the administration, the best kind of Jewish student was a man who in no way or form made his Judaism public.

In 1946, Colgate invited George Weaver, director of the Congress of Industrial Organizations Committee to Abolish Discrimination, to speak on campus about the use of quota systems in college admissions. The Congress of Industrial Organizations Committee to Abolish Discrimination was created in 1943 in order to combat racial discrimination and prejudice in the labor movement and the war effort.[73] Weaver told a *Colgate Maroon* reporter that, "changing conditions, in college enrollments make the quota system a poor one for improving racial and religious discrimination conditions."[74] In response to a Colgate official's claim that removing racial and religious questions from college entrance applications would serve no good purpose as those questions could be easily answered by personal interviews, Mr. Weaver agreed that it might be true for smaller institutions like Colgate where personal interviews are possible. However, Weaver argued that removal of these questions would "serve a good purpose" for larger universities like Columbia and NYU which could not guarantee all applicants a personal interview.[75]

Although Mr. Weaver discussed discrimination in college admissions, a topic that should have sparked the interest of Colgate students, few viewed his visit as worthy of their time and attention. Dave Davies, class of 1949, wrote the *Colgate Maroon* editor, deriding him for the fact that only 85 students attended Mr. Weaver's talk, a talk which he described as, "one of the most informative and thought provoking of lectures held [at Colgate]."[76] Davies blamed lack of publicity, poor planning, and, proffered the idea that, perhaps, Colgate men "lack the intelligence to take advantage of a chance to hear . . . one of the most brilliant men ever to come on this campus."[77] From Davies's letter, it is apparent that the issue of religious and racial discrimination in Colgate's admissions process was not of great concern to the student body.

Without pressure from Colgate students, faculty, and staff, the university had no reason to change its admissions process; clearly, articles in the *New York Times* and *The American Mercury* were not enough to instigate change either. It would take a New York State law—the Austin-Mahoney bill—to convince Case and his administration that a quota system was outdated, discriminatory, and incompatible with Colgate's goals as an institution of higher learning.

A Legislative End to Discrimination?

In January 1947, the New York State Legislature proposed the Austin-Mahoney bill, "to amend the education law, in relation to the elimination and prevention of practices discrimination in education because of race, religion, color, or national origin."[78] Introduced by Assemblyman Bernard Austin (D-Brooklyn) and Senator Walter J. Mahoney (R-Buffalo), the bill gained support from the American Jewish Committee (AJC) and the New York State Committee Against Discrimination in Education (NYSCADE), but gained the derision of the Executive Committee of the Association of Colleges and Universities of the State of New York.[79]

Father Robert I. Gannon of Fordham University served as the titular leader of those private colleges and universities that opposed the introduction of an anti-discrimination bill. Like President Case, Father Gannon espoused the view that not every American was worthy or capable of benefitting from a college education, especially not the liberal arts model that both men held as its ideal form.[80] Case and Gannon were joined by Eugene G. Bewkes of St. Lawrence University, Edmund E. Day of Cornell University, and President Frank Fackenthal, Provost Albert C. Jacobs, and William J. O'Shea of Columbia University to make up the Executive Committee of the Association of Colleges and Universities of the State of New York. Father Gannon served as its president with John C. Adams of Hofstra University as its secretary-treasurer.[81]

Unlike Case and Gannon, Fackenthal was outspoken in his views about Jews and African Americans—groups he referred to as the "tyrant minorities."[82] Fackenthal believed that America was approaching the end of the Christian Era, a time where man "finds himself trapped."[83] Fackenthal stood against the Fair Educational Practices Act for New

York, which he attributed to "a minority which uses its balance of power to compel special legislation that endangers the welfare of all."[84] Although Father Gannon and President Case were not as vocal about their distaste for minorities, it is clear that they viewed Fackenthal as a valuable ally in the fight against the Austin-Mahoney bill.

Gannon and his buddies disapproved of the bill's two most important goals: an end to discrimination in higher education based on race, religion, or national origin and the creation of a state university.[85] New York's private colleges and universities opposed any anti-discrimination measure because the quota system then in use protected their colleges from an unwanted invasion of Jewish students. To make matters worse, the establishment of a state university was viewed as a direct economic threat that would increase competition and threaten existing public subsidies.[86] Father Gannon voiced his disapproval of the measure and explained his strategy to "appoint a committee, see that it has intelligent members, and depend on the eloquence of the situation to prevent the creation of this absurdly expensive Jewish university."[87]

In a letter to Father Gannon, President Case appeared to take a more liberal stance, emphasizing that "society has an obligation to see that all educational opportunities at every level are available to qualified students irrespective of their racial, religious, or national background."[88] Discriminatory practices, he continued, were symptoms of prejudice and ending prejudice was a worthy mission. His conclusion, however, puts him in complete alignment with Gannon. As ending prejudice in America could not be accomplished overnight, any legislation created for that purpose had no chance at success. In fact, Case reasoned that such legislation could "provoke reactions quite opposite of those which it intends."[89] In place of the Austin-Mahoney bill, he proposed "research into the area of inter-group tensions; joint promotion of programs for intercultural education; and a critical scrutiny of admission procedures with particular reference to discriminatory policies or practices."[90] Case did not elaborate on how universities like Colgate and Fordham could implement such programs, nor what they would do for the returning veterans who wanted to go to college and commence their lives.

In February 1947, Case received a telegram from John C. Adams, the secretary of the New York State Association of Colleges and Universities, urging Case to join in opposing the Austin-Mahoney bill. Adams labeled the bill "premature and prejudicial."[91] Three days later, President Case responded with his approval of Adams's proposal.[92] Soon thereafter, Lindsay Bradford, a Barnard trustee, wrote to Case admitting that he did not expect the Austin-Mahoney bill to gain enough traction to make it out of committee, but expressing concern that he might be wrong.[93] In his letter to Case, Bradford enclosed a copy of a letter he had written to Governor Thomas E. Dewey imploring him to oppose the bill on the grounds that "the independent control of our private educational system is a subject that politics should never be allowed to interfere with it."[94]

Case, claiming that he had misplaced Gannon's letter, replied two months later. Again, he couched his opposition to Austin-Mahoney as resulting from his concern for minorities: "In my judgment, it is a very fortunate thing for the cause of tolerance and the situation of the minority groups that they are spared the reactions which the passage of such a measure would certainly have provoked."[95] The sincerity of Case's concern for minorities is doubtful; what is apparent is his understanding of the legislation as an attack on American values.

In March 1947, Austin-Mahoney failed to pass, mainly due to opposition from the Catholic Archdiocese, which believed that the bill was "un-American" and infringed "on the fundamental rights of parents," adding that it would "seriously affect the freedom of all educational institutions in the State." However, Austin-Mahoney's supporters did not view the bill's failure as a final defeat. Protestors from the AJC and NYSCADE held a sit-in at the state capitol, pushing for the state legislature to reconsider.[96]

In response to rumors that Austin-Mahoney was not dead, Father Gannon hoped to launch a propaganda campaign that would incite greater public opposition. Gannon wrote to Case suggesting that the larger colleges and universities "pool their resources for a campaign of public relations, designed, of course, to influence the Commission indirectly."[97] Case was typically more cautious: in his response to Gannon, he voiced his concern over any large-scale campaign of public relations, fearing that paid advertisements would do more harm than good.[98] Trying, as always, to paint his opposition in milder terms, he proposed a program that would educate the public on the issues without seeming too incendiary or propagandistic.[99]

The result was a handbill, created and distributed by the Republican Club of Forest Hills and Kew Gardens Inc., that highlighted specific passages from the Austin-Mahoney bill and offered critical commentary. The pamphlet argued that the bill would result in "civil rights lost" and "politically appointed one-man hearings" where nothing would be confidential. Overall, it aimed to undermine public support for the proposed legislation by claiming that it violated individual rights and liberties and posed a danger to American democracy.[100] The pamphlet was a slick move: in the aftermath of World War II, Americans were exceptionally proud of the liberties and rights that made American democracy superior. By questioning the constitutionality of the Austin-Mahoney bill, Case and his associates were priming Americans to view it negatively.

Governor Thomas E. Dewey visited Hamilton on June 14, 1947, and gave an informal speech over dinner to Colgate alumni. In his speech, Dewey addressed the struggles faced by higher education in the postwar years, as well as its promise. American education, in his view, could "produce a people with an unshakable faith that the worth of the individual transcends every other material and earthly objective."[101] But he also warned about "the spirit of indoctrination" and "over-sized statism" which turns individuals into slaves."[102] Dewey, like Case, saw freedom and individualism as key principles of American democracy—principles that, though he didn't say so directly, were under threat from Austin-Mahoney.

President Case also spoke at the June 14th alumni dinner, including, among those other bedrock freedoms, the idea of academic freedom."[103] From there, without naming it, he moved to a direct attack on the proposed legislation. The virtue of a private academic institution lay in its ability to decide what is best for the university, without government pressure. Curtailing the freedom of private colleges, such as Colgate, would strike a devastating blow "at every freedom we prize."[104]

On October 6, 1947, Fackenthal sent Case a copy of the first draft of an analysis of the amended draft of the Austin-Mahoney bill, in which he criticized the bill for embodying "serious Constitutional questions." The bill, he warned, might "overturn the public policy of the State and seriously destruct, if it would not destroy, the services of these great New York Institutions."[105] The analysis called allegations of discrimination at New York's colleges and universities "either totally or largely erroneous, " the result of "misunderstanding on the part of candidates for admission who could not be admitted by reason of insufficient academic facilities."[106]

On behalf of the Association of Colleges and Universities of New York State, Case prepared a letter to the Governor's Commission on the Need for a State University that voiced the association's concerns. Case warned that Austin-Mahoney would indirectly undermine the freedom of the association's member institutions to select their student bodies; in effect, Austin-Mahoney would invalidate the achievements of successful applicants and force universities to accept minority applicants instead. Though there is no record of Case ever discussing the Austin-Mahoney with minority groups, he nonetheless spoke on their behalf, suggesting that they too reject the bill for its coercive nature and its ability to create an unfair, "special privilege."[107] Consistent with arguments in the association's previous letters and appeals, Case appealed to the patriotism of the commission and implored its members to reject Austin-Mahoney on the grounds that it would destroy "that academic freedom which undergirds so many of the freedoms all Americans hold dear."[108]

Despite the Association's implacable opposition to Austin-Mahoney, its strategy changed in late November 1947.[109] President Edmund E. Day of Cornell University wrote to the head of the Commission for a State University, Owen D. Young, suggesting that the association was ready to go along with "practically all" of the Commission's proposals. Young was a popular Democrat and a successful lawyer. But what made him most valuable to the association was the fact that he was Case's father-in-law. The relationship between Case and Young enabled the association and the commission to informally share opinions, concerns, and information through letters and telegrams.

In a letter to his father-in-law, Case voiced criticism of the association's strategy, regretting that each institution had not instead advertised how it had progressed and diversified in the past fifty years without government intervention. Had the association pursued this reasoning, it would have revealed

> as no state's survey can the enormous progress we have made voluntarily in opening our doors to youth of every creed and race and origin. For example, in 1900 sixty per cent of our entering class were Baptists, and with negligible exceptions all the rest were Protestants. Today, the Catholics far outnumber the Baptists, and the Jews are not very far behind . . . I suspect in effect that during that period assimilation at the colleges has progressed at a more rapid rate than in the social structure of the nation generally.[110]

With his father-in-law as the head of the commission, Case was in a unique position to voice his personal concerns. He wanted his father-in-law to understand that anti-discrimination legislation was not needed at Colgate, in the hopes that Young would leave each institution to its own devices.

Despite the association's decision to cooperate with the commission, individual members occasionally stepped out on their own. On

February 11, 1948, Case received a telegram from Vic Hamerslag of the *Newark Star Ledger* inviting him to comment on a recent statement made by Father Gannon. Gannon was quoted saying that a third of college students were "useless lumber" and colleges should drop the bottom third of students to make it more difficult to enter college.[111] Not surprisingly, Case was unable to comment as he was "away from campus" and "not expected to return for several days."[112]

By March 1948, Austin-Mahoney splintered off into three separate bills: two creating SUNY and its associated community colleges and the third establishing fair educational practices.[113] On April 4, 1948, after years of fierce debate, Governor Dewey signed all three bills, creating a modest state university and banning discrimination in higher education. However, Case was right: prejudice could not be eradicated overnight. When Colgate could no longer discriminate against applicants due to race, religion, or national origin, discrimination took on new but potent forms. Jewish students who entered Colgate after 1948 in greater numbers were excluded from conventional forms of social life. They struggled to find an accepting and welcoming community at Colgate, a university whose Baptist heritage ran deep. Several decades would pass, and with them multiple acts of resistance and self-affirmation, before a Jewish community would take root and thrive on campus.

Endnotes

1. George B. Cutten, "The Reconstruction of Democracy," *School and Society* 16 (1922): 478.

2. "Mr. James C. Colgate States College Ideals," *Colgate Maroon*, October 18, 1922.

3. Howard D. Williams, *A History of Colgate University, 1819–1969* (New York: Van Nostrand Reinhold, 1969), 2.

4. Williams, 2.

5. "Dr. George Barton Cutten Now Head of Acadia College Chosen President of Colgate." *Colgate Maroon,* May 24, 1922.

6. Williams, *History of Colgate,* 295–298.

7. "President Speaks on Ideal of Education," *Colgate Maroon,* October 1, 1924.

8. Dan W. Dodson, "Religious Prejudice in Colleges," *The American Mercury* 63 (July 1946): 11–12.

9. Jerome Karabel, *The Chosen: The Hidden History of Admission and Exclusion* (Boston: Houghton Mifflin, 2005).

10. This paragraph draws on the insight of Jason Petrulis and his findings presented to a faculty meeting in November 2016.

11. George B. Cutten, "Nature's Inexorable Law–Inequality," *New York Times,* July 1, 1923.

12. Cutten, "Nature's Inexorable Law–Inequality."

13. George B. Cutten, "Shall We Abandon Religion?" *New York Times,* April 15, 1928.

14. Cutten, "Shall We Abandon Religion?"

15. "Education: Cutten's Reaction," *Time Magazine,* January 23, 1939.

16. Cutten, *The Reconstruction of Democracy,* 26.

17. Cutten, *The Reconstruction of Democracy,* 26.

18. "First College Vesper Service Well Attended," *Colgate Maroon,* December 20, 1922.

19. "First College Vesper Service Well Attended."

20. "First College Vesper Service Well Attended."

21. Ronnie A. Grinberg, "Neither 'Sissy' Boy Nor Patrician Man: New York Intellectuals and the Construction of American Jewish Masculinity," *American Jewish History* 98, no. 3 (2014): 131. doi:10.1353/ajh.2014.0030.

22. Karabel, *The Chosen,* 91.

23. Karabel, *The Chosen.*

24. "Calling the Bluff," *Colgate Maroon,* February 14, 1923.

25. "President Speaks on Ideals of Education," *Colgate Maroon,* October 1, 1924.

26. "15 Added to Faculty Under 'Colgate Plan,'" *Colgate Maroon,* August 5, 1934.

27. "2 More Books Out On 'Colgate Plan,'" *New York Times,* January 5, 1941.

28. George B. Cutten, *The Threat of Leisure,* (New Haven: Yale University Press, 1926), 40.

29. R. X. Graham, "The Spirit of a Small College," *Colgate Maroon,* 1924.

30. Clifford M. Weinberger, son of Herald Weinberger, personal communication to Rabbi Dena Bodian.

31. "Calling the Bluff."

32. KWB to Rockefeller Foundation, January 14, 1938. Collection GEB, Folder 6530, Box 618, Series 1, FA058, General Education Board records (GEB), Rockefeller Archive Center.

33. Williams, *History of Colgate,* 304.

34. Karabel, *The Chosen*, 94.

35. Karabel, *The Chosen*, 94.

36. Karabel, *The Chosen*, 94.

37. Colgate University Special Collections and University Archives, A1003, Box 47, Folder 2035, Colgate University Library.

38. Karabel, *The Chosen*, 94.

39. Ruth Gay, *Unfinished People: Eastern European Jews Encounter America* (New York: W.W. Norton, 2001), 64.

40. Sander Gilman, *The Jew's Body* (New York: Routledge, 2009), 22.

41. Pamela Rice, "A Legislative Attack on Educational Discrimination," *The Journal of Negro Education* 23, no. 1 (1954): 106. doi:10.2307/2293261.

42. "President Speaks on Ideal of Education."

43. Sydney M. Schoenberg to Orrin R. Judd, June 15, 1931, Colgate University President's Office records, Special Collections and University Archives, A1002, Colgate University Library.

44. Schoenberg to Judd, June 15, 1931.

45. Orrin R. Judd to George B. Cutten, June 18, 1931, Colgate University President's Office records, Special Collections and University Archives, A1002, Colgate University Library.

46. George B. Cutten to Sydney M. Schoenberg, June 20, 1931, Colgate University President's Office records, Special Collections and University Archives, A1002, Colgate University Library.

47. Cutten to Schoenberg, June 20, 1931.

48. Cutten to Schoenberg, June 20, 1931.

49. Heywood Broun and George Britt, *Christians Only: A Study in Prejudice* (New York: Da Capo Pr, 1974), 87–88.

50. "Trustees Choose Everett Case Colgate Head," *Colgate Maroon*, February 20, 1943.

51. Everett N. Case to James Case, June 15, 1945, Everett Needham Case Papers 1913–1982, Colgate University Special Collections and University Archives, A1015, Colgate University Library.

52. Karen B. Sacks, *The GI Bill: Whites Only Need Apply* (Philadelphia: Temple University Press, 1997), 310.

53. Sacks, *The GI Bill*, 310.

54. "Who We Are," Anti-Defamation League (ADL), https://www.adl.org/who-we-are.

55. Meier Steinbrink to Everett N. Case, August 1, 1945, Office of the Provost and Dean of the Faculty 1928–2012, Colgate University Special Collections and University Archives, A1003.1.2, Colgate University Library.

56. Steinbrink to Case, August 1, 1945.

57. Everett N. Case to Meier Steinbrink, August 1, 1945, Office of the Provost and Dean of the Faculty 1928–2012, Colgate University Special Collections and University Archives, A1003.1.3, Colgate University Library.

58. Lawrence E. Spivak to Everett N. Case, September 6, 1945, Office of the Provost and Dean of the Faculty 1928–2012, Colgate University Special Collections and University Archives, A1003.1.4, Colgate University Library.

59. Spivak to Case, September 6, 1945.

60. Edward J. Van Dyke to Everett N. Case, September 6, 1945.

61. Van Dyke to Case, September 6, 1945.

62. Hubert Reynolds to Everett N. Case, February 2, 1946, Office of the Provost and Dean of the Faculty 1928–2012, Colgate University Special Collections and University Archives, A1003.1.9, Colgate University Library.

63. Reed Alvord to Edward J. Van Dyke, February 7, 1946, Office of the Provost and Dean of the Faculty 1928–2012, Colgate University Special Collections and University Archives, A1003.1.9, Colgate University Library.

64. Adam Clayton Powell to Everett N. Case, April 30, 1947, Colgate University President's Office records 1851–2010, Colgate University Special Collections and University Archives, A1002.1.23, Colgate University Library.

65. Everett N. Case to Adam Clayton Powell, May 11, 1947, Colgate University President's Office records 1851–2010, Colgate University Special Collections and University Archives, A1002.1.23, Colgate University Library.

66. Case to Powell, May 11, 1947.

67. Case to Powell, May 11, 1947.

68. Dan W. Dodson, "Religious Prejudice in Colleges," *The American Mercury* 271 (July 1946): 5–13.

69. Robert D. Leigh to Everett N. Case, June 5, 1947, Office of the Provost and Dean of the Faculty 1928–2012, Colgate University Special Collections and University Archives, A1003.1.29, Colgate University Library.

70. Everett N. Case to Robert D. Leigh, June 16, 1947, Office of the Provost and Dean of the Faculty 1928–2012, Colgate University Special Collections and University Archives, A1003.1.29, Colgate University Library.

71. Case to Leigh, June 16, 1947.

72. Emerson Reck to Everett Needham Case, October 28, 1946, Office of the Provost and Dean of the Faculty 1928–2012, Colgate University Special Collections and University Archives, A1003.1.11, Colgate University Library.

73. William Townsend, "Citizen CIO," *The Crisis* (October 1943): 299.

74. "College Use of Quota System for Entries Vetoed by Weaver" *Colgate Maroon,* March 12, 1947.

75. "College Use of Quota System."

76. Dave Davies, "Letter to the Editor." *Colgate Maroon,* March 12, 1947.

77. Davies, "Letter to the Editor."

78. Frank D. Fackenthal to Everett N. Case, October 6, 1947, Office of the Provost and Dean of the Faculty 1928–2012, Colgate University Special Collections and University Archives, A1003.1.42, Colgate University Library.

79. William B. Leslie, John B. Clark, and Kenneth Paul O'Brien, *SUNY at Sixty: The Promise of the State University of New York*, (Albany: SUNY Press, 2010), 22.

80. Thomas J. Shelley, *Fordham, A History of the Jesuit University of New York: 1841–2003,* (Oxford: Oxford University Press, 2016), 136.

81. John C. Adams to Everett N. Case, October 14, 1947, Office of the Provost and Dean of the Faculty 1928–2012, Colgate University Special Collections and University Archives, A1003.1.21, Colgate University Library.

82. Report, "The Tyrant Minorities," Frank D. Fackenthal, October 13, 1947, Office of the Provost and Dean of the Faculty 1928–2012, Colgate University Special Collections and University Archives, A1003.1.4, Colgate University Library.

83. Fackenthal, "The Tyrant Minorities."

84. Fackenthal, "The Tyrant Minorities."

85. Leslie, Clark, and O'Brien, *SUNY at Sixty*, 22.

86. Leslie, Clark, and O'Brien, *SUNY at Sixty*, 22.

87. Robert I. Gannon to William F. Cahill, January 28, 1946, Fordham University, Robert I. Gannon Papers, Box 3, File 26.

88. Everett N. Case to Robert I. Gannon, January 28, 1947, Office of the Provost and Dean of the Faculty 1928–2012, Colgate University Special Collections and University Archives, A1003.1.15, Colgate University Library.

89. Case to Gannon, January 28, 1947.

90. Case to Gannon, January 28, 1947.

91. John C. Adams to Everett N. Case, February 21, 1947, Office of the Provost and Dean of the Faculty 1928–2012, Colgate University Special Collections and University Archives, A1003.1.21, Colgate University Library.

92. Everett N. Case to John C. Adams, February 24, 1947, Office of the Provost and Dean of the Faculty 1928–2012, Colgate University Special Collections and University Archives, A1003.1.21, Colgate University Library.

93. Lindsay Bradford to Everett N. Case, February 26, 1947, Office of the Provost and Dean of the Faculty 1928–2012, Colgate University Special Collections and University Archives, A1003.1.20, Colgate University Library.

94. TL, enclosure, Lindsay Bradford to Everett N. Case, Thomas E. Dewey, February 26, 1947, Lindsay Bradford to Everett N. Case, February 26, 1947, Office of the Provost and Dean of the Faculty 1928–2012, Colgate University Special Collections and University Archives, A1003.1.20, Colgate University Library.

95. Everett N. Case to Robert I. Gannon, March 13, 1947, Office of the Provost and Dean of the Faculty 1928–2012, Colgate University Special Collections and University Archives, A1003.1.22, Colgate University Library.

96. Leslie, Clark, and O'Brien, *SUNY at Sixty,* 22.

97. Robert I. Gannon to Everett N. Case, April 23, 1947, Office of the Provost and Dean of the Faculty 1928–2012, Colgate University Special Collections and University Archives, A1003.1.24, Colgate University Library.

98. Everett N. Case to Robert I. Gannon, April 30, 1947, Office of the Provost and Dean of the Faculty 1928–2012, Colgate University Special Collections and University Archives, A1003.1.24, Colgate University Library.

99. Case to Gannon, April 30, 1947.

100. Handbill, Austin-Mahoney Bill, 1947, Office of the Provost and Dean of the Faculty 1928–2012, Colgate University Special Collections and University Archives, A1003.1.28, Colgate University Library.

101. "Fight for Ideals is Urged by Dewey" *New York Times,* June 15, 1947

102. "Fight for Ideals is Urged by Dewey."

103. "Fight for Ideals is Urged by Dewey."

104. "Fight for Ideals is Urged by Dewey."

105. Frank D. Fackenthal to Everett N. Case, October 6, 1947, Office of the Provost and Dean of the Faculty 1928–2012, Colgate University Special Collections and University Archives, A1003.1.42, Colgate University Library.

106. Fackenthal to Case, October 6, 1947.

107. Draft, Association of Colleges and Universities, October 6, 1947, Office of the Provost and Dean of the Faculty 1928–2012, Colgate University Special Collections and University Archives, A1003.1.49, Colgate University Library.

108. Draft, Association of Colleges and Universities, October 6, 1947.

109. Eugene G. Bewkes to John C. Adams, November 4, 1947, Office of the Provost and Dean of the Faculty 1928–2012, Colgate University Special Collections and University Archives, A1003.1.50, Colgate University Library.

110. Everett N. Case to Owen D. Young, January 28, 1948, Office of the Provost and Dean of the Faculty 1928–2012, Colgate University Special Collections and University Archives, A1003.1.58, Colgate University Library.

111. Vic Hamerslag to Everett N. Case, February 11, 1948, Office of the Provost and Dean of the Faculty 1928–2012, Colgate University Special Collections and University Archives, A1003.1.63, Colgate University Library.

112. Reed Alvard to Vic Hamerslag, February 11, 1948, Office of the Provost and Dean of the Faculty 1928–2012, Colgate University Special Collections and University Archives, A1003.1.63, Colgate University Library.

113. Leslie, Clark, and O'Brien, *SUNY at Sixty,* 28.

2

The Evolution of Jewish Identities

Kim Ravold

Hindus and Parry: Self-Erasure

The journey of Jewish identity at Colgate begins with Maurice Hindus, a Russian immigrant who became a well-known journalist. Hindus's books, novels, and essays would cover the cataclysmic turns of Soviet politics in the 1930s, documenting various subjects which included the collectivization of peasants, the show trials, and World War II. Unlike so many of the western journalists covering the Soviet affairs of his day, Hindus had an innate understanding of the subject matter and authority over the language, and although he leaned left politically, he was ambivalent about Bolshevism. Hindus also wrote an autobiography that documented, among other things, his daily life as the first Jewish student to pass through the doors of Colgate University.

Hindus speaks little about his Jewish home life in his autobiography, mentioning briefly the three Jewish families that lived alongside his own.[1] Most Eastern European Jews lived in cities or small towns; rural Jews like Hindus were an anomaly, particularly in the Russian Empire, which explains the few Jews that lived in Hindus's village. This small Jewish community didn't seem to have much of an impact on Hindus. He claims to have never noticed any anti-Semitic attitudes from the Belorussian Christians he lived among, citing the shared burdens of poverty as the reason for the village's tolerance toward Jews. Likewise, he believed his upbringing in Bol'shoe Bykovo protected him from the anti-Christian bias that he noticed among Jews from towns and cities. The accuracy of the picture Hindus paints is up for interpretation. It's unlikely that the Jews and Christians of the village lived in harmony in late nineteenth-century Russia when, as a result of government action and general anti-Semitism, the already precarious situation of Jews had deteriorated further.[2] While Jews may have shared "universal experiences with their neighbors: the birth of children, the pleasure of friendship, the pain at the lost of a loved one. . . . Jews were also saddled with legal disabilities that marred their quality of life and impeded their aspirations for greater civic rights."[3]

Hindus did not often refer to anti-Semitism in Russia, still less to the anti-Jewish riots known as pogroms. There is no mention of either in his autobiography, written in 1971. Surprisingly for someone who kept his origins under wraps, he seems to have been less controlled while at Colgate. A piece he wrote for an oratorical essay contest (in which he won second place), mentions both, and holds the Russian Church responsible. The essay uses the Jewish situation to showcase tsarist oppression, and also, quite surprisingly given his populist (pro-peasant) views, is startlingly clear-sighted about peasant motivations:

> The peasant may have no animosity toward the Jew; he and the Jew may be very good friends. But when the priest tells him that the Lord's blood is crying for revenge, and that he himself had heard the cry—the stupid peasant forgets his friendships. He becomes a veritable savage—frenzied and furious. If, as it sometimes happens, the peasants are vacillating, their consciences seemingly disapproving of bloody persecutions, and neither threats nor exhortations on the part of the priest can prevail against them, then the doors of some saloon are thrown open, and what threats and exhortations fail to accomplish, liquor achieves—it stifles the voice of the *moujik's* conscience, it deadens his reason, it smothers the cry of his soul . . . Such is Russia, a great but unfortunate country, a land where justice is

> a cruel jest, where lust is law, where rights, liberties, and privileges of man are myth, where the government fosters, rewards and abets the perpetration of heinous crimes. Tolstoy called his fatherland a government of executions. That is just what it is—a government of pillage, plunder, and persecution.[4]

Hindus's clear distaste for the Russian Orthodox Church never carried over to the Baptist Church. His fondness for the Baptists, acquired in his years in Madison County, was likely a major contribution to his happiness at Colgate.

By the time Hindus immigrated to America in 1905, the small village of Bol'shoe Bykovo was long behind him, and the grand city of New York was his to explore. It wasn't long before his English became fluent enough to attend high school.[5] He chose to attend Stuyvesant, then, as now, a prestigious school with a highly selective enrollment. The principal, in Hindus's recollection asked about his schooling in Russia and declared himself pleasantly surprised by the caliber of the young man's education and "the extraordinarily high academic quality of those Czarist schools."[6] The Stuyvesant principal was, however, flummoxed by Hindus's chosen ambition: farming.[7]

Hindus's longing for a life in agriculture was not dissimilar to that of many Russian Jews who sought a personal and national transformation that would take them out of traditional Jewish life (urban and artisanal or entrepreneurial) and into farming. Am Olam was one such movement, which sought to create agricultural communes for Jewish immigrants in America. Hindus, though, was motivated less by his abandoned Jewish ties and more by his political leanings. Encouraged by the Socialist Revolutionary party, a group that looked toward agrarian socialism and the purity of the soil as an attractive ideal, Hindus set his sights on the vast farmland of upstate New York, specifically the rolling hills of North Brookfield, Madison County.[8] He applied to a farm agency in search of a job, a unique move for a Jewish boy who had just been accepted by an elite high school in Manhattan. Hindus certainly drew a few questions from the agency manager, who was afraid that this city boy would tire of farm work in a few days' time and grow homesick for metropolitan pleasures. Hindus assured the manager that he had no reservations about leaving the city, and when asked about his farm experience, admitted that he had none, but he had seen his father plow and his mother milk cows and was certain that he could learn to do the same. After he convinced the agency manager of his pure intentions, he was hired by a farmer named Jim Moore in exchange for room, board, and fifteen dollars a month.[9]

Hindus would remain immensely fond of his time spent working as a farmhand, milking cows, plowing fields, and eating a great assortment of delicious meals he had not yet encountered. Always cognizant of his village past, he was startled by the amount of food that American farmers ate. He was thankful to be taken in as part of the family, working alongside his employer instead of under him.[10] Most of all, he was thankful for the education that farm life gave him:

> [Jim Moore] flung open the doors of a new world for me, taught me a new way of farming, inculcated in me a set of priceless disciplines, introduced me to a new humanity, and gave me an insight into an America I never should have discovered had I stayed in the city and even gone to college there. Working for him and living in his home was an education I never could have acquired from school teachers or textbooks, an education that in later years, when I began to write articles and books on Russia, proved a sounder guide to the understanding of some of the whys and wherefores of the Soviet revolution than all the works of Marx and Engels or Lenin and Stalin.[11]

Hindus was certain that farming was the work he wished to do for the rest of his life, and in a way, it deeply impacted his career after he decided to change directions and pursue writing. His experiences with rural life in both America and Russia gave him and his commentary an unusual vantage point that distinguished him from other western writers of the subject. His time on the Moore farm opened his eyes to how different farm life could be in America. In the American economy, writes Hindus, Jim would be what Russians would call a *bedniak*, a poor man, but compared to the Russian poor man, Jim was living in luxury.[12] The food Hindus enjoyed with his employer and the land that his employer owned was a stark contrast to a collective farm in the Soviet Union, where "Soviet Russian standards would have invoked on its hard-working and always cash-poor owner the epithet of 'kulak' and would have rendered him subject to liquidation."[13]

Yet, at this point in his journey, writing had not even occurred to him. After three years spent working with Jim Moore, Hindus applied to the Cornell State College of Agriculture with dreams of owning and working a farm of his own someday. It would take a few more pushes to guide him toward a new career path.[14]

The first push came from Cornell, and the second from the local church preacher. Hindus was rejected from Cornell because he lacked the required number of class credits. He had completed three years of high school and had taken fourth year classes under the instruction of a local teacher. Cornell was not satisfied with this arrangement, and though Hindus wrote back to the registrar offering to take the required courses while completing his first year at Cornell, the registrar would not be moved. If Hindus completed an additional year of high school, he would be admitted—a solution that was quite unappealing to the then twenty year old.[15]

It was the local Baptist preacher, Elder Mattison, who pointed Hindus in the direction of Colgate University. Hindus's first acquaintance with the Baptist faith was the community in North Brookfield, which invited him to take part in the services as if he were part of the congregation.[16] His curiosity about his new neighbors would not let him stay away, and though unmoved by the sermons, he loved the songs, a bit of music in an unmusical world.[17] It was here that Hindus met Elder Mattison, a fount of optimism and advice, and—having long cut his ties with Judaism—found a refuge in the Baptist faith. In Hindus's distress over being denied entry at Cornell, he sought solace from Elder Mattison, who knew exactly how Hindus should proceed. Colgate, he said, would have a "proper Christian understanding" when reviewing his application.[18]

Hindus followed the Elder's instruction and applied to Colgate. Though Colgate, too, was wary of accepting a student missing credits, once again Hindus's persuasive talents won out over mere academic standards.[19] Thus, the first Jewish man entered the Colgate community, likely without the school's knowledge, and likely a moment gone unrecognized by Hindus himself. Not only was he the first Jewish student enrolled, he was enrolled despite not being as qualified as his peers, a situation that would not be repeated later. There's no indication that either the admissions board or his peers knew about his Jewish identity—and Hindus was smart enough to keep this part of his life hidden.

The third push toward Hindus's career in writing came from Professor Thomas, who suggested that with his rich and varied experiences as a Russian immigrant and his thoughtful and well-written compositions, Hindus might become a writer rather than a farmer.[20] Hindus had his doubts of course. He couldn't imagine a life that would take him away from the pastoral scene of the farm. He had planned on transferring to Cornell after his first year at Colgate and eventually owning his own land, an aspiration that was already far and beyond anything he could have achieved in Russia. But once again, a Baptist intervention changed his mind. During one Sunday school class, which Hindus seems to have attended voluntarily, the head of the English Literature department, Dr William Crawshaw, substituted for the usual preacher, Professor Thomas. Hindus found Dr. Crawshaw to be a captivating speaker, imparting new meaning to the prayers he was reciting weekly. Hindus determined to take every class Dr. Crawshaw taught.[21] Hindus decided to stay at Colgate, putting himself on the path toward writing.

His change of career path was not the only instance of Hindus's romance with the Baptist church in Madison County. Just before classes at Colgate started, Hindus set out to find work on a farm closer to Colgate than Jim Moore's. Farmer Bronson, a rather reserved man, was distinguished by his love of baked apples and solo hymn-singing late at night. Awakened by the music, which he found pleasingly familiar, Hindus went to investigate. Bronson retrieved a second hymnal and the two voices went on singing in the dead of night.[22]

Life at Colgate proved to be an unexpected contrast to his education in Russia, particularly when it came to the academic habits of his fellow students. Hindus felt strange in this new world full of double standards perpetuated by his peers, who "pretended to be frivolous when they were serious, as though being serious was an offense against good taste. . . . Even when they studied hard, they would not admit it . . . yet [they] were proud of their high marks and of their professor's praise of their scholastic achievements."[23]

His peers' rowdiness was especially alarming when juxtaposed against the discipline of the Russian students of his past life. The disciplined and respectful members of the Russian intelligentsia, writes Hindus, would never have tolerated the behavior of Colgate students. Hazing seemed especially foreign and unnecessary, and isolated him from his peers. The TNEs, a secret sophomore society designed to keep freshmen in check, were especially bothersome:

> I was shocked and scared. My preconceptions of college were rudely shattered. I had pictured it as a place where the intellectual youth of the country—as students were regarded in Europe and especially in Czarist Russia—gathered to pursue their studies in a cloistered atmosphere of high thinking and serious living, and here were the TNEs, a self-appointed gendarmerie,

> enforcing the observance of absurd and humiliating customs on helpless freshmen. Had I come to the wrong college?[24]

What never seemed to set him apart was his Jewish background. Just as in his Russian village, he discerned no hint of anti-Semitism or prejudice against him because of his immigrant status. Again, he attributes this to the rural setting of the school, especially when compared to his past and future home in New York City:

> I could only feel grateful for the instinct that had prompted me at a very young age to flee to the upstate country side, where I would never hear of nor suffer from the snubs and social humiliations. . . . Nor had I encountered them at white Anglo-Saxon Protestant Colgate. Maybe it was because at the time I was a senior there were only four students of immigrant origin there—a Persian, a Lebanese, a German, and myself. There may have been students who thought themselves superior to these foreigners but if so, they kept their sentiments to themselves.[25]

Although it is unknown if Hindus's account of an inclusive, welcoming student body can be trusted, his perception is, at the very least, consistent with the way he chose to remember life in Russia. Perhaps he learned to ignore and steel himself against the prejudices of others. Perhaps students were careful to keep their hateful comments out of Hindus's earshot. Perhaps there really were no such comments made—but one thing that's clear is his belief that if there were biases against him, it would be because of his immigrant status, not because of his minority religious or ethnic roots. Here and throughout his memoir, Hindus separates the Jewish identity he was born into from the Russian identity he grew into and identified with. The student body would have no reason to suspect he was Jewish—Hindus went to church with the rest of his peers, and though he never sought to hide his Russian

Albert Parry, at map, with students and Alexander Kerensky. Kerensky led Russia's Provisional Government following the Revolution of February 1917. He was overthrown by the Bolsheviks in October. Courtesy of Tom and Jim Parry.

background, he had no reason to link it with his Jewish past. There were no Jews at Colgate apart from him, and likely no occasion to test the attitudes of his fellow students to the group he had been born into. Anti-Semitism was not on his radar because it did not affect the way his peers looked at him—so long as his connection to Judaism remained uncovered. He was very aware of the need to keep that part of his life, small as it was a secret.

Enter Albert Parry. The similarities between Parry and Hindus are great in number. Both emigrated from Russia in their youth, both came from a Jewish background, and both found their way to Colgate, Hindus as a student and Parry as a professor. Both wrote about Russian politics and culture. Their paths crossed a few times as can be seen from the postcards they exchanged and it is likely they were friends.[26] It is no coincidence that both Hindus and Parry—and countless other Jews in that generation—changed their names. In Russia, Hindus, born a Yiddish "Moyshe," Moses, became a Russified Moisei. In America, he left the bible behind and became Maurice. Albert Parry, born Avrom (Abraham) Poretsky, abandoned both his first and last names.[27] It's unclear why Hindus didn't change his last name—he might have thought no one would recognize it as a Jewish matronym (Hindes; from the family of Hinde). Parry, on the other hand, left nothing to chance. He wanted nothing to do with his Jewish background or with any religion at all.

Parry, the founder of Russian Studies at Colgate, was born in the city of Rostov in 1901, at an increasingly instable period in the Russian Empire. He watched every person in his mother's extended family leave except for his mother, who didn't want to become a refugee. The Bolshevik Revolution took place in 1917, when Parry was an adolescent, and led him into a early life very different from the tranquility of Madison County. Immediately after the revolution came the civil war, with dizzying changes of power. In 1919, Parry was conscripted by the Whites. He deserted immediately, returned to Rostov with semi-false papers, and hid himself by becoming a printing plant employee for the Reds.[28] When the Whites came back to Rostov, Parry and his brother traveled north with a battalion of Reds. The next morning, the village they had stayed in was surrounded, overwhelmed with White soldiers. One moment, they were sleeping peacefully, believing to have escaped the Whites. The next moment, Parry, his brother, and 58 other civilians and Red soldiers were lined up to be shot and killed.[29] They were marched to the cemetery, each step bringing them closer to death. Hazy, weak, and scared, Parry decided that he would not be among the casualties. He, his brother, and a handful of battalion members took off running through the deep snow, and though they were shot at, the bullets missed.[30] The lot of them would live to see another day.

Eventually he became a writer and photographer for ROSTA, the Bolshevik press agency.[31] It's easy to see why Parry wanted to leave Russia at this point. There was "too much filth, too much sickness, too much uncertainty, savagery, stupidity. [He] longed to go abroad and study in some quiet, clean city, amid cultured, polite people, away from drunken Whites and fanatical Reds, from typhus, from ill-smelling peasants in crowded trains."[32] Russia was suffocating him, and despite his family's wish for him to remain in his home country, Parry sought refuge elsewhere.

Before being drafted by the Whites, Parry had met a young man named Boris Ruzhansky, the son of a Jewish ship captain and shipper of grain. Now Boris told Parry that he and his father were about to sail for Constantinople. "Despite his being a Jew," writes Parry, "Captain Ruzhansky was widely respected and even loved by Russian sailors in all the ports of the South." The idea of a daring, skillful Jewish ship captain was unusual enough to captivate the future professor, who would not otherwise spend much time in his autobiography talking about Jews.[33] At the time, the destination combined with the reputation of the man leading the journey was incredibly tempting. Parry asked Boris if he could sail with them. The younger Ruzhansky agreed to his proposal, saying—in an unexplained reference either to Jews or intellectuals, "I'd love company of my own kind."[34]

The refuge wasn't permanent. Parry stayed only a few months in Constantinople before returning to Rostov, then moving from city to city in hopes of evading the draft.[35] Parry had had enough of Russia. It was time to make his exodus. But by 1920, the coasts of Russia had been blockaded, so there would be no sailing to Constantinople as he had done before. He would have to cross into a non-communist country first, then make his way from there. He used his job at Rostov and a recent illness to facilitate his leave, transferring to the Caucasus before crossing over to Georgia and manipulating the system to gain the proper passport he would need to reach Britain.[36] From there, he would return to Constantinople and then, the great prize at the end of a long and stressful journey: America. It took him a total of ten months, but in 1921 he finally stepped on American soil.[37]

Parry seemed to have always been at odds with religion. At the age of 12, he says, he refused to prepare for a bar-mitzvah, and in his youth he and his friends had little use or appreciation for traditions. His specific discomfort with, and sometimes, according to his sons, hatred of Jews, has an unclear origin. He told them that it came from the legal restrictions placed on Jews in the Russian Empire—though it would be more logical to hate the Russian government—and from the restrictions Jews placed on themselves due to scarce resources. It was an emotional and to a great extent illogical response.[38]

So great was Parry's distaste for his background that he did not tell his own children, Tom and Jim, about his or his wife's Jewish heritage. Parry moved to Hamilton, and Colgate, in 1947. He and his wife, Louise—who had earlier converted to Unitarianism, although she did not go to church—raised their children as Christians. They celebrated Easter and Christmas and the boys were sent to Baptist Sunday School, an attempt on their mother's part to make sure they fit in. Growing up, Jim and Tom had not reason to doubt their Christian backgrounds, an illusion the Parrys maintained by negotiating with the maternal grandparents to make sure that there would be no Jewish friends around when the children came to visit. It wasn't until the 1960s that a family friend told Jim, by this time married with children, that his mother was a Jew.[39] Following this encounter, Jim called his father, and when Albert Parry picked up the phone, Jim asked, "Dad, am I half Jewish?" "Not half," the elder Parry replied. Tom remembers a wry and humorous note to his voice, a tone that suggested, perhaps, a note of pride in the number of years Parry had been able keep the secret.[40] Now, the farce was over. The curtain was dropped. But the real theatrics had only just begun.

Of course, Parry was hiding his Jewishness not only from his children, but also from the Colgate community. In that, he had good reason. Both Parry and Jerry Balmuth refer to a rumor that a music professor was denied tenure because he was Jewish.[41] For Parry, hiding his Jewish background was, among other things, an act of self-preservation. His Russian identity was a different matter. Parry founded the department, often said to be the first such department in an undergraduate institution, and lectured on Russia's history, politics, language, and literature. He also paved the way for generations of Colgate graduates to work for the government, and in particular, the Central Intelligence Agency.

Parry's connection to the CIA was yet another secret he kept from his children until just before his death. His work with intelligence agencies was, however, of long standing. It began with the Office of Strategic Services (OSS) (the precursor to the CIA). As World War II broke out in Europe, he was assigned to keep an eye on the German-American community in the upper Midwest by going undercover as a lecturer and traveling around the region looking for anything out of the ordinary.[42] Then came his work with MI6, which made him part of a covert program to convince the United States to join the war, in part, apparently, by setting up a fake advertising agency.[43] Later, according to his sons, he joined a CIA program that paid academics to write books that would shape American readers' opinions about the Soviet Union.[44]

In addition to his Jewish past and his connections to the CIA there was another secret Parry kept from his children and from the Colgate community: his family. Though Parry presented himself as a man whose Russian-Jewish past was cut off from his American present, he maintained family ties that were as intense as they were distant. During the Russian famine in the early 1920s, Parry not only kept in contact with his family in Russia without his American family's knowledge, but also sent food packages to his mother, father, and siblings still in Rostov. He advised them to make their way westward across the border where Parry would send money and American visas. He managed this successfully for everyone except his mother, who refused to leave.[45] In 1931 the secret police charged her with the crime of private trading and being a "socially harmful element."[46] She was sentenced to three years of exile in Siberia, a sentence that might have led to her death.[47] Parry, remarkably, engineered her release by calling in favors from American leftists like Upton Sinclair, who were well-regarded in the Soviet Union, and by intermediaries in the USSR itself.[48] The end is not completely triumphant: after all she went through in the prisons and after the lengths Parry went to orchestrate her release, his mother decided that she would still rather stay in Rostov. The last years of her life—she died soon after—and Parry's attempts to help her are an emotional focal point of his autobiography, but it is not a story that he ever shared with his sons.

Parry's father had landed in America in 1926 after a grand adventure funded by Parry, again without anyone's knowledge.[49] One year prior, his father's textile business had been destroyed by the government, then transitioning to socialism. The government seized the store. The next day, Parry's father broke in and removed some of his valuables. With the police after him, he fled. Later, when Parry met up with his father in 1926, his father recounted his story:

> "The problem was, where was I to flee? The nearest borders to Leningrad were those of Finland, Latvia, and Estonia. But surely these were the very frontiers where the secret police would be looking for me—to grab me, try me, and either shoot me or at the very least deport me to the labor camps of Siberia. Where wouldn't they be looking for me? In Siberia, of course." So, with faked documents under another name, Father traveled east to Siberia, almost to the end of it, and several months later had the wit and the luck to cross the border into Manchuria.[50]

There, he sent a cable to Parry in New York, who, with his brother and sister in Los Angeles, secured the finances and visa needed for his journey to America.[51] Always the benefactor, Parry helped his father secure a living, but while he was generous with his money, he was always frugal with his words. Nobody on the east coast knew what he was doing.

Maintaining all the while that everyone close to him had perished in Russia, Parry went on to bring other family members from Russia to California. He continued to send money to this family—this was, according to his sons, the likely purpose of the paycheck he received from the CIA. One secret helped him keep another. It was not until 1972 that he brought Tom to see the rest of the family, telling him only the day before the visit that he had close relatives who were alive and in the United States. Parry called his son, a freshman in college, and asked him to come with him to California over winter break. On the plane to Los Angeles, Tom asked, "What is the purpose of this trip?"

"We're going to visit family," Parry replied.

"What family?"

"My family."

"Dad, you said all of your family had perished."

"I never said that."

"So, are these some distant cousins?"

"No, we're going to visit my sister, my niece, and my cousins."

Tom hardly had the chance to get over the shock of finding out his father's family was alive before having lunch with his newly resurrected aunt and cousins, while the Star of David, wrapped in Christmas lights, twinkled above them.[52]

All of this is to say that Parry was an enormously complicated man. He was exceptionally well-connected—even more so when one is reminded that he arrived in America with nothing. It was by his own hard work that he climbed the ranks he did, making a place for himself in secret agencies and top-tier schools. It was also his decision to lead a divided life, not permitting the pain and worry he must have felt at his mother's imprisonment and father's near arrest to spill over into his day-to-day professional life. His children thought of their paternal grandfather as dead. Parry must have preferred that to the idea of him being alive and Jewish.

The emotional toll of keeping his family separate, telling his cousins about his sons but never telling his sons about his cousins, must have been immense. Parry went to great lengths to try to erase his Jewish identity from his life, yet these family members were a constant, significant reminder of that identity and the religion he despised. Caught between a duty to his family and his antipathy for the heritage they shared, Parry could think of no other solution than to keep his Jewish self and his Russian-American self separate, engaging with his students one day and catching up with his relatives another. Parry did not simply reinvent himself as Hindus did; he created a duality within his life. It was a messy, imperfect solution.

But we should not be deluded into thinking that Hindus had all the answers. He, too, had a mind that was divided, constantly comparing his American life to his Russian one, yearning for a life of farming that he never tried to live (as his New York City, West 67th Street address can attest, he certainly had the money to purchase a piece of Madison County and plow the soil to his heart's content).[53] His work and writing should not have been an excuse: other writers and editors, like E.B. White and Katherine White, lived the rural life and corresponded with New York offices by mail. Perhaps his dream had dissipated by the time he was able to live it out. Perhaps it was easier to go into the countryside on vacation rather than commit to the hard labor day after day.

Parry's inner conflict is particularly stark in his unpublished autobiography. He makes no outright mention of his Jewish background and clearly does not want to reveal it to his readers. At the same time, he refers to his father as a successful businessman in Los Angeles—an unlikely landing for anyone but an immigrating Jew. He also talks about his mother as a businesswoman, which, in the Russian context, points quite squarely to a Jewish milieu. Perhaps he didn't think that his American readers would catch the social context, or perhaps the detail would have been discarded in a later draft, leaving his Jewish identity better concealed.

At around the same time as Parry, Colgate hosted one other, very famous, Jewish instructor: poet Louis Zukofsky, who taught for one or two summers including the summer of 1947. Noting Case's disinclination to have a Jew on the faculty, retired University Archivist Carl Petersen says that "they had to slip [him] in the back door."[54] We don't know what Zukofsky, whose upbringing on New York's Lower East Side left him highly attuned to issues of assimilation, thought of Colgate from that particular biographical perspective. His attitude toward Colgate more broadly can be guessed from the poem below, in which campus references are coded in what Margaret Maurer pinpoints as the "diction and archaic spelling" of the sixteenth-century English poet Sir Thomas Wyatt: [55]

LESE-WIAT, FROM CAUL GATE

Caul Gate, Farewell, that hath me bound
And with an ointment laved my teethe
Until mine own voice tired, the sound
A quiet wasting summer's breath

Babylon his flood is stilled
Babel her tower doeth tie my tongue
In the willow path there it hath swilled
My spirit, His case, and young.[56]

Beyond the easily decipherable toothpaste, summer (when Zukofsky taught), and Willow Path, we see references to Case himself and Case's wife Josephine Young Case. Petersen helpfully describes her as "a poet Z would have loathed," the more so that "Everett passed out her books to any writer who came through campus." "Swilled," continues Petersen, "may refer to Case's perpetual round of faculty cocktail parties, attendance mandatory according to Howard Williams. Z was a teetotaler."[57]

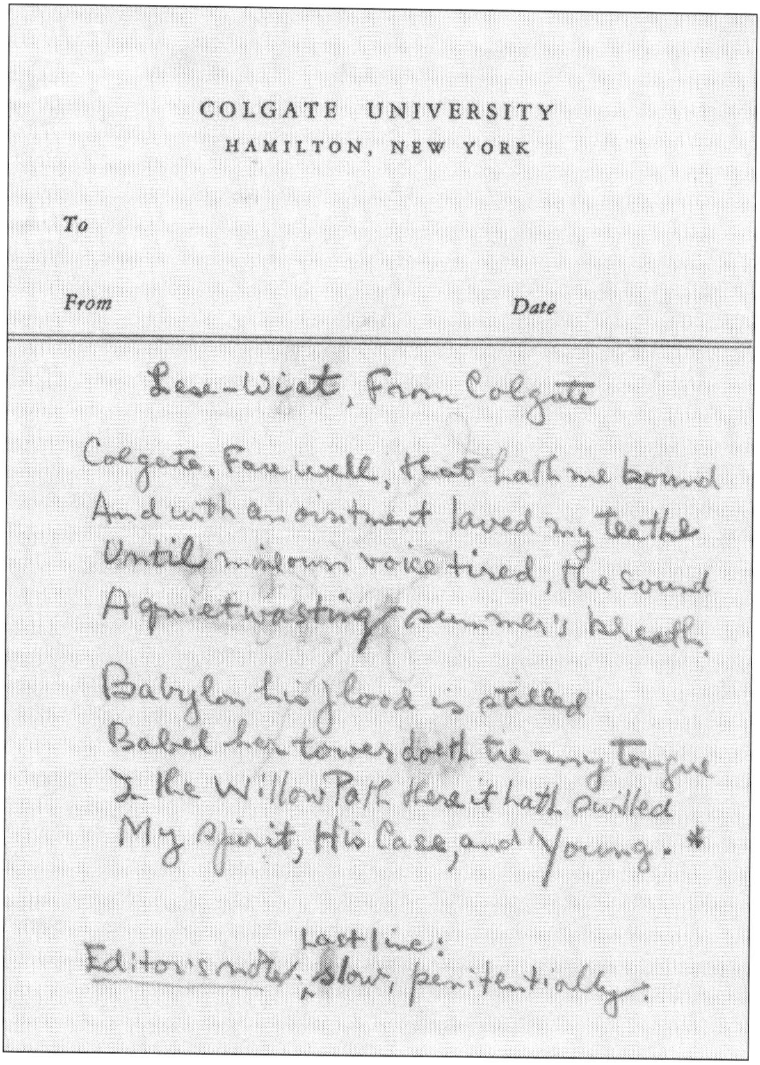
COLGATE UNIVERSITY
HAMILTON, NEW YORK

To

From *Date*

Lese-Wiat, From Colgate

Colgate, Farewell, that hath me bound
And with an ointment laved my teethe
Until mine own voice tired, the sound
A quiet wasting summer's breath.

Babylon his flood is stilled
Babel her towers doth tie my tongue
In the Willow Path there it hath swilled
My spirit, His Case, and Young. *

Last line:
Editor's note: slow, penitentially.

Louis Zukofsky's poem "Lese-Wiat, from Caul Gate" on a Colgate pad. Courtesy of Harry Ransom Center, The University of Texas at Austin.

Zukofsky, on campus only briefly, had no particular need to blend in. Hindus and Parry did, making them an excellent example of how Jews at Colgate and elsewhere reinvented themselves in order to succeed in the American educational elite. Their stories are not uncommon, but they are significant. Jewish self-erasure must be recognized and remembered as the first stepping stone on the path to a strong and positive Jewish identity on Colgate's campus.

Later, it would not be necessary.

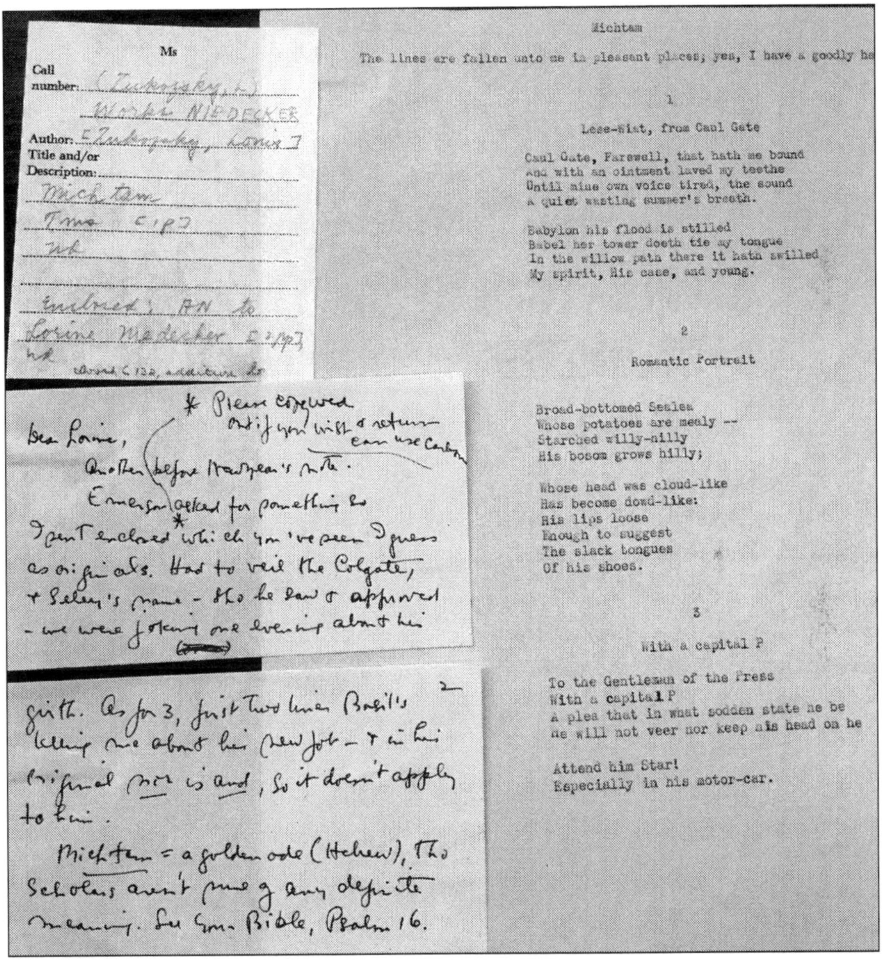

Ms
Call number:
Author:
Title and/or Description:
Michtam

Michtam

The lines are fallen unto me in pleasant places; yea, I have a goodly he

1

Lese-Wiat, from Caul Gate

Caul Gate, Farewell, that hath me bound
And with an ointment laved my teethe
Until mine own voice tired, the sound
A quiet wasting summer's breath.

Babylon his flood is stilled
Babel her tower doeth tie my tongue
In the willow path there it hath swilled
My spirit, His ease, and young.

2

Romantic Portrait

Broad-bottomed Sealea
Whose potatoes are mealy --
Starched willy-nilly
His bosom grows hilly;

Whose head was cloud-like
Has become dowd-like:
His lips loose
Enough to suggest
The slack tongues
Of his shoes.

3

With a capital P

To the Gentleman of the Press
With a capital P
A plea that in what sodden state he be
He will not veer nor keep his head on he

Attend him Star!
Especially in his motor-car.

Dear Lorine,

Michtam = a golden ode (Hebrew), tho scholars aren't sure of any definite meaning. See Jew. Bible, Psalm 16.

"Lese-Wiat," typed, with an explanation of a Hebrew reference. Courtesy of Harry Ransom Center, The University of Texas at Austin.

Perspectives on Anti-Semitism

Many years passed before a significant Jewish presence was felt at Colgate, a consequence of an admissions process that made it difficult for

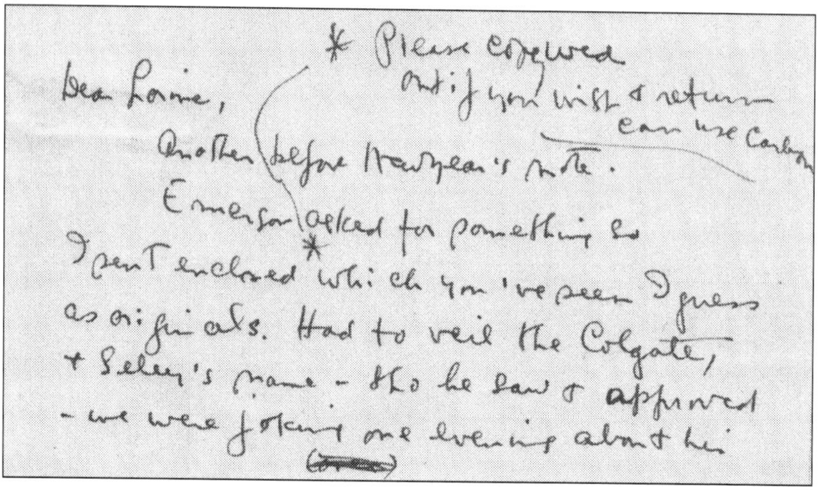

* Please copy word
Dear Lorine, out if you wish & return
can use Carbon
Another before New year's note.
Emerson asked for something so
I sent enclosed * which you've seen I guess
as originals. Had to veil the Colgate,
& Seeley's name - tho he saw & approved
- we were joking one evening about his

A letter from Louis Zukofsky to Lorine Niedecker, explaining that he needed to conceal some Colgate references. Zukofsky's office was 311 Lawrence. Courtesy of Harry Ransom Center, The University of Texas at Austin.

Jews and other minorities to be accepted to the institution. As quotas were dropped and Jewish students grew in number, a new age emerged—in the phrasing of longtime philosophy professor Jerome Balmuth, "the age of Non-Semitism."

At the time of his retirement in 2010, Jerry Balmuth had taught at Colgate and observed Jewish life for 56 years. When he arrived in 1954 he knew of only one other Jewish member of his department. Balmuth saw his hiring as a necessity driven by Colgate's struggle to accommodate the influx of students resulting from the G.I. Bill. If the administration had it their way, Balmuth said, they would not have hired Jews.[58] Officially secular, the campus was still Baptist in heritage. Administrators did not recognize Jewish holidays, nor were they inclined to include Jewish perspectives in campus-wide events such as graduation. Balmuth summarizes the situation this way:

> One didn't talk about one's Jewishness . . . you may have talked about your Christian commitments, which were connected to

Jerry Balmuth.

> the Baptist Church downtown. . . . In fact, the Baptist church and the Baptist minister, at the time, would give the Baccalaureate, systematically, and also would give the invocation for the opening at the Convocation. It took a certain degree of subsequent influence to let him know that not all of the students were Christian, and not even all of the faculty [members] were Christian. It never dawned on him that in giving the kind of benedictions that he did, which were intimately connected with his Baptist origin, that he was effectively leaving out people or excluding people—so there was a sense of non-awareness, of there being diffusion of various backgrounds in the university, that more than anything else, accounted for the fact that Jewish students felt left out in many ways.[59]

Non-Semitism, then, was something like a campus-wide obliviousness, a generally accepted assumption that there was no such thing as a community member who was not Christian. This obliviousness manifested itself in a lack of physical space for Jewish activities, a lack of discussion of Jewish concerns, and a simple failure to recognize that Jews were in fact part of Colgate. This phenomenon is distinct from anti-Semitism in that, in Balmuth's view, it was not driven by outright hostility. There was simply a failure to include Jews and a desire to preserve the image of a Baptist institution. Balmuth's "non-Semitism" is a milder form of the willful self-erasure practiced by Hindus and Parry, but it shares a pervasive Jewish reticence to stand out in a Christian community. "Jewish students never identified themselves at that time," says Balmuth:

> It was always thought to be something to be avoided, that one saw oneself as a minority in the institution. So Jewish students tended to go along, and Jewish faculty, too, went along without raising the question of how to identify themselves.[60]

Only later would Balmuth recognize a few run-ins with faculty members as anti-Semitic instances. As he sees it now, these faculty members seemed to be jealous of the pay Balmuth received for his work with the Carnegie Foundation, a pay they saw as "over and above" and that confirmed their stereotype as a Jew as someone who was always seeking money.[61] Another faculty member who was friendly with Balmuth told him he would never send his daughter to a school in New York City because "they were filled with Jews who were always grasping for grades." Perhaps there was no overt anti-Semitism, but the faculty and administration were still threatened by the mere presence of a Jew amongst their ranks, afraid that these "outsiders" would change the character of the university.[62]

It was for good reason that the benign picture Balmuth painted during his days at Colgate was not shared by everyone who existed within that era. We have only a few accounts from Jewish alumni who were on campus in the 1950s—and these dispute both Balmuth and each other. It is, at this late date, impossible to reconstruct a general picture. The alumni stories discussed below represent individual viewpoints on the domain of student life, each one a telescope focused on a singular or small group experience of Colgate's social and religious climate at the time.

While some students encountered something like Balmuth's non-Semitism, others shared experiences that were closer to the anti-Semitic clashes among the faculty. For Steve Greenleigh, Peter Greenwald, and Al Pasternak, Jewish members of the class of 1957, anti-Semitism was an open part of Colgate social life. At a time when social life revolved around fraternities, Jews could not pledge. The situation at Colgate was markedly different, and worse, than what they had had expected. Peter Greenwald remembers that until his years at Colgate, he had never come into contact with anti-Semitic behavior. It was at Colgate that he was introduced to this attitude, and he cites fraternities as being the driving force behind it.

Fraternities were not the only source of offence. Greenleigh remembers an incident in his freshman year dorm, Stillman Hall, of a fellow classmate looking at his head and saying in serious bewilderment, "You know it's funny. You don't have horns. I don't understand it."[63] (The reference was to the idea that Jews have horns because of their close relation to Satan.) Greenleigh remembers being the only Jewish student in a Philosophy and Religion class, and being nicknamed "Yahweh" as a result.[64] Not only did this name-calling ostracize Greenleigh, but the offense was emphasized by the use of the name of God, which is not pronounced by Jews (the fact that it can be pronounced outside a religious context was probably lost to both Greenleigh and his antagonists, who all understood the move as offensive). Greenleigh also recalls taking an economics class with a professor who had a reputation for being anti-Semitic. Although there were no tests or other graded assignments, Greenleigh received a B, while, he says, every other student was given an A.

Outside of the classroom, in a social scene dominated by fraternities whose charters had restrictive clauses against Jews, Jewish students had even more trouble navigating. Greenleigh, Greenwald, and Pasternak think that as many as 25 Jews enrolled as freshmen in 1952. At the end of this year, they believe, up to eight students dropped out because of the difficult social situation they found themselves in.[65] A handful of Jews managed to pledge to one of the more accepting fraternities, but the remaining students were left to fend for themselves.[66] Although, as we will see in Chapter 4, a non-fraternity living arrangement called the Colgate Commons Club was available to non-affiliated men, Greenleigh found the lack of options unacceptable. As a member of the Student Senate representing unaffiliated men, he strove to change things.

Joined by a few of his affiliated colleagues in the Senate, Greenleigh proposed a bill to eliminate restrictive clauses in fraternity charters preventing minority populations from pledging. This bill was proposed during Greenleigh's senior year, and gave fraternities a timeframe of ten years to eliminate restrictions. Although he would never get to benefit from the policy change, he did have the gratification of working with affiliated members of the Senate to pass the bill, and Pasternak confirmed that the majority of the Student Senate was in favor of it. However, the bill also had to be approved by the Alumni Interfraternity Council. It is unclear if the council ever did.[67]

The three friends agree that while they enjoyed the academic challenges that Colgate had to offer them, their social options were decidedly underwhelming. Pasternak says that he felt like an "outcast," and would not go out of his way to attend a class reunion because he did not feel that he was truly a part of the Colgate community.[68] However, Pasternak, Greenleigh, and Greenwald remain good friends to this day, and regularly make time to have lunch together. There's something to be said for the strength of friendships formed in adversity.

No single representative story can possibly encompass the experience of every Jewish student or faculty member. Hidden in between the anti-Semitism experienced by Steve Greenleigh, Peter Greenwald, and Al Pasternak, and the non-Semitism proposed by Jerry Balmuth lies yet another story, another lens to look through. Jerry Berkson, class of

1958, was very aware of the policies restricting Jews from pledging to a fraternity, but he also has strong memories of positive experiences on campus. A member of the Colgate Commons Club, he has no recollection of any anti-Semitic insults of the type experienced by Greenleigh. He says instead that he and his Jewish peers became friends with Christian students, something he had thought was likely to happen in a community that was both predominantly Christian and geographically isolated.

Berkson attributes the Jewish dimension of his positive experience to the Reverend Robert V. Smith, the campus minister from 1952 to 1988 and a teaching member of the Department of Philosophy and Religion. Berkson describes R.V. Smith as a man with a "very warm personality," a pastor who took care of everyone, regardless of religious affiliation.[69] Balmuth agrees, though in somewhat more qualified terms, calling him "tolerant—a Midwestern tolerant—of Judaism."[70] Berkson, on the contrary, views Smith as his Colgate mentor. Although the Colgate Hillel Foundation was founded in 1948, Berkson did not feel the presence of a Jewish organization, but he had the Reverend and the chapel services he gave. Berkson went to the Sunday services often and remembers them fondly. The sermons, he says, were given in a manner that was as non-sectarian as possible, and afterwards, participants had hot cider and donuts in the chapel basement.

Jerry Berkson met the Reverend Smith on his first day during his very first class, fortuitously a class in in Religion. He remembers Smith pointedly covering the basic elements of Judaism, saying to his students, "You must understand that everybody in this class is Jewish first. . . even if you think you're not," and making it clear that if one is going to understand Christianity, it must be understood from the beginning—from Genesis.[71]

Berkson's gratitude is at once heartfelt and emblematic of a huge curricular emptiness. The Jewish topics that R.V. Smith covered were mostly likely the basics of the Old Testament, and his "Jews" the equivalents—however positive—of Old Testament Hebrews. Smith did what he could to teach his students about Judaism from his Christian standpoint. He was a resource for students who wanted validation of themselves as Jews, but a resource of a very limited, singular kind. No other classes were offered on Jewish sacred texts or religious traditions, and there was no rabbi. Boxed in by Colgate's curriculum, Berkson wasn't aware that there could be an alternative. He was happy with the one presented to him, happy to have the Jewish tradition taught in class in a respectful way, happy to be taught about his religion at all. The topics discussed in class resonated with him years later, making Judaism, as conveyed by this Baptist minister, and his own Jewish identity very much a part of his academic career.[72] Smith even encouraged him to become a rabbi—a path that he considered but ultimately did not follow.

The effect of the non-Semitism Balmuth describes was not limited to faculty and administrators. It started to transform student experiences in the late 1960s, as anti-Semitism gave way to apathy. Thomas Baker, class of 1969, did not experience any anti-Semitic acts or attitudes, but he did notice a lack of courses related to religious life. The disinterest in this aspect of religious experience was not limited to Jewish life, as it affected other religious communities as well. In Baker's view, not only was Colgate non-Semitic, but it seemed to be generally non-theistic:

> There was no institutional Jewish life. . . there were no Friday night or Saturday prayers, no synagogue, no Rosh Hashanah days off or even special services or Yom Kippur. There were a couple of clubs that catered to Christian interests, but none of the Christians belonged to them either. So the entirety of the student body was assimilated and secular. I would say there was almost nobody who even pretended to be interested in religion at all, Jewish or otherwise.[73]

According to Baker, the student body seemed comfortable with formally being largely secular. Although he says he might have participated in Jewish life had it been present, he never felt its absence. Universities, it seemed to him, were places to study. They were meant to be secular.[74]

Students' apathy toward religious life mirrored their apathy—or at the very least, removal—from world events during the 1960s, like the Cold War. While the school did invite speakers to lecture on related topics, and while *Maroon-News* articles were written about world events, student activism was largely absent. Rural isolation made it easy to ignore the world beyond. In this respect, Baker differed from the majority of his peers. He cites milestones connected to world events that helped him recognize his Jewish identity during his time at Colgate. One of these events was the publication of *Babi Yar*, by the Russian poet Yevgeny Yevtushenko, a shattering poem about the Holocaust. The publication of the poem was extraordinary, considering the fact that the topic was, at the time, unmentionable in the Soviet Union. Yevtushenko made a visit to the United States to read his poem at several institutions, and while it is unclear if he visited Colgate, a copy of his poem appeared in the Fall 1961 edition of *The Caliper*, a literary journal published by Colgate.[75] Yevtushenko's poem helped Baker become aware of the fact that he was not simply an American, but a Jewish American.[76] This feeling resurfaced again during the aftermath of the Six Day War, when he received a letter from his roommate congratulating him "on [his] terrific victory."[77] His roommate's words helped Baker understand that the outside world viewed all Jews as homogeneous, whether Israeli or American. This realization seems to have instilled within Baker a sense of kinship with other Jews.[78]

Mark Krinsky, class of 1967, is another Jewish student who immediately noticed the lack of Jewish life at Colgate. Although there was a Hillel, it didn't have much of a presence, which explains why Baker and other students were unaware of it. When Krinsky first joined, there were only six or seven members. There were no Shabbat services or dinners. The club's involvement seemed to be limited to sponsoring a bagel breakfast once a year during parents' weekend.[79] All of this changed when Krinsky, realizing that no one else was stepping forward, somewhat spontaneously asked to take over the club. Under his leadership, Hillel invited a student rabbi to come to Colgate once a month to hold Shabbat services.[80] Membership slowly grew until as many as 20 students attended Shabbat. Krinsky also helped reinstitute a seder, and while it was not the first one to be held at Colgate (which happened in 1949), it signaled a revival of Jewish religion and culture.[81] Judaism slowly began to be a presence among the students.

Though student attitudes during the 1950s and 60s varied, it was clear that there was a growing desire for a Jewish community in the most basic traditional sense—that is, a community headed by a rabbi, or at least someone who knew Jewish texts and Jewish practice. The person to push for this change, breaking through the non-Semitism, anti-Semitism, and mediation through a Baptist minister like Reverend Smith, was Jerry Balmuth.[82]

By this point, twenty years had passed since Balmuth arrived on campus. The population of students who were not Baptist was growing, and they too needed a religious community. As Balmuth remembers it now, while Catholic students had St. Mary's Church nearby, isolated Hamilton had no resources for Jewish students. Among Jews—including, at this point, a new generation of young faculty—the desire to be recognized began to outweigh the social awkwardness of that same recognition. Faculty hoped to have holidays acknowledged, if not officially then at least unofficially. With this in mind, Balmuth campaigned within the Department of Philosophy and Religion for a position that would combine an academic and mildly rabbinic ("counselor to Jewish students") role. He succeeded: department members, he said, were aware of "the religious dimension of the cultural life."[83] It was a step in the right direction, providing leadership and support to a Jewish population that otherwise had none.

Acceptance, Activism, and (mostly) Normalcy

The transition to a sustainable Jewish community didn't happen overnight. The Hillel that Krinsky revived had its starts and stops, which likely stemmed from a dwindling membership or a lack of effective advertising. Not even ten years had passed by since Krinsky's efforts to expand the Hillel membership that Nancy Grossman, class of 1974, arrived at Colgate. She was not made aware of any Jewish community on campus, though she admits that, at the time, she was not looking for a community.[84] This did not stop her from signing up for the 1973 study group to Israel, the year the Yom Kippur War broke out. Grossman and the rest of the group were given the option to return to America to avoid the conflict but chose to stay instead. Despite the uncertainty and danger, Grossman describes the experience as positive and moving.[85] She was not the only one. Susan Stone, class of 1974, participated in the Israel study group with Grossman as one of ten non-Jewish students. Stone says that she never felt uncomfortable as a Christian in Israel who, until that point, had not known any Hebrew.[86] On the contrary, she considered her semester abroad to be an amazing experience that helped her to be more empathetic to her Jewish friends. The 1973 Israel study group was an invaluable experience that positively affected perceptions of Jewish identity across religions. Not only were Jewish students growing into their identity, but students of other religions were acknowledging their identity as well.

One of the most telling signs of the shift toward a Colgate that was accepting of Jews was the hiring of Neil Grabois, Colgate's first Jewish president, in 1988. The fact that he was Jewish, he says, did not come up in the hiring process at all. He knew that the Board was aware of his religion, but they did not seem to find it relevant.[87] The Colgate that hired Grabois was a long way away from the Colgate that had hired Cutten and Case. In a span of 46 years, Colgate's president changed from a man who tried at all costs to keep Jewish students out of the university, to a man who was himself a Jew. As president of Colgate, Grabois was not only a symbol of changed times, he was a man who himself sought change. Grabois's presidency saw the beginnings of the Jewish Studies department and the installation of the Saperstein Center.

Marilyn Thie, a nun and professor of Philosophy and Religion, helped move this change along. She approached Grabois and shared her worries that the university did not have a Jewish Studies department. At Colgate, students could study a variety of Christian subjects, and Islamic Studies was being added to Colgate's curriculum. It was only right, she argued, to make room for the study of Jewish subjects as well.[88] With this in mind, Grabois asked Colgate's Jewish alumni for help in laying the department's foundation.

The alumni refused. Grabois understood them as "a vestige of the earlier Colgate, because these were wealthy Jews who had—in whatever way—made it at Colgate, and were fearful that if Colgate got a reputation for affirmatively wooing Jewish students, that it would come back to haunt [them]."[89] It was an unfortunate side effect of the previous generation's experience at Colgate and in the larger world. But if Grabois could not give Jewish students a place within academic life, he would give them a place outside of it. He secured a space, later named the Saperstein Center, finally giving Jewish students a home on campus that recognized them as a group with a specific religious and cultural profile.

The changes made to support Jewish life on campus had a great impact. In only a few decades, the Jewish community at Colgate, at one time barely acknowledged and rarely celebrated, became the most satisfied religious group on campus according to the results of the Campus Life Survey conducted in 2009.[90] Where once students were discriminated against, subjected to anti-Semitic remarks, and left without a support system of any kind, now students were not only active in their Jewish community, but accepted in the wider Colgate community. This massive shift of contentment was the subject of a sociology and anthropology senior thesis by Rebecca Blake '10. She posited that there were four factor that enabled Jews to integrate into the student body while still maintaining their Jewish identity: the implementation of the Jewish Studies program, the construction of the Saperstein Jewish Center, the acquisition of strong Jewish leadership in the form of both a rabbi and Jewish educators, and the enrollment of enough Jewish students to make the community sustainable.[91] The first three of these factors created a community that prospective Jewish students would find desirable, encouraging a greater number of Jewish students to enroll and in turn fulfilling the fourth.

For students and the parents of students like Suzanne Brock, class of 2001, no college was complete without an active Jewish community. While Brock herself didn't feel the need to seek out information on Colgate's Jewish community, Brock remembers her parents searching through a college catalogue outlining each institution's Jewish aspects.[92] Having grown up in a very Jewish area, Brock initially felt uncomfortable at Colgate after realizing that the Jewish community at Colgate wasn't as big as she was used to:

> I remember my freshman year getting here, and on my hallway not only were there no Jews, but one of the girls who lived across the hall [was] shocked that I was Jewish and had never met a Jewish person before. And, you know, nothing wrong, just ignorant and asking, like, really kind of odd questions.[93]

However, once Brock attended Rosh Hashanah dinner, she made friends and found her place in the Jewish community. Brock has especially fond memories of Shabbat dinners, and considered them to be "a little bit of home, a little bit of calm."[94] She would look forward to cooking Friday dinners with her friends, who would arrange their class schedules every semester to give them time to prepare dinner. It was a highlight of the week.

Joshua Strom, class of 2002, was also looking to go somewhere with a strong Jewish presence.[95] Strom's father was a rabbi, and his Jewish background was an important aspect of his life, so a strong Jewish community was a priority in his college search. Strom was excited to attend his first Shabbat, but found himself to be disappointed. The framework for a strong Jewish community was there, but the student participation, in his view, was lacking, and the services were different than he expected. He felt as though there were more people attending services out of obligation than there were people who genuinely wanted to be there. Strom started thinking about the changes he would make to encourage student participation if he were the rabbi. While he had thought about following in his father's footsteps for a long time, his experiences at Colgate cemented his desire to take that step. The low participation of his peers only inspired him to participate more. One of his most memorable experiences was during his semester abroad in London. Strom led the Passover seder for the students on the trip, and though not every student was Jewish, every student attended the gathering.[96]

Jordie Slutsky Kattan, also class of 2002, offers a different perspective on Jewish life of those same years. To her, the community was a warm and active. Although she was not sure how to get involved at first, she quickly found her footing once her friends convinced her to attend her first Shabbat dinner. She became a member of the CJU's board and made it her personal mission to let the students of the school know that the Jewish community was a place for everybody—regardless of one's level of observance.[97] Together with the other board members, including Joshua Strom, Slutsky Kattan brainstormed for more ways to make the CJU more present and inclusive. This initiative gave birth to Tuesday movie and board game nights, giving the community a place to interact with in a more secular setting.[98]

Before Rebecca Blake, the student who wrote the senior thesis on Jewish contentment at Colgate, arrived on campus, she had not been a religiously active Jew. Because of this, she felt out of place at services but kept going anyway. Blake had a strong desire to connect with her Jewish identity, so when the rabbi at the time, Rabbi David Levy, invited her to go on a Birthright trip to Israel with 45 other Colgate students, Blake jumped at the opportunity.[99] Her parents were less thrilled with the idea:

> They said "Israel is dangerous. You're not going." So I told Rabbi Dave. . . he called [my parents] and my dad, who's

> Jewish, tried to 'out' me, saying "You know her mom's not Jewish, right? She's not really Jewish. She can't go." And Rabbi Dave was like, "Actually, she's the perfect kind of kid we want on Birthright because we want kids who are trying to explore their Jewish identity and maybe don't know much about Israel. That's a perfect candidate for Birthright.[100]

Her parents finally relented, and Blake went to Israel the summer following her freshman year. In a huge shift from the situation a few generations earlier, not only was the community at Colgate accepting of Jewish students, but Jewish leadership was playing an active role in the growth and development of students who were not rooted in their Jewish backgrounds already. Colgate's support was an opportunity that students like Blake took full advantage of. By the end of the trip, she had a renewed desire to connect to her Jewish background. She took classes in Hebrew during the remaining three years of Colgate, minored in Jewish Studies, and wrote the senior thesis just noted, examining the shifting state of Colgate's Jewish community from a sociological perspective.[101]

Like students, the latest generation of Jewish faculty members has also found a more accepting community at Colgate. Noah Dauber, a professor of Political Science, enjoys life at Colgate. In other places like the suburbs, Dauber says, people tend to go home after the day is over instead of sticking around and interacting with one another.[102] He sees Colgate's rural location as facilitating community because colleagues from work with are never far away. He finds the Jewish community very welcoming, and as an observant Jew who does not drive on Shabbat, appreciates being in a place where he can manage easily without that.[103]

When Lesleigh Cushing, a professor in both the Religion and Jewish Studies departments, accepted her double appointment in 2002, she was aware of the somewhat unsettled community—during her first few years, there were a number of different rabbis rotating through—

but she felt confident in joining the community and, like Noah Dauber, has made it work for her.[104] Unlike Dauber, however, Cushing—who has been at Colgate nearly a decade longer—caught the tail end of a distaste for Jews radiated by a few older colleagues. One of them, about to retire, left volumes on the Bible (Cushing's field) to someone else, reserving for her a book with the title "You Bring the Bagels, I'll Bring the Gospel: Sharing the Messiah With Your Jewish Neighbor."[105] In a different instance, after a short lecture she gave in town about the Hebrew Bible and America, she received, from a colleague already retired, a letter questioning her knowledge of the "Old Testament" and insinuating that, as a Jew, she did not have the right to teach local Christians about this text. Although Cushing found these incidents off-putting, she feels that they were isolated events which have not repeated. She sees her department now, with its representatives of many religious traditions, as a place of mutual respect.[106]

With recognition from the University and a support system in place for Jewish students, Jewish identity is able to thrive now in ways it wouldn't be able to before. Problems can still arise, particularly with the calendar. Rebecca Blake finished her senior thesis the same semester that Colgate held its first annual Diversity Week in 2009. Nobody was paying attention to the Jewish community—or the calendar, on which religious holidays are listed—and so the keynote speech was scheduled for Rosh Hashanah. Blake was interested in documenting this case because she found it to be "evident that Jews are not considered one of the minority groups making up this 'diverse' community."[107] For all of the steps Colgate has made to recognize its Jewish community, administrators still sometimes fall back into the attitudes of non-Semitism. Yet as this book was being written in the spring of 2017, a candidate for Dean of Faculty was slated to speak during the first night of Passover. Jewish faculty objected, not expecting anything to change. But, at some cost, the faculty committee, President Casey, and the candidate all shifted the schedule. This was not the Colgate of Balmuth, or Greenleigh, or Parry and Hindus.

With the addition of Jewish spaces in both academic and social life, as well as strong Jewish leadership, Colgate has made itself an attractive option for Jewish prospective students and established an ongoing community. Jewish students are no longer expected to erase their identity in order to conform to Colgate's mainstream culture. Although it took decades, Jewish students finally have "a little bit of home, a little bit of calm" at Colgate.

Endnotes

1. Maurice Hindus, *A Traveler in Two Worlds* (Garden City, N.Y.: Doubleday, 1971), 35.

2. Antony Polonsky, "Relations between Jews and Non-Jews: Historical Overview," *The YIVO Encyclopedia of Jews in Eastern Europe* (Yale University Press: 2008) http://www.yivoencyclopedia.org/article.aspx/Relations_between_Jews_and_Non-Jews/Historical_Overview, accessed May 10, 2017.

3. Chaeran Y. Freeze and Jay M. Harris, eds., *Everyday Jewish Life in Imperial Russia* (Waltham: Brandeis University Press, 2013), 47.

4. Maurice Hindus, Oratorical Essay, 1914, box 3, folder 410, coll. A1014, Student Oratorical and Essay Contests, Special Collections & University Archives, Colgate University.

5. Hindus, *A Traveler in Two Worlds,* 52.

6. Hindus, *A Traveler in Two Worlds,* 53.

7. Hindus, *A Traveler in Two Worlds,* 53.

8. Jonathan Dekel-Chen, "Agriculture," *The YIVO Encyclopedia of Jews in Eastern Europe* (New Haven: Yale University Press, 2008) http://www.yivoencyclopedia.org/article.aspx/Agriculture, accessed May 10, 2017.

9. Hindus, *A Traveler in Two Worlds,* 58.

10. Hindus, *A Traveler in Two Worlds,* 59.

11. Hindus, *A Traveler in Two Worlds,* 58.

12. Hindus, *A Traveler in Two Worlds,* 60.

13. Hindus, *A Traveler in Two Worlds,* 61.

14. Hindus, *A Traveler in Two Worlds,* 120.

15. Hindus, *A Traveler in Two Worlds,* 125.

16. Hindus, *A Traveler in Two Worlds,* 86.

17. Hindus, *A Traveler in Two Worlds,* 86.

18. Hindus, *A Traveler in Two Worlds,* 126.

19. Hindus, *A Traveler in Two Worlds,* 126.

20. Hindus, *A Traveler in Two Worlds,* 151.

21. Hindus, *A Traveler in Two Worlds,* 153.

22. Hindus, *A Traveler in Two Worlds,* 129.

23. Hindus, *A Traveler in Two Worlds,* 138.

24. Hindus, *A Traveler in Two Worlds,* 131.

25. Hindus, *A Traveler in Two Worlds,* 214.

26. Postcard, Albert Parry to Hindus, September 12, 1968, box 2, folder 49, coll. M4038, Maurice Hindus papers, Special Collections & University Archives, Colgate University.

27. Tom and Jim Parry (sons of Albert Parry), interview by Alice Nakhimovsky, January 2017, interview in possession of the author.

28. Albert Parry, "Ask That Your Way Be Long" (unpublished manuscript, n.d.), PDF, 1.

29. Parry, "Ask that Your Way be Long," 4.

30. Parry, "Ask that Your Way be Long," 11.

31. Parry, "Ask that Your Way be Long," 67.

32. Parry, "Ask that Your Way be Long," 21.

33. Parry, "Ask that Your Way be Long," 56–57.

34. Parry, "Ask that Your Way be Long," 57.

35. Parry, "Ask that Your Way be Long," 64.

36. Parry, "Ask that Your Way be Long," 108.

37. Parry, "Ask that Your Way be Long," 57; 110.

38. Tom and Jim Parry, interview.

39. Tom and Jim Parry, interview.

40. Tom and Jim Parry, interview.

41. Tom and Jim Parry, interview; Jerry Balmuth, interview by Richard April and Alice Nakhimovsky, December 2009; videotape in possession of the author.

42. Tom and Jim Parry, interview.

43. Tom and Jim Parry, interview.

44. Tom and Jim Parry, interview.

45. Parry, "Ask that Your Way be Long," 265–267.

46. Parry, "Ask that Your Way be Long," 383.

47. Parry, "Ask that Your Way be Long," 384.

48. Parry, "Ask that Your Way be Long," 404.

49. Parry, "Ask that Your Way be Long," 265.

50. Parry, "Ask that Your Way be Long," 268.

51. Parry, "Ask that Your Way be Long," 269.

52. Tom and Jim Parry, interview.

53. Postcard, Albert Parry to Hindus, September 12, 1968, box 2, folder 49, coll. M4038, Maurice Hindus Papers.

54. Carl Petersen, e-mail message to Alice Nakhimovsky, May 18, 2017.

55. Margaret Maurer, personal communication to Alice Nakhimovsky, May 17, 2017.

56. Louis Zukofsky, *Anew: Complete Shorter Poetry* (New York: New Directions, 2011) 121–122.

57. Carl Petersen, e-mail message to Margaret Maurer, May 12, 1999.

58. Balmuth, interview.

59. Balmuth, interview.

60. Balmuth, interview.

61. Balmuth, interview.

62. Balmuth, interview.

63. Steve Greenleigh, Peter Greenwald, and Al Pasternak, interview by Rachel Cohen, 2017. Recording in possession of the author.

64. Greenleigh, Greenwald, and Pasternak, interview.

65. Greenleigh, Greenwald, and Pasternak, interview.

66. Greenleigh, Greenwald, and Pasternak, interview.

67. Greenleigh, Greenwald, and Pasternak, interview.

68. Greenleigh, Greenwald, and Pasternak, interview.

69. Jerry Berkson, interview by Rachel Cohen, January 12, 2017.

70. Balmuth, interview.

71. Berkson, interview.

72. Berkson, interview.

73. Thomas Baker, interview by Emily Kahn, January 2017.

74. Baker, interview.

75. Literary Journal, Colgate University, 1961, box 1, folder 3, coll. A1125, the Caliper, Special Collections & University Archives, Colgate University.

76. Baker, interview.

77. Baker, interview.

78. Baker, interview.

79. Mark Krinsky, interview by Emily Kahn, December 2016.

80. Krinsky, interview.

81. Notices, *The Colgate Maroon*, April 13, 1949, http://diglib.colgate.edu/cdm/compoundobject/collection/ColgateNP04/id/24716/rec/1.

82. Balmuth, interview.

83. Balmuth, interview.

84. Nancy Grossman, interview by Emily Kahn, January 2017.

85. Grossman, interview.

86. Susan Stone, interview by Emily Kahn, January 2017.

87. Neil Grabois (former Colgate University President), interview by Alice Nakhimovsky, January 2017.

88. Grabois, interview.

89. Grabois, interview.

90. Rebecca Blake, "From Marginalized to Most Satisfied: The Segmented Assimilation of Jews at Colgate University" (undergraduate thesis, Colgate University, 2009), 2.

91. Blake, "From Marginalized to Most Satisfied," 3–4.

92. Suzanne Brock, interview by Chelsea Mohr, October 2016, recording in possession of the author.

93. Brock, interview.

94. Brock, interview.

95. Joshua Strom, interview by Emily Kahn, January 2017, recording in possession of the author.

96. Strom, interview.

97. Jordan Slutsky-Kattan, interview by Alice Nakhimovsky, January 2017, recording in possession of the author.

98. Slutsky-Kattan, interview.

99. Rebecca Blake, interview by Emily Kahn, January 2017, recording in possession of the author.

100. Blake, interview.

101. Blake, interview.

102. Noah Dauber, interview by Amy Balmuth, March 2017, recording in possession of the author.

103. Dauber, interview.

104. Lesleigh Cushing interview by Marit Vangrow, March 2017, recording in possession of the author.

105. Cushing, interview.

106. Cushing, interview.

107. Blake, "From Marginalized to Most Satisfied," 26.

3

Starting Over . . . and Over . . . and Over

| Religious Life and Religious Space |

Dominic Wilkins

No Jewish history can be complete without understanding Jewish religious life, and the story at Colgate is no different. Given the extremely small number of Jewish students, brought about primarily by the difficulty that Jewish students had gaining admission, it is little surprise that there was no formal Jewish religious life or community at Colgate prior to the 1950s. Similarly, the rural character of the Village of Hamilton and surrounding Madison County had not changed much, if at all, since Maurice Hindus first set foot on campus in 1911. As Vanessa Ochs explains, "Hamilton, if you're talking Jewish geography, is nowhere."[1] Though we have seen quotas relaxed over the tenure of Everett Case and Jewish enrollment rise substantially during subsequent presidential administrations, Jewish religious life still had no foothold at Colgate or within Madison County.

While there was an active Hillel hosting events and speakers on campus dating back to 1948, religious practice, as well as institutional support for it, was lacking.[2] The extremely low number of Jewish faculty, one of the only ways outsiders come to Hamilton and Colgate, similarly stymied the creation of any Jewish religious community. Jewish faculty who were present at the time were uninterested in Jewish life, exhibiting the kind of self-suppression and rejection of Jewish identity characteristic of a certain kind of assimilation-minded Jewish immigrant (and particularly exemplified by the case of Albert Parry). Those who suppressed their Jewish identity believed that they had legitimate reason to as we saw in Chapter 2, rumors circulated that one professor was denied tenure in the early 1950s on suspicion of being a Jew. For all these reasons, there was little, if any, faculty assistance in establishing Jewish religious life before the 1970s.[3]

This absence was not necessarily intended or forced, but stemmed from the invisibility of and lack of administration concern for Jewish students on campus. It is part of what Jerry Balmuth describes as "non-Semitism," an arrangement under which Jewish identities simply were not addressed, were ignored and not thought of.[4] Jewish alumni from that period have described an ingrained subtext of hostility toward Judaism. The lack of Jewish community and the foreign nature of the dominant culture at Colgate created a space where Jewish worship and practice felt foreign and out of place.[5]

Beginning in the late 1940s, as the Jewish population began to grow into a sizable minority on campus, this void slowly began to fill. There are records of Passover seders in both 1949 and 1951—though after that there is no mention for almost 15 years—and the first organized Shabbat service occurred in 1951.[6] Charles Winetsky '58, recalled that at his arrival on campus there was nothing, "no spiritual advisor, no organization and no facilities," no synagogue, and no religious life.[7] By his graduation, very sparsely attended Friday night services were held in the formerly Baptist Chapel at the center of Colgate's campus, and school trips were made to celebrate the High Holidays at a synagogue in Utica, New York, roughly 30 miles from campus.[8] By 1967, Mark Krinsky, as president of Hillel at Colgate, helped organize more regular Shabbat services and Passover seders on campus.[9] Around the same time, students and faculty began a push to create a position for a Jewish chaplain whose time would be split between duties as a counselor to Jewish students and as a professor within the core curriculum.[10] This push would eventually culminate in the hiring of S. Daniel Breslauer as the first formal institutional marker of Jewish religious life.[11]

These developments coincided with the development of Chapel House by now Emeritus Professor John Ross Carter. Opened in 1959 and directed by Professor Carter, the space was designed to allow students and community members to explore religious life of many varieties.[12] Specifically mentioning that it aims to create a space for any religious tradition, Chapel House serves as a strong message from the university that religious exploration regardless of tradition can be a valuable part of the Colgate experience.[13] Over its history, the space has struggled to attract student involvement, and increasing the role it plays within the community has long been an aim of religious life leaders on campus.[14] Perhaps most noteworthy within our discussion of Jewish religious life is the omission of Chapel House from the interviews we conducted. Though it has played a part in the experiences of some students and faculty, it was all but a non-factor in the religious life of the Jewish alumni we talked with.

Despite advances over the 1950s and 60s, Jewish religious life still faced significant hurdles at Colgate. Services were small, sparse, and run by students without institutional support. Worship took place within a church that the students took over for only an hour or so each week, where the ambience and architecture was entirely Christian.[15] A space imbued with the worship character of one religious tradition hardly makes for an ideal location for worship in a different religious tradition, yet at this point in Colgate's history, that was the only religious outlet for Jewish religious practice.[16]

It was in 1971 that Colgate as an institution formally began responding to the need for a religious leader for Jewish students through the hiring of S. Daniel Breslauer as "resident rabbi" and instructor in Philosophy and Religion.[17] Rabbi Breslauer came to Colgate with the intent of fostering an active religious community from among the several hundred Jewish students at the university, and saw Colgate as a natural place for Jewish students to discover their religious identities.[18] He spoke of prayer and worship as coming from within an individual, and that he saw himself more as a facilitator for what the community desired rather than as the leader and director of Colgate's Jewish life.[19] He certainly wanted to assist students in their spiritual journey and development and saw Colgate as a place where that vision could be realized. Despite this positive vision at the outset, there was not a strong focus on religious development during Breslauer's rabbinate.[20] He remarked that Colgate "emphasizes personal, private religion rather than public religiousness," and that the Colgate Jewish Union (the Jewish student group then affiliated with the chaplaincy and abbreviated CJU) was far more a cultural and political organization rather than somewhere to explore Jewish religious identity and find spiritual fulfillment.[21]

Jewish religious life would not truly start to carve out its own space on campus until years later with the arrival of Peter and Vanessa Ochs in 1979. Peter, fresh from finishing his dissertation, came to Colgate to fill a split position as both assistant faculty and Counselor to Jewish Students, while Vanessa taught writing courses in what is now "Writing and Rhetoric."[22] It was under the Ochs' leadership that Jewish religious life, both among students and faculty, began to truly exist at Colgate and the surrounding area. They were fundamental in creating the Jewish community and in engaging public Jewish religious life with the non-Jewish dominant community at Colgate.[23] Interestingly, Peter Ochs's position as counselor to Jewish students was funded by the university, rather than by Hillel or another outside organization as is the case at most institutions.[24] Over time this has meant that, at Colgate, Jewish religious life has been a much larger part of the broad religious life at the university than is common at U.S. colleges and universities.

The Ochses came to Colgate contemporaneously with number of other younger Jewish faculty, all under pressure in a tough academic job market to take whatever position was available.[25] These families coalesced to form the core of Jewish life during that period, and it was through their work that a Jewish community began establishing itself in Hamilton.

When the Ochses arrived, they found a Hamilton largely unchanged from that of Hindus's day; the rural, small-town character of the village had remained constant over the years. Vanessa describes it as having felt like Camelot, in a way, as somewhere that was not a real place, somewhere that existed in an idyllic fairytale, cut off from the world. Yet this halcyon vision of Colgate had its darker side. The isolation and emptiness felt by the arriving Jewish faculty was all too genuine, for the idea of Jewish space for religious practice was absent from the broader community.[26]

This isolation did not prevent a small, vibrant community from growing. There was initially no space for Jewish worship or practice. What it boiled down to was that there was no space for the expression of Jewish identities without feeling on display or necessitating continuous explanation.[27] So the young faculty did what they could to create one.

This effort to allow space for Jewish life in the area became the Colgate Hamilton Jewish Community (CHJC), formed in 1979 by the Ochses and other families as a way to connect as Jews.[28] At its height, there were around 35 families, ranging from faculty members to local doctors to farmers from the surrounding villages. All came together to celebrate festivals, discuss various elements of Judaism, and provide support for one another in a very non-Jewish area.[29] Meeting in living rooms—for there was no synagogue or other dedicated space for Jewish religious life (though there was short discussion of establishing a synagogue in the apartment over the village pizzeria)—the CHJC began to create religious life.[30] They began a Hebrew school for about 20 or so children that met in the Colgate Chapel Basement and was staffed by members of the CJU.[31] After a few years, bar and bat mitzvahs began to occur and the community was filled with a vibrancy and vivacity that had never before been seen in the lives of Jews at Colgate.[32]

Vanessa Ochs, in an essay titled "A is for Autopsy, B is for Burial," published in *Moment Magazine* just as the Ochses left Colgate, provides a wryly comic take on crafting this community in Hamilton, in particular hypothesizing responses to a potential death in the community.[33] There was no synagogue, there was no rabbi, and since many of the older Jewish faculty had not strictly kept to traditions, there was no established history of practice.[34] The story of how the CHJC responded to funerary concerns is the story of establishing the Jewish community in Hamilton.

The essay begins at a meeting of the CHJC one evening in the early 1980s in the living room of Dr. Rich Cohen, a local doctor and long-time Kol Nidrei singer at Colgate.[35] As host for the evening, it fell to Dr. Cohen to select the topic of discussion, for which he chose death and Jewish burial as he explained the particular minutiae required should a tragedy strike their local community.[36] Despite the morbid topic, the discussion was lively, and at the evening's end several attendees formed a committee to discuss in more detail how to respond to a death.[37]

This committee (participants originally named it the Committee on Death and Dying but, finding that overly depressing, adopted the traditional Hebrew *Chevra*) prepared protocols to support community members to whatever degree necessary based on their particular circumstance.[38] The Chevra was able to function quite effectively when it first was called on, providing the religious support to the Jewish community that, even five years before, would have been entirely unimaginable.[39] With the creation of the Chevra, the CJHC was able to provide support to its members when they faced death and mourning.

Even still, one question remained for Chevra: how to conduct a burial in Hamilton. As Jewish practice does not require a specialized building for day-to-day Jewish worship, the CJHC had not had a need to construct or formalize one. Jewish burial practices were another story altogether, as the centrality of burial practices to Judaism has meant that the presence of a Jewish cemetery is a traditional marker that a permanent Jewish community has been established in a particular area.[40] The Chevra took on the important task of investigating how and where a Jewish cemetery could be established, a significant mark of the degree to which things had changed.[41]

The students of the 1970s were not quite so concerned with death and dying as the faculty, yet public Jewish life and religious expressions was similarly becoming reality for them through both secular and religious organizations. The Colgate Jewish Union grew as a group within which Jewish students could unabashedly embrace Jewish identity, and the group has generally flourished since then.[42]

The Ochses focused on creating a strong, formal, and visible religious community for Jewish students on campus. Emblematic of this rise in public worship were the open seders offered by the Ochses in the center of Colgate's campus. These seders, which occurred at various times in both the O'Connor Campus Center and Merrill House, brought together Jewish and non-Jewish students and faculty in public celebration.[43] Peter and Vanessa were able to use these events to show "Jewish ritual life to be something really attractive and beautiful and relevant to everyone's lives"; the efficacy of this approach was such that these seders were used by the Introduction to Religion courses as a way of explaining both lived religious life and concepts of ritual.[44]

Yet there was still a lack of formal space for Jewish religious practice, or any place at Colgate that Jewish students had to call their own. The only space set aside for their religious activity was the chapel basement, with the occasional exception of the main chapel for use on high holidays.[45] There was no synagogue within 25 miles of the University, and there was no nearby rabbi to support religious learning. Peter Ochs, though he cared deeply for students and supported them, was split between his role as counselor and as a faculty member, and could not solely provide adequate support for the increasing Jewish student population at Colgate in such a role, for he lacked the formal training to really succeed as a religious counselor.[46] Apart from Ochses, there was a lack of any institutional support for Jewish life, even though the formal institutional discrimination faced by earlier generations of Jewish students had diminished. The Jewish community that formed in the

Students lighting Shabbat candles in the kosher kitchen in the Student Union. From left to right: Sydney Scheinman, Howard Liebman, unknown, unknown, Neal Rosenberg, Howard Sayetta, unknown, Ken Grossman. Colgate Salmagundi, 1974.

CJU developed closeness, but in the context of the wider university, Jewish students who typically engaged in fraternity and more mainstream social life at Colgate kept their Jewish identity under wraps—not so stringently as before, but as something that was just easier to leave behind and not talk about.[47]

Keeping kosher in particular was difficult at Colgate, especially given the communal nature of collegiate dining at an institution not geared toward kosher food preparation and the lack of any kosher butchers. Though not a concern for every Jewish student, those who wished to keep kosher found it practically impossible. It became somewhat easier in 1968 when the National Conference of Young Israel worked with Colgate to provide a separate kitchen and dining facility for Jewish students. Though initially they did charge $500 per year, this charge had been dropped by 1973.[48]

Very few students used the kitchen facilities, which may initially have had to do with their location in Reid Athletic Center, relatively far distance from most residential facilities.[49] Once the kitchen had moved to the Student Union, it was still not often used, likely because it served as a definitive marker of Jewish identity that students may not have been comfortable embracing.[50] Alternatively, the students may have been put off by the $200 price tag for dinners only per semester.[51] Perhaps it was not important to some of the Jewish students at that point, or it may have been a combination of a variety of factors. Elements reflecting a Jewish identity among the student body had begun to emerge at Colgate, yet this happened only for a few students as the choice to participate was still very much a publicly known. The feeling among students at the time was that it was better for one's social life not to be known as Jewish, and this may have closed off options for spiritual fulfillment for the far larger number of Jewish students who did not participate in religious life.

While Peter and Vanessa Ochs did what they could to help establish a Jewish community among the students and faculty, and their efforts were quite successful, they could not remain at Colgate forever, and this in no small part had to do with the inescapable burden of being and representing a minority. Vanessa articulates this when describing the sense of relief that washed over her when she left Colgate, when she was able to throw off the facade of being the model Jew and address her own personal doubts about Judaism. She was "yearning for a place where Jewishness didn't have to be explained," and Hamilton was not that.[52] Both Vanessa and Peter experienced a sense of isolation, and a sense that, in Peter's words, "it was an odd place for Jews to find themselves."[53] They had given what they could to Colgate, had sparked the Jewish students and faculty and begun to build a Jewish community, yet this community, though at Colgate, was not *of* Colgate and thus required a great deal of effort to create and lead, effort that the Ochses could not maintain within Hamilton without intense effort. And so, replicating the high turnover characteristic of collegiate institutions, a new chapter in Jewish religious life at Colgate began.

(For those wondering, despite the strides in establishing a Jewish community made over the course of the Ochs' tenure, there is as of yet no Jewish cemetery in Hamilton or for many miles in any direction.)

The departure of the Ochses in 1986 was a major shift in the story of Jewish religious life at Colgate, though its unintended magnitude would not be fully visible for several years. Peter and Vanessa had been such major forces that their departure left a vacuum seemingly impossible to fill—yet a replacement had to be brought in. On the recommendation of Vanessa Ochs, the person chosen for this task was Susan Schnur.[54]

Vanessa had first become interested in Schnur as a possible replacement after reading an opinion column she had written in the *New York Times*.[55] Schnur's column touched on growing up, coming of age, and discussed the complexities of being a Jewish woman within Judaism.[56] These topics deeply resonated with Vanessa's own struggles with Judaism, and Schnur was hired in 1986.[57] She held a similar position as Peter Ochs, teaching half time in the Department of Philosophy and Religion and serving as counselor to Jewish students.[58] Unlike Peter, however, Schnur did not yet have a PhD. She had been ordained as a rabbi and had successful experience before Colgate expanding Jewish congregations.[59]

Schnur experienced immediate success developing a community at Colgate, both in her teaching and ministerial roles. Her class on Genesis in the fall of 1986 was incredibly popular, and the following spring her class exploring Jewish self-identities so affected students that she is still in touch with many of them now, some thirty years later.[60] She also taught a course over the now-discontinued January term that brought Jewish students (and one non-Jewish student) to New York City to explore urban Jewish identities, and she describes that January experience as enlightening for the students and for herself in uncovering their place in the non-Jewish world.[61]

This exploration of Jewish identities was very much tied to her pastoral role at Colgate. Schnur believed that the most necessary thing for the students when she was at the university was having a place to test their Jewish identities.[62] She felt that, apart from her own efforts, there was nothing at Colgate to help these students.[63] But she did think that the administration was at least tacitly supportive of what she was doing.[64]

Despite her ability to identify student needs, Schnur felt that she was not personally equipped to meet them.[65] She was also not vocationally called to serve as a congregational rabbi, a realization that came as a result of her exploration of her own identity within Judaism over her year at Colgate.[66] Though well liked—even adored—by the students and faculty, and able to continue the community established by the Ochses, Schnur's path diverged from Colgate at this point. In 1987 she left Colgate to pursue a career writing and editing for the prominent Jewish feminist magazine *Lilith*, eventually rising to the position of senior editor before retiring in 2016.[67]

Colgate too moved on, but without immediate success. Rabbi Susan Einbinder faced many of the same pressures but lacked the charismatic vibrancy of Peter and Vanessa Ochs and Susan Schnur. She could not craft a community among students or connect with the Jewish community in Hamilton. Her job was certainly made no easier when the entire board of the Colgate Jewish Union resigned during orientation her first semester at Colgate, and in 1988 Einbinder left Colgate.[68]

Thus in the spring of 1988 Colgate was searching for its fourth counselor to Jewish students in three years. The Jewish religious community that had sprung up while the Ochses were at Colgate had fallen apart in only a few short years.[69]

Some Jewish faculty, distressed that Einbinder had been appointed with no input from the Jews she had been hired to serve, went to see Coleman Brown, University Chaplain and Professor in Philosophy and Religion. A man of surpassing empathy and moral sense, Coleman is a recurring figure in Jewish memories of this period. In this instance, he understood that something had to be done to select a counselor who could support both students and faculty.[70] As the counselor's position included teaching responsibilities in Philosophy and Religion, professors in that department, which included two other Christian ministers in addition to Coleman, had up to this point sole responsibility for the hiring—even though whoever the counselor was had to get along with Jewish faculty and students, especially the CHJC.[71] In the aftermath of Einbinder's ill-fitting year at Colgate and with Coleman's intercession, input from Jewish students and community members was considered in the hiring process for the first time.[72] It was after these changes that Moshe Gresser arrived at Colgate in 1988.[73]

When he arrived at Colgate, Gresser found a community of Jewish people that was not truly a Jewish community. The CHJC would host holiday events with Colgate students a few times a year, but most of the time it provided little support for its members.[74] The students similarly had very little programming and a minimal budget for speakers and events, and though they wanted a more robust life, they felt as if they had nowhere to turn.[75] Jewish religious life existed but not in the way Gresser envisioned that it could, or should.

Moshe Gresser's arrival was a catalyst for change within Colgate and particularly Jewish religious life. A former rock musician, Gresser was completely different from anyone who had been previously seen at Colgate, and he embraced his role as the very public face of Judaism. After finishing his dissertation examining the intersection between psychology and religion at the University of Chicago's divinity school, Gresser had traveled to Israel where he completed his personal return from a secular Jewishness to a strong, lived religious Judaism.[76] Alongside his extensive academic and religious training, his time spent traveling with a rock band gave him the performative experience necessary to succeed in the difficult public role he would find at Colgate.[77]

It was not just that Gresser was intensely Jewish: he was fervently affixed to his Judaism.[78] His beard and kippah made him distinctly visible as a proponent of lived Judaism within the secular and Christian Colgate scenes. Gresser aimed to create space for Judaism to be

Moshe Gresser on the first night of Hannukah, Hamilton village green, 1990s. Courtesy of Matt Berkowitz.

practiced in public, sensing a general feeling shared by both Jews and non-Jews that even if it was allowable to be a Jew, it was somewhat shameful.

One of his first opportunities to publicize Jewish religious life came when he was asked to write a letter to the faculty and administration outlining the Jewish holidays and explaining their place within Jewish religious practice.[79] He wrote four pages describing the proper observance of a great many Jewish holidays, many of which had either not been part of Colgate's religious holiday policy or, in the case of Rosh

Hashanah, had only been observed for one day rather than two.[80] This letter met with disagreement from both Jewish students who had never observed, or in some cases even heard of, some of the holidays as well as faculty who felt that Gresser was overstepping his boundaries in insisting that all of these holidays be observed.[81]

Gresser's push to make Jewish religious life more publicly acceptable was not restricted solely to the students. Hanukah had long been a time when the CHJC had been most active, and over the years they had constructed a large menorah.[82] One Hanukah after Gresser had been able to settle into Hamilton and bond with the adult Jewish community, he cajoled them to hold a public lighting of the menorah on the Hamilton Village Green.[83] The village every year put on a large display in celebration of Christmas, and Gresser wanted to use the menorah lighting as a way to make the town a far more pluralistic rather than a predominantly, if subconsciously, Christian space.[84] The lighting ended up being quite successful and drew a large crowd from both the Hamilton and Colgate communities; Gresser describes it as a "coming out of the closet" and a way to let all know that it was acceptable to be Jewish and to be proud of that identity.[85] There is perhaps no greater example of the effect Moshe Gresser had on galvanizing Jewish life at Colgate than that an unprecedented four students from the Classes of '91, '92, and '93 entered rabbinical training following graduation.[86]

Though Gresser was central to the creation of Jewish life and loved by many students, his disruption of Colgate's normal patterns did not come without resistance.[87] The letter concerning Jewish holidays pushed the envelope and caused clashes with faculty—clashes that continued as Gresser continued to attempt to carve a space in which Judaism could be openly practiced without embarrassment or shame around non-Jews.

Gresser's emphasis on public display and on his interpretation of lived Judaism caused frequent strain with the broader Colgate Jewish community.[88] Early on in his tenure, Jewish students who felt that the CJU was overly religious formed the Association of Jewish Students as a social alternative where religion was not an emphasis.[89] His insistence on celebrating what students saw as minor holidays, on constantly talking about Judaism, on dressing and acting and eating in a manner strictly consistent with Jewish law, marked him as someone who was anathema to stereotypical Colgate culture. This caused discomfort among those in the Jewish community who were reluctant to publicly identify or push against the status quo.[90] Many Jewish alumni at the time were uncomfortable with Gresser's interpretation of lived Judaism and felt disconnected from his understanding of how Judaism should be practiced.[91] Gresser pushed Jewish life in a way that was quite foreign to Colgate and to much of American Judaism, and consequently discord sparked as to the 'correct' way Judaism was to be practiced at Colgate and in Hamilton.

The non-Jewish community at Colgate also pushed back against Gresser's public Judaism. The primary debate Gresser had within the university was over the role of religion in public space.[92] Gresser envisioned a pluralistic Colgate where a variety of different religious traditions each were able to express themselves, yet the dominant vision throughout the various strata of the university envisioned space as ideally independent of any religious character.[93] Gresser's major rebuttal to this point, apart from his own argument that pluralism was generally better for all members of a society, was that Colgate, due to its heritage as a Baptist school, the perspectives of its former presidents, and the dominant social culture within the university, was at its core still tacitly a Christian space, even if official affiliation had dissolved.[94] Gresser held that, without outward and public expressions of Jewish religious life, the institutional non-Semitism and invisibility traditionally found at Colgate could not be resolved.[95]

The clash over the permissibility of religion in Colgate's space came to a head when Gresser and the CJU wanted to construct a sukkah on the Quad to celebrate Sukkot.[96] Though there had been a sukkah on campus in the past, it had always been on the old golf course, far from the heart of campus—Gresser wanted to change that and to bring Jewish celebration to the center of Colgate.[97]

Colgate students split campus into two distinct categories: there is "up the hill," where first and second-year students live, classes are taught, and most community and religious activities happen, and there is "down the hill," dominated by upper-class residential and social life and separate from "official Colgate" as an academic university. The Jewish students wanted their religion to be "up the hill" and constructed a sukkah on the side of the old Baptist chapel where Jewish life at the time was housed.[98] This construction met with little formal resistance, and Professor Steven Kepnes brought his classes on Jewish philosophy and world religions to the sukkah as an example of practiced and lived Judaism.[99]

The next year Gresser wanted to bring Judaism more to the fore and constructed the sukkah on the academic quad at the center of Colgate's communal life, where it could not be missed by anyone. For some members of the Colgate community, this pushed public religion and Judaism too far beyond where they felt it belonged. Many people felt that Gresser was "Judaizing" communal space, while Gresser saw the construction of the sukkah as a way to make Judaism publicly acceptable and to show Jews at Colgate that they could take space for their religious practice—that they could have a religious community and be part of the broader Colgate community at the same time.[100]

Jewish religious life is necessarily influenced by events affecting the broader university, and on occasion these larger events combine to dramatically change the broader narrative for Colgate's Judaism. It was during Moshe Gresser's time at Colgate that one such series occurred, and it in no small part defined his time at the university. Afterwards Jewish life at the university would never be the same.

The first of these events was a lecture given by Kwame Ture (born Stokely Carmichael) in January, 1991. Though active in a number of civil rights movements both within the United States and across Africa,

Ture gave a number of speeches during the 1990s that took rather antagonistic views toward Judaism and toward Zionism.[101] Over the course of that decade these speeches drew the ire of the Anti-Defamation League in New York, and he became widely known for his anti-Semitism in addition to his work for civil rights.[102]

When Colgate's Jewish students learned that Ture had been invited to speak, many were shocked and scared by the idea that one of his notorious lectures would take place at Colgate. For the CJU, letting Ture's presence pass unnoticed was not an option.[103] They coordinated with the African American Students' Association to place CJU student leaders in the front row of the lecture. A number of other students and faculty, both Jewish and non-Jewish, came to Ture's lecture with a similar mindset of opposition. As the lecture drew near, the campus had become quite tense.

Those who feared that the lecture would take a controversial and antagonistic stance toward Judaism saw their presuppositions fulfilled. During the talk, which will be discussed at length in Chapter 5, Ture spent a great deal of time focusing on his belief that Zionism was "an enemy of the people."[104] He framed Judaism as originally African and saw its modern practice as a corrupted, pervasive extension of Western imperialism.[105] In the talk Ture took a negative view of Israel, argued that Jews were not a people, reduced Judaism to a form of idolatry, and contended that Zionists had colluded with Hitler.[106]

As Ture began taking questions, the room became a shouting match over his position on Judaism. Matt Berkowitz, who at this point was president of the CJU, describes the "utter shock and paralysis that this was happening" reflected in the faces of many in attendance.[107] The event had turned into an ugly mess of anti-Zionism and anti-Semitism that rocked the Jewish community to its core.[108]

The impact was immediate. Tensions among Jewish students, alumni, faculty, and administrators that had sprung up over the proper place of Judaism on campus largely subsided as the community focused on how best to respond to this aggressive display. Jewish students and alumni convened to discuss the future of Jewish life on campus and what was needed to foster a stronger community.

The response took the form of a rather lengthy list of the ways in which Jewish life could be improved at Colgate. At the very top, however, and far more important than the remainder of the points, was the need for a Jewish space on campus. Matt Berkowitz recollects that the general tone of all at the meeting was that "we need a home . . . we need Jewish space."[109]

With the necessity for such a space for Jewish community and religious life established, the community debated the best way to proceed. Gresser and many of the students wanted to immediately move forward and do as much as possible. While they were initially met with concern from some alumni and other members of the Colgate community who argued that moving so quickly would hamper their efforts, the side pushing for immediate change won out. They were pleading for a space to call their own, a space where they could be themselves.

This group reached out to President Neil Grabois, who though by no means as public about his Jewish background as Gresser or Ochs, was able to support the students in their efforts to find a home. Though not active in religious life, he was at ease with his Jewish identity and sympathized with those students who felt left in the lurch. Grabois saw the creation of a space as a way in which Jews at Colgate could begin to feel more secure.

Much of the push for a Jewish space from the Jewish community found support from people at Colgate who were not Jewish. Principal among them was Marilyn Thie, a Catholic nun and longtime professor in the Philosophy Department. In conversations with Grabois before the Ture lecture, she had been pushing for a Jewish Studies professor, and in the lecture's aftermath, she expanded her lobbying to push for a Jewish space on campus.[110] Her urging on both of these issues bolstered the cries from within the Jewish community and helped convince Grabois that addressing these concerns had to be a central issue for the university.[111]

Grabois, who had been in contact with a number of Jewish alumni while trying to develop a Jewish studies program, reached out to see if a principal donor could be secured for a new Jewish center. He initially was met with a great deal of reluctance from many alumni who felt that publicizing Jewish life would diminish Colgate's reputation rather than enhancing it.[112] Grabois was eventually able to convince Michael Saperstein '62 to take the lead, and they decided to convert an old equipment shed that had been used for a number of cultural organizations into this space for Jewish students. In 1992 the process of creating the center began.

In January 1993, Jerry Balmuth wrote an article in the *Colgate Scene* describing the future of Jewish life in light of the new center. Central to the article—though he does not use the term here—is his idea of "non-Semitism." As he puts it here, while Jewish identity was permissible within the university, "young people, for all their talk otherwise, don't take easily to being different," and being Jewish at Colgate was a major difference.[113] The Jewish center helped "contribute to the insistence that differences and commonality are not incompatible." It was a move toward the formation of a Colgate community that celebrated both inclusion and the uniqueness of each constituent part.[114]

Dedication ceremonies for the Saperstein Center were planned for the weekend of April 16–18, 1993. The planning committee for the center had crafted it be the heart of Jewish life on campus, serving the "religious, academic, social and communal needs" of the Colgate and Hamilton Jewish communities.[115] All forms of Judaism were to be encouraged. It had taken only two years since Kwame Ture's lecture for the Jewish community to carve out a space on Colgate's campus solely dedicated to its religious and communal life.

In preparation for the opening ceremony, in March 1993 the Jewish community published the first volume of *Kol Gate* (Hebrew for

"Voice of the Gate"), a newsletter focusing on Jewish life at Colgate. Many of the influential voices within Colgate's Jewish community contributed an article, beginning with Neil Grabois, who wrote that "when Jews come together to praise God, they are reinforcing the ties that bind the community." Steven Kepnes discussed the ongoing process of developing a Jewish Studies program that by this point was well underway. Matt Berkowitz and Robin Schaer, both Class of '93, describe their experience at Colgate as "continually explaining what it meant to be Jewish." Arriving on campus, they found themselves "adjusting to life at Colgate on two fronts—both to fit in as first-years and to reconcile our Jewishness at a predominantly Christian institution." They hoped the center would provide a home for future generations of Jewish students and allow them to feel part of the Colgate community without facing pressure to conform and forfeit their identity.[116]

When April rolled around and the center had been completed, it was time for a celebration of Jewish community. Invitations were sent to Jewish alumni around the world, and many made plans to return to Colgate. The Ochses made the journey back to speak about the history of Jewish life at Colgate. Chaim Potok, a prominent rabbi and eminent Jewish author, came to the university to speak at the dedication and discuss Jewish life and especially Jewish studies.[117]

Thomas Dine '62, who at that time was the executive director of the American Israel Public Affairs Committee (AIPAC) and a leading member of the Colgate Jewish alumni community, was the featured speaker at the dedication dinner. Dine began by speaking about how the Saperstein Center allowed the community to have a permanent presence on campus for the first time. Like so many others, he recalled his time at Colgate as permeated by "an emptiness in my encounter with my Jewish identity, " but anticipated that the center would allow the Jewish community at Colgate to thrive in ways that he had not previously thought possible. Touching on how "being Jewish without support often turns people away from the faith," Dine saw this center as a place where Jewish religious life would be able to flourish in a permanent space rather than a Christian space temporarily set aside for Jewish worship.[118]

Dine also spoke more broadly about establishing a community that would endure regardless of external pressures—though he did not specify what those might be. Dine pushed the Colgate Jewish community to continue establishing their formal presence on campus in five major ways. He argued that developing a Jewish Studies program, fostering pro-Israeli activism, increasing campus programming alongside collective community action, and starting a Jewish Studies summer institute for high school students would be the benchmarks on which the establishment of Colgate's Jewish community would be measured. While Dine's use of Israeli activism as a necessary standard is difficult to separate from his position at AIPAC, the other four pillars directly stem from his time as a Colgate undergraduate. As we will see in the following chapters, some of Dine's goals were quickly met; others were not.[119]

The emotional height of the celebration came when the Torah scroll was carried across campus to be placed in the Center for the first time. Installing a new Torah in any place involves dancing, singing, and celebration as the scroll is brought it, for it signifies the Jewish religious nature of the space. At Colgate, the celebration included a recognition of the weight of past history and the university's remarkable reorientation. Indeed, when the time came for Michael Saperstein to lead the procession, he was almost unable to. Overcome with emotion, Saperstein began to cry as he brought the scroll into its new home. So much had changed since his days at Colgate—Judaism, long encapsulated by a sense of absence and embarrassment at the university, now had a place to call its own. No longer were Jews interlopers in Christian space. At least within the Saperstein Center, Judaism was unabashedly part of Colgate.[120]

President Brian Casey, speaking with the writers of this book in Spring 2017, made an interesting observation about Colgate's history: when groups that that had no space succeed in fighting for one, they have often been given spaces in basements. At present, the Saperstein Center is on the first floor of a building dominated by Human Resources, the Center for Women's Studies is in the basement of East Hall, the organization for LGBTQ students on campus occupies a similar sort of space, and the chapel basement today functions as the meeting space for Buddhist, Hindu and Muslim groups in the same way it functioned for Jewish students in the past.

Though the opening of the Center owed a lot to Moshe Gresser's work, his time at Colgate was drawing to an end. Gresser and his family made good on a plan they had postponed during the Colgate years, and left for Israel later in 1993. His time at Colgate had seen significant changes for Jewish religious life, many of them for the better, and he left a Jewish community far more vibrant, energetic, and established than when he arrived. Though the impetus for this change had been building up for well over a decade, it was in the early 1990s that Colgate's Jewish community saw a paradigmatic shift into the life of mainstream Colgate.

Since 1993, Jewish religious life at Colgate has been far more visible as a crucial part of the campus's religious experience. This has paralleled a shift throughout the broader university toward more ecumenical religious experience, with many different faiths hosting joint events and openly discussing religious questions. Judaism is far more public and unabashed than it was thirty years ago. The vibrancy of the community still fluctuates depending on who is leading the community, but the presence of the Saperstein Center means that even when the community has lacked a charismatic leader there has been a sense of religious community. A Colgate without Jewish religious life is at present unimaginable, which is a dramatic shift from before when it could only be found among strangers temporarily occupying Christian space.

It is easy to see the effect that "the Sap" has had on stabilizing Colgate's Jewish community. Rachel Lutwick-Deaner '97 remembers her social life revolving around the center. It afforded her a community that "added a lot of warmth and love" to her time at Colgate.[121] Caryn

Fields '08 thought of Jewish religious life as a crucial part of her collegiate experience but not as something that completely took it over. Fields recalls that the Jewish students she knew were all mostly invested in non-Jewish social groups, but the Sap stood out as a place where they could come together and find a home.[122] No longer did students have to spend all of their time reinventing Jewish community on campus in order to have some connection with their religion. Such a group would be there whenever they wanted it, but it would no longer disappear if one student stepped away for whatever reason.

The remainder of this chapter will tell some stories about this more ecumenical Colgate. Though these anecdotes cannot capture every detail from the past twenty years, together they represent the broad arc of recent Jewish religious life.

Rabbi Joan Friedman, who served at Colgate from 1994–2000, helped guide the Jewish community as it moved into this ecumenical modality. Over her time at Colgate there were around 600 Jewish students on campus, but only a few dozen were frequently involved in Jewish religious life.[123] It was difficult for them to acquire kosher food, which had to be ordered from Albany—a practice that continues to this day.[124] There were difficulties with caterers and interactions with members of the Colgate community who simply did not know much about Judaism. Yet despite these challenges, Jewish life at Colgate was in a relatively comfortable and stable position.

Friedman remembers developing interfaith life, especially with the Catholic community on campus. While Gresser's pluralistic vision for Colgate had helped enliven the Jewish community, his emphasis on developing Judaism resulted in interfaith concerns being somewhat overlooked. Friedman instead turned outward and attempted to develop a strong connection to other religious life communities. Despite this, when she left in 2000, she felt that there was still a gulf between Jewish life and Colgate's Christian communities that had not been bridged.[125]

As Friedman could not maintain the Jewish community herself, she relied on support from several students. Key to those efforts was Noah Wintroub '98, who Friedman remembers as having raised Shabbat dinner attendance to an average of fifty students per week when he was leading the CJU.[126] Wintroub's influence helped develop Jewish life, but after he graduated regular attendance dropped to its present norm of roughly thirty students per week.[127] Religious life flourished through the work of exceptional student leaders. Yet when these leaders could not be found—or were more invested in other facets of campus life—religious life maintained itself at a comfortable baseline, whereas in the decades before it would have been all but non-existent.

The epitome of the changes surrounding Judaism at the university can be seen in a story from the mid-1990s. Lauren Braun '98, a former president of the CJU, was a major figure in Jewish life over the course of her time at Colgate. In the fall of her sophomore year, she met Sean Costello '97, whom she began dating the following semester. Because he was Catholic and she was Jewish, she did not expect the relationship would lead to anything serious. When they continued dating over the course of her semester abroad the next fall in Geneva, Braun and Costello began seriously discussing what their life would look like if they did end up marrying.[128]

As they began this discussion, Braun and Costello reached out to Rabbi Friedman and Father John Donovan, the Catholic chaplain. Both campus ministers believed that it would be better not to split the household religiously, and Braun and Costello agreed. Realizing that Braun was deeply rooted in her Jewish identity while Costello had lapsed away from Catholicism, Father Donovan suggested that, if he was going to remain in this relationship, Costello ought to convert to Judaism for the benefit of any future children they might have. "I know we've lost you," he said.[129] Though he did not immediately take Father Donovan's advice, Costello did eventually convert, and he and Braun remain married to this day.[130]

A Catholic priest suggesting to a Catholic student that he leave Catholicism in order to raise a family within Judaism is an unlikely scenario today, and would have been unthinkable even in the recent past. That this happened at the university shows both the development of an interfaith community that would have sent Colgate's Baptist founders spinning in their graves and the degree to which Judaism had become part of that communal fabric.

The roots of this ecumenism can be traced to Coleman Brown and his work decades before to crease a supportive community among Colgate's chaplains. Realizing that their vocation was incredibly trying, especially at somewhere as isolated as Colgate, Brown frequently brought the chaplains together to discuss common challenges.[131] As a major force at Colgate from the time his arrival in 1970 until his death in 2014, Brown shaped the university and counseled students and faculty from all traditions. He is the one figure who comes up again and again in conversations with presidents (Neil Grabois), chaplains (Peter Ochs) and students privileged to know him. In a memorial essay, Douglas Lavine '72 wrote about Brown's deep reverence for Judaism, and how he inspired the Jewish students he taught to explore their religion.[132] Brown, first and foremost, wanted students to have a home and a place to be secure in themselves, and he set the tone that allowed Colgate to develop what is now a strong interfaith community.

Mark Shiner, who became the Catholic campus minister in 2004, has continued fostering the interfaith community at the university. The first non-Protestant to lead Colgate's religious life, Shiner instituted the concept of a rotating chaplaincy under which primary leadership alternates among Catholic, Protestant, and Jewish chaplains.[133] This rotation has helped to break apart the subconscious hierarchy prioritizing Christianity to the exclusion of other traditions and has helped give Jewish religious life a more central role within the university.[134] The strong interfaith community has allowed many more students to benefit from religious life than would have happened had communities had remained separate.[135]

Support for the interfaith community has continued ever since. Rabbi David Levy, who was at Colgate for four years beginning in 2007 and was a galvanizing presence for both students and faculty, also played a major role in developing Jewish interfaith ties. Rabbi Dave's aim was not to ignore differences between the traditions but to have them come together through shared religious values. He and the other chaplains helped organize a "Faith Week," when students would go to events hosted by other religious communities and participate in "their thing." Levy saw this as an opportunity for students in their own religious communities to come together as valuable constituent parts of the broader Colgate community.[136]

The vitality of the interfaith community was particularly evident in February of 2008. Shabbat only falls on the 29th of February once every three decades, and Levy helped organize a special Shabbat to commemorate the occasion. The CJU rented out space in the ALANA Cultural Center and packed in hundreds of students, Jews and non-Jews alike, for Shabbat and a broader discussion about what the Jewish community at Colgate was about. Like the massive seders organized by the Ochses, Leap Year Shabbat was primarily an exercise in "public space Judaism." It had the intention, and the effect, of raising awareness of Judaism throughout the Colgate community.[137]

There have been notable structural changes in how the Jewish community fits into Colgate's religious life. Beginning just over a decade ago, the Heretics' Club was established by the presidents of religious life organizations as a forum for discussing general questions about religion. It now hosts a weekly lunch series, in which speakers from the Colgate community and the world at large discuss their religious traditions and experiences in an explicitly interfaith setting. The Heretics' Club has strong support from all religious life organizations on campus, and serves the collective community in ways that an organization tied to a particular tradition cannot. In a similar way, interfaith activity was on display in the early 2010s when the chaplaincy organized a student bus to New York City to protest the ongoing tragedy in Darfur.

The shirts they wore bore the slogan "Many Faiths, One Belief: Stop Genocide."[138]

Colgate's religious life is remarkable among higher education institutions in the United States as the university employs the chaplains and funds the various clubs and organizations. At many universities this happens through Hillel, the national Muslim Students' Association, or another group, and as a result there is very little overlap between religious organizations. Colgate's funding of religious life provides an opportunity to bring together people who likely would not interact with each other, and it creates a lively and connected interfaith community.[139]

Related to this internal funding has been the broadened role of the rabbi across the university. For over than a decade, a Jewish chaplain has at times served as an administrative leader for the Muslim, Hindu, Buddhist, and secular student associations.[140] They help the Muslim students procure Halal meat, assist in organizing ongoing lunch speaker series, and have helped organize many of the major celebrations across religious traditions.[141] The leadership by a Jewish chaplain of other religious life organizations is a far cry from the days in which Jews at Colgate had to rely on Christian ministers for their own religious guidance. These organizations are in a similar situation to Jewish students half a century ago, and are working to carve out their own niches at Colgate. They face many of the same struggles (low numbers, limited funding, reliance on ever-changing student leadership) as Jewish students did historically, yet the progress made by Jewish life suggests at least a possible road forward. The path taken by Jewish life is not the only one, and we hope that the path these groups take is not filled with the same negative experiences that have historically plagued Colgate's Jews. Yet the similarities between these groups as outsiders at the university are noteworthy, and it is a mark of how much the situation of Jewish religious life has improved that the rabbi is now called upon to help guide them.

The overall level of interfaith activity, and the participation by all of Colgate's religious groups in it, is far higher than might be expected at somewhere like Colgate, and Judaism has a major part of that community.[142] Judaism is somewhat separated from the rest of the religious life communities since Jewish students have the Sap and do not spend as much time in the Chapel basement, but they do spend time and do attend events hosted by non-Jewish religious groups.[143] Spirited interfaith life has brought about a far deeper sense of community and connection among religiously-oriented students than could have been imagined before. In that respect, Jewish and non-Jewish students alike have had the opportunity to benefit and grow at Colgate.

Even despite this, problems persist in Jewish life at Colgate. One of the most common concerns from alumni has been the small size of the Jewish religious community on campus, even as roughly 12% of the university's student population is Jewish.[144] In the buildup to his first Shabbat dinner as a new student at Colgate, Joshua Strom remembers looking forward to finding a lively community filled with many students from all over the university.[145] Yet when he arrived for dinner, Strom was shocked and disappointed by paucity in attendance.[146] Numbers did creep up at points, and on occasion around fifty students would attend, but this was still a far cry from the few hundred Jewish students at the university.[147] In the late 1990s and early 2000s, the CJU was not able to put on much programming apart from weekly Shabbat dinners, observation of the High Holidays, and the occasional bagel brunch. There was a Jewish religious community, but not as much a social one.

Due to the small size of the active community, and general ignorance about Judaism among faculty, students and staff, unintentional conflicts persist. As we will see in Chapter 5, there have been issues with catering bringing in non-kosher food and conflicts over scheduling during religious holidays.

Outside of the campus, Colgate and Hamilton still have very little in the way of formalized Jewish religious life. The nearest synagogues are in Syracuse and Utica; to find a kosher butcher or a synagogue, you have to travel very far.[148] Jewish professors at Colgate mostly leave to celebrate the holidays, which are often, quite inconveniently, mid-week.[149] While non-student Jews no longer confront a structural system that actively works against Judaism, they do face loneliness and lack of community.[150] The activities of the CJU and presence of Colgate's rabbi do not necessarily provide sufficient religious outlet for Jewish residents who seek a deeper and more stable community—or who simply have different concerns than Colgate's students.

The low level of Jewish participation is not particularly abnormal when compared to that of other religious life organizations at Colgate or colleges across the United States. Over the past several decades, religious practice within elite colleges and universities has become far more private and far less central to daily life.[151] Religiously unaffiliated universities function primarily as secular institutions even when the vast majority of faculty at the institution are religiously affiliated themselves.[152] As religion declines in importance for quotidian life, religious life organizations can similarly expect lower attendance and less active participation.[153]

This trend can also be seen broadly in the declining religious affiliations of college-aged U.S. students. Data gathered in 2014 by the Pew Research Center has shown that, among those born between 1990 and 1996—basically, among Colgate's student body in 2017—religion is only "very important" to 38%.[154] This is a sharp decline from previous generations of students, though it is represented as a general trend within the survey's data.[155] Alongside this, the overall percentage of American adults who identify as religiously affiliated has dropped by seven percentage points even since 2007.[156] The decline in both religion's importance and religious affiliation may together explain the low numbers of active students within Colgate's religious life communities over the past decade. The problems faced by Jewish life at Colgate are the same ones that confront collegiate religious communities across the United States. No longer are they evidence of the lack of institutional support that proved so challenging to Colgate Jews historically.

I do not want to give the wrong impression of the current state of religious life at Colgate. There are still vibrant communities for any students who chose to participate. For those invested in Judaism, Colgate provides the facilities, budget, and broad support necessary for their success.[157] Students are constantly moving in and out of the Sap, the weekly Shabbat dinners and monthly bagel brunches are well publicized and have consistent attendance, and on the high holidays a large number of Jewish students come together. The CJU allows students to grow in their faith as well as allocating space for them to practice practical skills, whether keeping kosher or serving on a synagogue board as CJU leaders, that will allow them to successfully participate in a Jewish community following their graduation.[158] Jewish students participate alongside other religious traditions in interfaith dinners and their contributions are welcomed within the broader community of religious life. Judaism is no longer an exceptional or abnormal religious tradition at the university—it is part of the dominant narrative of Colgate's religious life. It is just that Colgate's religious life overall is now smaller than it has been in the past. Jewish students are able to grow and connect with their tradition, and even if they do not actively participate in religious life, its presence in the background adds security and a sense of comfort to far more than just the active membership.[159]

The status and prominence of Jewish life at Colgate has dramatically increased over the past half century. Forty years ago, for all intents and purposes there was nothing, no support or place for anyone at the university, even for those who wanted it. Through the intense effort and leadership of far more men and women than we could mention in this chapter, Jewish religious life has gained a foothold at the university. There are of course still difficulties that spring up, and both Colgate and the Village of Hamilton remain predominantly Christian spaces. Yet the Jewish members of the Colgate community have been able to make the university a home for however long they remain here, and while it may not be a perfect home, it has become a place where Judaism can exist with pride.

Endnotes

1. Vanessa Ochs, "A is for Autopsy, B is for Burial," *Moment Magazine* (1986): 42.

2. "The Hillel Foundation. . . ," *Colgate Maroon*, March 16, 1949.

3. Jerry Balmuth, interview by Alice Nakhimovsky and Richard April, December 2009, videotape in author's possession.

4. Balmuth, interview.

5. Gilbert Simon, interview by Emily Kahn, February 16, 2017.

6. "The Hillel Foundation. . . ," *Colgate Maroon*, April 13, 1949, "Colgate Hillel to Hold Sunday Service at Inn," *Colgate Maroon*, April 18, 1951, and "Hillel Sponsors First Friday Eve' Services at Colgate," *Colgate Maroon*, March 7, 1951.

7. Charles Winetsky, personal communication with Dena Bodian.

8. Winetsky, personal communication.

9. Mark Krinsky, interview by Emily Kahn, December 27, 2016, recording in author's possession.

10. Balmuth, interview.

11. Randi Glickberg, "Colgate Acquires First 'Resident Rabbi'; To Teach Core 170, Hebrew Scriptures," *Colgate Maroon News*, September 14, 1971.

12. "Chapel House Vision Statement," last updated April 27, 2015, http://www.colgate.edu/about/facilities-at-colgate/chapel-house/about-chapel-house/vision-statement.

13. Rabbi David Levy, interview by Dominic Wilkins, April 28, 2017.

14. Levy, interview.

15. Winetsky, personal communication.

16. Balmuth, interview.

17. Glickberg, "Colgate Acquires. . . "

18. Glickberg, "Colgate Acquires. . . "

19. Glickberg, "Colgate Acquires. . . "

20. Susan von Hoffman, " 'Is God Dead?' Not at Colgate Religious Organizations Active," *Colgate Maroon News*, February 25, 1975.

21. Von Hoffman, "Is God Dead?"

22. Peter Ochs, interview by Alice Nakhimovsky, January 6, 2017, recording in author's possession.

23. Chris Vecsey, interview by Alice Nakhimovsky, February 7, 2017, recording in author's possession.

24. Levy, interview.

25. Vanessa Ochs, in discussion with the author, April 27, 2017.

26. Balmuth, interview.

27. Rabbi Vanessa Ochs, interview by Alice Nakhimovsky, January 6, 2017, recording in author's possession.

28. Richard April, interview by Dominic Wilkins, February 13, 2017, recording in author's possession.

29. April, interview.

30. Vanessa Ochs, "A is for Autopsy, B is for Burial," 42.

31. April, interview.

32. April, interview.

33. Vanessa Ochs, "A is for Autopsy, B is for Burial," 42.

34. April, interview.

35. Ochs, "A is for Autopsy, B is for Burial," 42–43.

36. Ochs, "A is for Autopsy, B is for Burial," 43.

37. Ochs, "A is for Autopsy, B is for Burial," 43.

38. Ochs, "A is for Autopsy, B is for Burial," 43–44.

39. Ochs, "A is for Autopsy, B is for Burial," 44.

40. Ochs, "A is for Autopsy, B is for Burial," 45.

41. Ochs, "A is for Autopsy, B is for Burial," 45.

42. Barbara Brooks, "Colgate Celebrates 60 Years of Jewish Life." *Colgate University*, November 28, 2008, http://news.colgate.edu/2008/11/colgate-celebrates-60–years-of.html/.

43. Vecsey, interview.

44. Vecsey, interview.

45. Vanessa Ochs, interview.

46. Peter Ochs, interview.

47. Peter Ochs, interview.

48. David Wall, "Kosher Kitchen Enables Jewish Students to Observe Dietary Laws," *Maroon News*, April 3, 1973.

49. Peter Ochs, interview.

50. Wall, *Maroon News*, 1973.

51. Wall, *Maroon News*, 1973.

52. Vanessa Ochs, interview.

53. Peter Ochs, interview.

54. Vanessa Ochs, interview.

55. Vanessa Ochs, interview.

56. Chris Vecsey, *Jews and Judaism in the New York Times* (Lanham, Maryland: Lexington Books, 2013), 151.

57. Vanessa Ochs, interview.

58. Susan Schnur, interview with Dena Bodian, January 13, 2017, recording in author's possession.

59. Schnur, interview.

60. Schnur, interview.

61. Schnur, interview.

62. Schnur, interview.

63. Schnur, interview.

64. Schnur, interview.

65. Schnur, interview.

66. Schnur, interview.

67. Schnur, interview.

68. Dan Levin (former leader of the CJU), interview by Abe Benghiat, June 8, 2016, recording in author's possession.

69. Chris Vecsey, interview.

70. Alice Nakhimovsky, personal communication with the author.

71. Chris Vecsey, interview.

72. Nakhimovsky, personal communication.

73. Moshe Gresser (former Colgate counselor to Jewish Students), interview by Anat Guez, January 9, 2017.

74. Gresser, interview.

75. Levin, interview.

76. Gresser, interview.

77. Gresser, interview.

78. Gresser, interview.

79. Gresser, interview.

80. Gresser, interview.

81. Gresser, interview

82. April, interview.

83. April, interview.

84. Gresser, interview.

85. Gresser, interview.

86. Levin, interview.

87. Gresser, interview.

88. Gresser, interview.

89. Gresser, interview.

90. Gresser, interview.

91. Gresser, interview.

92. Gresser, interview.

93. Gresser, interview.

94. Gresser, interview.

95. Gresser, interview.

96. Rabbi Matt Berkowitz, interview by Anat Guez, January 9, 2017, recording in author's possession.

97. Gresser, interview.

98. Gresser, interview.

99. Gresser, interview.

100. Gresser, interview.

101. Abraham H. Foxman, "Black Activist Disparages Jews," *New York Times Opinion Pages*, March 11, 1996.

102. Foxman, "Black Activist."

103. Berkowitz, interview.

104. Kwame Ture, public lecture, Colgate University, February 5, 1991, Colgate University Archives A1061.2.22, Colgate University Library.

105. Ture, lecture.

106. Ture, lecture

107. Berkowitz, interview.

108. Gresser, interview.

109. Berkowitz, interview.

110. Neil Grabois (13th President and first Jewish president of Colgate University), interview by Alice Nakhimovsky, January 10, 2017, recording in author's possession.

111. Grabois, interview.

112. Grabois, interview.

113. Jerry Balmuth, "Professor of Philosophy Jerome Balmuth considers the imminent prospects of a Jewish Center at Colgate" *Colgate Scene*, January, 1993, Colgate University Archives A1319.1.1, Colgate University Library.

114. Balmuth, "Professor of Philosophy Jerome Balmuth considers."

115. Saperstein Jewish Center By-Laws, 1993, Colgate University Archives, A1319.1.2, Colgate University Library.

116. *Kol Gate (Voice of the Gate)* 1.1, March 1993, edited by Jyll Lottner and Jennifer Markson, Steven Kepnes private collection.

117. Steven Kepnes to Chaim Potok, April 2, 1993.

118. Thomas Dine, "Saperstein Center Dedication," keynote address, dedication of the Michael Saperstein Center, Hamilton, NY, April 18, 1993, speech text in Steven Kepnes private collection.

119. Dine, "Saperstein Center Dedication."

120. Grabois, interview.

121. Rachel Lutwick-Deaner, interview by Emily Kahn, January 8, 2017.

122. Caryn Fields, interview by Dena Bodian, January 10, 2017.

123. Joan Friedman, interview by Dena Bodian, January 27, 2017.

124. Friedman, interview.

125. Friedman, interview.

126. Friedman, interview.

127. Friedman, interview.

128. Lauren Braun Costello, interview by Emily Kahn, January 3, 2017, recording in author's possession.

129. Braun Costello, interview.

130. Braun Costello, interview.

131. Vanessa Ochs, in discussion with the author, April 27, 2017.

132. Douglas Lavine, "Remembering Coleman Brown," *Colgate Scene* April 26, 2015, 4.

133. Levy, interview.

134. Levy, interview.

135. Levy, interview.

136. Levy, interview

137. Levy, interview.

138. Levy, interview.

139. Rabbi Dena Bodian (current Associate Chaplain at Colgate), interview by Emily Kahn, May 6, 2017.

140. Levy, interview.

141. Bodian, interview.

142. Lesleigh Cushing, interview by Marit Vangrow, February 17, 2017, recording in author's possession.

143. Bodian, interview.

144. Rebecca Blake, "From Marginalized To Most Satisfied: The Segmented Assimilation of Jews at Colgate University," (Honors Thesis, Colgate University, 2009).

145. Joshua Strom, interview by Emily Kahn, January 6, 2017.

146. Strom, interview.

147. Suzanne Brock, interview by Chelsea Mohr, June 7, 2016.

148. Carol April (founding member of CHJ), interview by Kim Ravold, March 16, 2017.

149. Noah Dauber, interview by Amy Balmuth, February 21, 2017, recording in author's possession.

150. Dauber, interview.

151. Neil Gross and Solon Simmons, "The Religiosity of American College and University Professors," *Sociology of Religion* 70.2 (2009), 124.

152. Gross and Simmons, 124.

153. Gross and Simmons, 109.

154. Pew Research Center, "America's Changing Religious Landscape," May 12, 2015, 5.

155. Pew Research Center, 5.

156. Pew Research Center, 4.

157. Jordan Slutsky Katan, interview by Alice Nakhimovsky, January 13, 2017.

158. Bodian, interview.

159. Levy, interview.

4

Fraternal Living without a Fraternity

| The Evolving Social Life of Colgate Jews |

Emily Kahn

World War II had been over for more than forty years, but at Colgate in 1988, a fraternity pledge could walk into a room that would transport him back to that time. Surrounded by flags from America, Great Britain, Japan, and Nazi Germany, Delta Upsilon pledges were confronted by a brother dressed as Adolf Hitler, complete with the infamous mustache drawn in ballpoint pen. By the 1980s, Jews had made strides in gaining admission to fraternities. Even Delta Upsilon had approximately five Jewish members.[1] But the cheerful repurposing of Nazi symbolism struck many Jews as a physical symbol of the decades of discrimination they had faced from Colgate's Greek system. Individuals at Colgate remained oblivious of a central fact of Jewish history, perpetuating the need for Jews to find social outlets beyond Greek fraternities (or eventually sororities). Many Jews joined quasi-fraternities, a term coined by Gilbert Simon '58 in reference to social organizations available to unaffiliated students.[2] Within quasi-fraternities, Jews could embrace their Jewish identity unabashedly while gaining social opportunities on Colgate's campus.

Fraternities

They were "outcasts."[3] At a school where more than eighty percent of the student body was affiliated with a Greek organization in the middle of the twentieth century, Jews were peripheral members of the community due to their exclusion from the fraternity system.[4] Literally, they had to live in off-campus housing away from the excitement of Broad Street, Colgate's fraternity row. Figuratively, they had very little social capital and remained unseen by the preppy, athletic fraternity men who dominated the campus.[5] Some Jews were content with their unaffiliated status. Peter Greenwald '57 was "unimpressed" by the "playboy" mentality of the fraternity men and saw his independence as a way to focus more on his studies.[6] Other Jews also chose work over play on a campus that valued play over work, caring more about getting into a good medical or law school than into a fraternity party.[7] Bernie Siegel '53 knew that his chances of admission were limited and chose not to waste his time trying: "You weren't persecuted, but you didn't exist. So you never got into a fraternity if you were Jewish. . . If you were just a Jewish student, you're not getting into a fraternity."[8] Jews settled for a social life of football games, eating, and driving off campus where they actually existed for parties and dates.[9]

Colgate was aware of the fraternities' discriminatory practices.[10] But there was little the institution could do: all of the Greek fraternities were owned by national chapters and were subject to national policies, many of which remain secretive to this day. Students, as we will see in Chapter 5, attempted repeatedly to eliminate discrimination from the Greek system in the 1950s and '60s. Most of these attempts failed to produce lasting change, as the administration and Board of Trustees had little control over national fraternity policies. Yet even if Colgate had possessed autonomy over the fraternities, the university's leaders seemed comfortable perpetuating the values of muscular Christianity within the Greek system.

According to a 1958 report by the Alumni Interfraternity Council, of the fifteen fraternities at Colgate, only six had no discriminatory clauses.[11] This was an improvement from the previous decade but was still not enough to instill confidence in Jews attempting to join the Greek system. Two of the most accepting fraternities were Tau Kappa

Epsilon and Phi Kappa Tau, both of which attracted Jewish students. At this time, four fraternities retained unit rules or gentleman's agreements—"an agreement that no charter can accept any person who is unacceptable to any single chapter in the national organization."[12] Jews, barely able to gain admission at Colgate, were barred from Colgate social life by the bylaws of dozens of non-Colgate charters. The remaining five fraternities had racial and religious restrictions, only permitting white Christian males to join.[13] Individual Jews managed to gain entry into these five fraternities, but, as a collective, Jews were excluded. Phi Delta Theta, the most discriminatory fraternity, had a house on one end and Tau Kappa Epsilon had a house on the other end of Broad Street, allowing the spectrum of acceptance to be visible from the top of campus.

Tau Kappa Epsilon (TKE) stood out for its inclusive policies. It was founded as a non-discriminatory local fraternity in 1952, less than two years before the Student Senate passed a resolution to eliminate fraternal discrimination within ten years.[14] In 1955, the Colgate chapter of TKE formally affiliated with the national organization.[15] TKE was more welcoming and transparent than any other fraternity at Colgate. In the first *Maroon-News* article published on TKE, vice president Jay Stoner '53 declared that the fraternity had no restrictive policies "either open or concealed."[16] TKE lived up to this statement. Mark Krinsky '67, who was instrumental in reviving Jewish life at Colgate, was a member of this "basket of liberalism and Jewish guys."[17] He recalls that about fifty percent of the men in TKE were Jewish and the majority of the African American population pledged TKE as well. In addition to its achievements in diversity, TKE was often the top fraternity house in academics and athletics: Krinsky and his fraternity brothers "were really proud to tell these all gentile jock houses that Jewish guys could play intermural sports also."[18] The year after Krinsky graduated, TKE became the first fraternity at Colgate to dissolve all required pledge activities and hazing.[19] Yet TKE's commitment to equality was ultimately its demise. In 1968, upon hearing about the Rutgers chapter's refusal to admit an African American student, TKE decided to disaffiliate from the national organization, fearing that it had strayed from its commitment to counter discrimination.[20] The loss of funds, housing, and resources that accompanied this disaffiliation caused TKE to dissolve entirely from Colgate in the early 1970s.

In 1959, Alpha Chi Epsilon (AXE) became the second local fraternity claiming to be founded on an anti-discrimination platform.[21] However, in its first year, some students questioned whether this fraternity was formed as a "spirited and bold student movement" or as a desperate attempt for a group of men who "couldn't make it anywhere else" to join a fraternity.[22] Ralph Arlyck '62, a member of the Colgate Hillel Foundation's Executive Board, was weary of some of the political actions of AXE leaders. Multiple AXE members served on the Student Senate and sided against a resolution to create a deadline for the elimination of all restrictive clauses in fraternities.[23] Arlyck was correct in his speculations. AXE affiliated with Alpha Delta Phi in 1963. Members supposedly sorted through the charters of all major national fraternities not already represented at Colgate to see which would best fit the beliefs of AXE. Five years later, in the immediate aftermath of the Phi Delta Theta sit-in (to be discussed shortly), this fraternity disaffiliated with ADP after realizing (or finally acknowledging) the restrictive policies within the national charter.[24] Neal Rosenberg '74, a member of Alpha Delt and the Colgate Jewish Union (CJU), claims this fraternity dropped its restrictive clauses in order to accept Jews.[25] More likely, it disaffiliated out of self-preservation in the wake of heightened activism against restrictive clauses. Nevertheless, during its last few years on campus Alpha Delt finally served as a non-discriminatory fraternity that benefited Jews, allowing the Colgate Hebrew Union to be formed inside its house.[26]

Some Jews who became members of fraternities, both those with and without discriminatory policies, chose to disaffiliate. Marvin Forland '54 was able to join Alpha Tao Omega (ATO) despite its policy to accept only white and Christian men, making him an exception.

Forland, however, did not realize he was an exception. He did not even realize ATO had discriminatory policies when he joined, as at least two other Jewish men were in the fraternity. At the start of his senior year, he learned that his fraternity brothers sent a letter to the ATO national saying he was "of Jewish origin but not practicing" in order to gain him admission. As an active Jewish leader and vocal proponent of eliminating fraternity discrimination clauses, Forland chose to disaffiliate. He recognized that the problem was national rather than local and remained "cordial" with his former fraternity brothers, but no longer felt comfortable within the community. Gilbert Simon '58 chose to disaffiliate for a different reason. He joined Phi Kappa Tau, one of the fraternities known to accept Jewish students. His spot on the wrestling team made him an "acceptable Jew" who was sought after by fraternities that usually excluded them.[27] A dedicated student on the premedical track, Simon joined Phi Kappa Tau because of its reputation of attracting the nerds and the student leaders. But even in this academically motivated fraternity, Simon felt he did not have enough time to study and "opted out."[28] He clarified that his Jewish identity did not impact his decision to disaffiliate, even in light of his father storming out of the house after his fraternity brothers naively served him pork on Parents' Weekend.[29]

Tensions regarding fraternity discrimination reached a zenith in April 1968. Four hundred students and forty faculty members occupied the Administration Building for a hundred hours to protest the blackballing of a Jewish student from Phi Delta Theta.[30] That student, Bruce Hunter '71, thought he had been accepted, but at the last minute did not receive a bid.[31] Outrage ensued, as it was rumored that he was the number one pick, but the opinions of two or three anti-Semitic members caused him to be excluded. For a Jewish student, not gaining admission to Phi Delta Theta would not be surprising. Phi Delta Theta's national policy, published by the *Colgate Maroon* in 1956, was a startling Nazi throwback: "Any male white persons of full Aryan blood not less than 16 years of age may be eligible for membership."[32] The policy relaxed over time, restricting Phi Delta Theta to members "acceptable" to every chapter in the country. Jews, once again, did not fit the description.[33] For members of the African American community, united as the Association of Black Collegians (ABC), this blackballing was the final strike in a recent series of injustices. Linden Summers, a professor who participated in the sit-in, recognized why the ABC rallied behind a Jewish student: "the incident at Phi Delt was a rallying point because, if a Jewish kid was blackballed, then a black had no chance at all."[34] Other events also helped spark the sit-in, including the assassination of Reverend Dr. Martin Luther King Jr. and a shooting hoax at Sigma Nu in which two white fraternity brothers fired blanks at African American students.[35] To the satisfaction of Jewish and African American students, the sit-in led to the suspension of Phi Delta Theta's charter.

The Phi Delta Theta sit-in heightened awareness of discrimination in fraternities. While minorities were able to gain entrance into fraternities in increasing numbers, racial and religious intolerance continued to exist. Still, at the time of Delta Upsilon's (DU) Nazi Room incident two decades later, remedies were applied that were not preceded by a 100–hour sit-in. A year after the incident, DU showed a documentary about the Holocaust, an action commended by members of the CJU.[36] Today, fraternities remain controversial on Colgate's campus, but have certainly improved since the middle of the twentieth century.

Sorority women were spared from many of the restrictive clauses of Greek life. Women were first admitted to Colgate just two years after the Phi Delta Theta sit-in and entered a campus that was cognizant of the need to reduce discrimination in Greek life. The first sorority, Gamma Phi Beta, was founded in 1982, although Phi Psi fraternity accepted women in 1978. By 1996, Kappa Alpha Theta, Kappa Kappa Gamma, and Delta Delta Delta had gained recognition at Colgate.[37] None of Colgate's sororities have ever had formal restrictive clauses; however, some have been more receptive to Jewish women than others. Prior to the turn of this century, most Jewish women at Colgate rushed either Gamma Phi Beta or Kappa Kappa Gamma.[38] Today, Delta Delta Delta has the most Jewish members.[39] Kappa Alpha Theta, removed from campus in 2008, was known as the least likely to accept Jewish women.[40] Individual women have experienced negative reactions on the basis of their Judaism in various sororities, but the old fraternity practice of collective exclusion never applied. Yet until the Pan-Hellenic Council stops scheduling recruitment on the Jewish High Holidays, Jewish women will still have to fight to get involved with Greek life.[41]

Quasi-Fraternities

Jews at Colgate have always been drawn to other Jews, as many share a similar background. Most Jews at Colgate, especially in the middle of the twentieth century, grew up either Reform or Conservative in the Northeast, more specifically New York City and its suburbs. Their social disadvantage was heightened because of the City's policy of accelerating high-achieving students, making many of them among the youngest in their class. Once at Colgate, their stories further aligned. It was likely that they would eat and live together off-campus or on the Hill due to their exclusion from the Greek system. The situation often led to lasting friendships. But prior to the appearance of quasi-fraternities, Jewish students had to plan the entirety of their social lives on their own. Often this meant traveling to neighboring universities.[42] With the advent of the Colgate Commons Club, Colgate Hillel Foundation, Colgate Jewish Union, and Blue Diamond Society, Jews had the option to participate in organized social life at Colgate. Their Colgate experiences no longer hinged on the restrictions of the Greek system. The choice was now their own.

The Colgate Commons Club (1927–1959)

The yearly initiation started like this: the doorbell would ring at West Hall. A member of the Colgate Commons Club (CCC) would open the door to a group of young men eager to join a community of outsiders. Anyone was welcome inside—that is, anyone who was willing to ring the bell. The CCC did not lead to social equality, as the organization was seen as an option only for those unable to join a fraternity. Members of the CCC would remain on top of the Hill, isolated from the lively and prestigious social life of Broad Street. No one rang this bell if he had other options. Still, Jewish underclassmen that took this step found hospitality otherwise absent for them at Colgate.[43] Even if not in the way they originally hoped, Jews in the CCC could enjoy the paradigmatic college experience of fraternal living.

The Colgate Commons Club was founded in 1927, two decades before the G.I. bill and Austin-Mahoney bill would bring to Colgate an influx of students who were neither white nor Protestant. Yet the idea of the CCC dates back to 1908, years before Maurice Hindus became the first Jewish student to step on campus. In that year, President George Edmands Merrill met with thirty-five unaffiliated students in what was called a "non-Fraternity Meeting." Two students, having observed the Commons Club at Wesleyan University—believed to have been the first of its kind—addressed the possibility of forming something similar at Colgate.[44] Seeing how the Wesleyan Commons Club was a "fraternity in every way, except that every non-frat man had the privilege of membership," the representatives of Colgate's one hundred unaffiliated men rejected the idea.[45] An organization so similar to a Greek fraternity would not satisfy men who simply had no desire to participate in this social scene. However, later on, a Commons Club would help fill the void for students who expressed interest in Greek life but were prohibited from participating.

The first three social organizations for unaffiliated students that emerged following the "non-Fraternity Meeting" failed to meet the needs of this disunified community. The 1915 Neutral Club, 1924 Non-Affiliated Club, and the first attempt at a Commons Club at Colgate in 1926 were all unable to create a cohesive group. Every student unaffiliated with a Greek organization was automatically a member of these clubs, regardless of whether he had expressed interest in joining.[46] The new CCC differed by accepting only those students who wished to join, a policy aimed at creating a community of members who genuinely wanted to be a part of the organization and would work to ensure its survival. So long as the CCC was a part of campus life, Jews were neither in an organization that encompassed every unaffiliated student nor unaffiliated by default. For the first time, they had the power to choose. It was up to an individual Jew to decide if he wanted to remain unaffiliated or to join an alternative to a Greek fraternity through pledging the CCC.

While the CCC attempted to mirror a Greek fraternity, its policy of self-selection made it much more egalitarian. It never implemented racial or religious restrictions. Bruce Evgood '54 reflected fondly on his experience in the CCC in a handwritten letter sent to the organization on its thirtieth anniversary:

> Our Club is more than a social club on this campus, and it is more than a living group with a common commitment to a constitution and club rooms. It is rather a voice ever vocal, holding up the ideals of equal membership opportunities to all students who wish to be identified with some unit on campus which is larger than the individual. Let us continue to oppose that type of organization which, I think, un-democratically rejects persons, not because they are of opposing ideas towards that group but merely they are of colored skin or non-Christian religion.[47]

The organization did become "larger than the individual," though it was up to the individual to get involved. A self-identified candidate for the CCC could join an active member base that upheld "the ideals of equal membership," embodied by the diamond logo pinned on the members' chests.[48] Once he had completed a series of pledging and initiation rituals, he would become a part of a brotherhood. The CCC was selective only in the sense that it limited its membership to dues-payers (although honorary members such as Albert Parry and George Barton Cutten were exempt).[49] The cost was lower than that of Greek fraternities.[50] Jews, often coming from urban public schools rather than the elite private schools many Colgate students attended, could feel socially and economically secure within the CCC. For a small fee, they could increase their social capital in an organization that recognized men of all backgrounds. But this social capital was intermediary, and CCC men remained socially bound in the middle of unaffiliated and independent men.

Like fraternities, the CCC fostered unity by serving as—in Evgood's words— a "living group."[51] For most of the club's time on campus, its members were housed in West Hall and held many of their social events in a meeting room on the first floor.[52] The 1951 Student Senate Committee on Physical Living Conditions understood the impact a residential space could have on social activities. Its report emphasized that living facilities were not solely meant for studying and sleeping, but also socializing and moral development: "it is here that the student receives his additional lessons in social responsibility. It is here, in a group, that the student's personality and character further grows and develops."[53] A Jewish student in the CCC had a bed and a group, a place to be a serious student, a place to relax at the end of the day, and a community where dorm-mates became brothers. This experience contrasted with that of Jews who remained unaffiliated with either Greek life or the CCC. Although such independent Jews formed lasting friendships with members of their freshman dormitories, they were forced into off-campus housing as upperclassmen and withdrew almost entirely from the campus social scene.[54] While the CCC members remained connected to the independent students living in neighboring dormitories, they experienced a drastically different social life and status.

The increased status helped attract individuals such as Noel Rubinton '43. According to his son, he was a "proud member of the Colgate

Colgate Commons Club members from the Class of 1943. Noel Rubinton is seated in the center of the bottom row. Courtesy of Colgate University Special Collections and University Archives.

Commons Club." Despite being blackballed from fraternities, he, like many of his peers, "always talked about how great the Commons Club [was] rather than [ruing] not getting into fraternities."[55] He made the most of his social situation, enjoying the opportunities provided to him. In a way, however, he was part of the fraternity culture at Colgate. The Interfraternity Council (IFC) classified the CCC as a local (as opposed to a national) fraternity.[56] Jews who by virtue of their non-fraternity status had been excluded from the IFC were now inside it, interacting with those who had rejected them from a position of some strength.

As the CCC technically was a "non-Greek but not anti-Greek" fraternity, many of its members had experiences similar to those of their peers in the Greek system.[57] Members competed with other fraternity men in intramural debate, song, and sports competitions. At the CCC itself, men could bring a date to a party or play Ping-Pong with their CCC brothers.[58] Rubinton won a CCC Ping-Pong championship, and he told his son that this achievement was one of his "proudest memories" from college.[59] By embracing the fraternity lifestyle and belonging to the IFC, CCC Jews became rebels in conformity. They were able to show men who had excluded them that they could have thrived in a Greek organization had they been given the chance. They were able to have the college experience that Jewish alumni who remained unaffiliated out of necessity longed for.

Many Jewish students chose to join the CCC to be in the company of likeminded people, both Jewish and non-Jewish.[60] Jerry Berkson, a member of the penultimate CCC class, says that he and his fraternity brothers were "wanting to have a good time, wanting to be serious."[61] The CCC struck the ideal compromise, with a tilt toward academic achievement and away from sports. CCC men won the Scholarship Cup, an annual award given to the campus group with the highest cumulative GPA, for at least twenty-eight of their thirty-two years on campus.[62] Not surprising for a group of unathletic Jews and similarly-minded gentile nerds, the CCC often faltered in intramural athletics, frequently coming in or near last place when competing with the Greek fraternities.[63] Professor Jerry Balmuth, indirectly experiencing the Colgate social scene from his office, described these men as "idiosyncratic, unusual students who did not choose to affiliate."[64] Jews united with others who embraced these idiosyncrasies, remaining outsiders but outsiders with a home.

By functioning as "half-fraternity, half-neutral," the CCC existed in limbo, constantly questioning its role on campus.[65] It suffered a perpetual identity crisis: should the Club serve primarily as a fraternity or as a dormitory? As a group primarily associated with fraternities or with the unaffiliated? Ultimately, the CCC never found the answer to these questions and in practice functioned on campus as a quasi-fraternity.

Despite wanting to remain separate from the campus independents, the CCC members lived on the Hill with them, often ate with them in the Student Union, and even invited them to banquets and parties.[66] Although belonging to the IFC, the CCC failed to obtain a house on Broad Street despite multiple attempts.[67] Jews in the Club were thus caught in the middle of Colgate's social hierarchy, asserting a misplaced sense of superiority over independent Jews but living in the shadow of Greek fraternities.[68]

Toward the end of its run, the CCC suffered a decline in membership. By 1957, the IFC had derecognized the group and the administration had forcefully relocated its members to Kendrick House, where they had to live with students who were unaffiliated.[69] The CCC disbanded in 1959.[70] On the eve of its twenty-fifth anniversary, Professor Sidney J. French praised the organization's success, unaware or unwilling to admit that its days were numbered:

> As America has been called a world melting pot, so you have served for Colgate. This is not only an honorable title; it is one which is so significant in the modern world that no prize could be more eagerly sought. Quietly you have done those things for Colgate which few other groups could do. Quietly, you have grown into a major factor for better things on the campus. Quietly, you have put your weight behind those movements which ensure that Colgate's doors will always be open to worthy boys whatever their creed, color, race, or economic status, and what is more, that they will find at Colgate the hospitable atmosphere which should be the aim of all human endeavor today.[71]

French was right; the CCC did lead to "better things," or rather different things, on Colgate's campus. When the Colgate Commons Club came to an end in 1959, its open door shut, but other opportunities would soon arise to take its place.

The Colgate Hillel Foundation (1948–1970)

In 1948, the founders of the Colgate Hillel Foundation (CHF) announced their Judaism to the community. In the same year, the Newman Community formed to address the needs of Catholic students. Colgate was shifting, or rather, through publicizing their beliefs, Jews (and Catholics) were forcing it to shift. These men risked further social isolation on the off chance that they could improve their situation, especially once a CHF picture was printed in the *Salmagundi* for the first time in 1950.[72] The impact was not immediate. Jews continued to get rejected from fraternities and discrimination did not dissipate. Yet the CHF gave Jews the ability to embrace their Jewish identity in a non-Jewish place. It let its members become a presence, albeit a minor one, on a campus where many did not acknowledge they existed.[73]

Contrary to what the name implies, the Colgate Hillel Foundation was not associated with the national Hillel at the time of its founding

First Row: Mittleman, Bettman, Bekoff, Strasser, President.
Second Row: Greene, Weiss, Golding.

Hillel Foundation

The Hillel Foundation, which is a national collegiate group of Jewish students, entered its second year at Colgate. In addition to observing religious holidays, the Hillel Foundation serves as a social and cultural club. This group under the leadership of Seymour Bekoff brought Jewish leaders to the campus and worked with the CRA on various projects.

130

First documented photograph of the Colgate Hillel Foundation (CHF), published in the 1950 yearbook two years after the organization's founding. The yearbook incorrectly associated the CHF with the Hillel Foundation. Colgate Salmagundi, 1950.

(the announcement of its creation in the *Colgate Maroon* was wrong).[74] It comes as no surprise that the unification of a misunderstood group of students would also be misunderstood, especially since the social, religious, and cultural emphasis of the CHF was reminiscent of that of Hillel. Although Rabbi Arthur Lebyneld, the National Director of the Hillel Foundation, spoke at Colgate in 1949, the CHF lacked one critical element necessary to get recognized by Hillel: a resident rabbi.[75] Many visiting rabbis assisted the CHF, but Colgate would remain without its own rabbi for another thirty years. More than fifty years would pass before the Colgate Jewish Union, the CHF's successor, would be recognized as a national Hillel.[76] Consequently, the CHF would remain without any financial assistance from the Hillel Foundation.

The CHF was also not funded by Colgate (unlike the University Church, Colgate's Protestant organization). Despite donations from parents, it did not have enough money to host a wide variety of events. The organization started small in regard to both social and religious programming. Members provided Sunday afternoon snacks in the Student Union, invited guest lecturers, and showed what they called "movie[s] on the Hill."[77] The CHF hosted the first Passover Seder at the Colgate Inn in 1949 and the first Rosh Hashanah services in 1950.[78] The first Friday evening Shabbat service was held in 1951 and would continue every week until at least 1953, laying the foundations for the CJU to make Shabbat a main priority.[79] Compared to the robust parties of the Greek fraternities, these events may seem trivial. However, the CHF gave Jews a sense of belonging and the ability to exert some control over their social life.

Social and religious programming helped increase the visibility of Jews at Colgate. At the end of his term as president of the CHF in 1952, founding member Stan Weiss '52 explained the purpose of the CHF to the *Colgate Maroon*: "It is not only to provide a cultural and social center for the Jewish students on campus, but also to disseminate information of the organization's activities to the rest of the campus."[80]

Students who had never met Jews before or thought Jews had horns were forced to confront Jewish life in the newspaper.[81] All Jewish events were open to the entire community to allow non-Jews to explore the culture firsthand.

The CHF sometimes provided alternatives to fraternity parties for its members and other Colgate students. The first mixer with another school was hosted in 1951. Twenty-five women from Cazenovia came for a party (or maybe speed dating) with the CHF in the Student Union.[82] A year later CHF men travelled to Syracuse University for a Chanukah dinner dance.[83] These parties occurred less frequently than fraternity parties but allowed Jewish students to experience a more traditional social life. Many men in the CHF still wanted to join a fraternity. The organization held a panel discussion entitled "How to Approach Fraternity Rushing" in 1961 to help Jews become successful in this endeavor.[84]

Although the CHF provided new opportunities for Jews, it was not always successful. Services and events in the mid-1950s were sporadic at best, although weekly Shabbat services resumed from 1958 until the very early 1960s.[85] Jim Oestreich '64 recalls that he had to travel to Utica for services.[86] Even with the installation of a yearly bagel brunch in 1958, an event now hosted monthly by the CJU, and a mixer with Carlton College, the CHF did not meet the needs of the Jewish students.[87] This organization secured a place for Jews at Colgate but did not guarantee that programming would exist to utilize the organization's potential.

Mark Krinsky '67 wanted to change this. When he arrived on campus in 1963, the main CHF event was a bagel brunch on Parents' Weekend.[88] "If you ate like a Jew once a year," Krinsky said, "then you had your Hillel."[89] Even though Krinsky had a social life through TKE, he did not feel as if he had his Hillel. Under Krinsky's leadership in 1965 and 1966, the CHF held Rosh Hashanah and Yom Kippur services.[90] He reinstated bi-weekly Shabbat services led by visiting rabbis.

The success of these services varied. Some weeks the CHF struggled to acquire a minyan while in other weeks, services attracted twenty to twenty-five students. Shabbat services, however, were not accompanied by dinner, causing Friday evenings to be less of a social experience than they would become under the CJU.[91] Krinsky also reinstated a Passover seder at the Colgate Inn in 1965 (he believed that this was Colgate's first).[92] He felt that Jewish students were proud that the CHF was "starting to be something of a bona fide organization on campus."[93] His success was tangible— the parents of John Rubinstein '66 donated a Torah to Colgate at the end of Krinsky's tenure as president.[94] Jews still did not have a full range of social opportunities, as evidenced by Shabbat services taking place on Winter Party Weekend.[95] Nevertheless, in the rejuvenated CHF, Jews could engage socially through religious practice (and bagel eating).

The CHF's newfound strength was fleeting. The year after Krinsky graduated, the Phi Delta Theta sit-in occurred. Most members of the CHF supported both this sit-in and the subsequent 1970 sit-in at Merrill House. In a time of political resistance, Jewish students needed an organization that could support not just the social and religious elements of Judaism but also the ideal of activism. On April 30, 1970, the fourteen founders of the Colgate Hebrew Union published a joint obituary for the CHF and birth announcement for the CHU:

> After a long illness, Colgate Hillel died at the Freedom Seder on Monday, April 19 because it neglected the needs of the Jewish community at Colgate. The moribund members of that community were infused with a new spirit of action; action meant to fill the voids to which Hillel never directed itself.[96]

Even without the sit-ins, change was inevitable, as the 1970s brought a new type of student to Colgate: women. The CHF did not disintegrate entirely. It just changed form in order to meet the demands of a rapidly evolving campus.

The Colgate Jewish Union (1970–Present)

Every Friday at Shabbat services, students share their highlight of the week. For many students, the Colgate Jewish Union (CJU) itself has been their highlight. The Colgate Jewish Union, originally called the Colgate Hebrew Union, was founded "to affect (sic) a closer link between Jews and their unique Jewish identity through political, cultural and religious action."[97] Even in its infancy, this organization was more lively than its predecessor, sponsoring an Israeli folk dance after Shabbat services, a "Knish-In" to feed and welcome freshmen to campus, hangouts and cooking in the Kosher Kitchen in the Student Union, and other community building events.[98] It was also more controversial, especially in the 1970s. Within its first two years on campus, it was accused of being too liberal or too radical.[99] Most of its events had been cultural or religious in nature, but two political events helped shape the perception: the CJU hosted a "Prayer for Silence" for Jews in the Middle East and four of its members attended a protest in Washington, D.C. against the treatment of Jews in the Soviet Union. Cary Goodman, the CJU Political Coordinator, was arrested at this protest, unintentionally jeopardizing the social position of this new organization.[100]

As any form of political action is bound to isolate some members of the community with opposing views, the CJU's partial emphasis on politics was guaranteed to make some Jews uncomfortable. In 1971, Kerry Baker, one of the founders of the CJU, recognized that it was difficult to be a Jew at Colgate and that it was the role of the CJU to provide a range of options for as many types of Jews as possible:

> The CJU does not pretend to speak for each of the 350 students who, in response to a questionnaire, indicated that they are Jews. It represents only its members, though it does believe in the necessity of defending the interests of all Jews at Colgate, whether Zionist or non-Zionist, Kosher or non-Kosher, politically or non-politically oriented.[101]

Nearly a decade later, Peter Ochs recognized the "range of different tastes and articulations of being Jewish, but non-apologetically."[102] He identified the athletic and fraternity Jews, the intellectual and classroom Jews, and the Jews who saw the CJU as their "primary home."[103] Despite these differences, Ochs described the Colgate Jewish population as having a "collective character."[104] These students were not deeply observant, did not reject their Jewish identity, and were not self-isolating, allowing any Jew to find a "niche" in an organization that was diversely homogenous.[105]

Under Peter Ochs's leadership, the CJU became more inclusive.[106] Technically all CHF and CJU events always had been open to the entire Colgate community.[107] Nevertheless, these events often failed to attract Jews. Ochs's attention to interfaith matters helped CJU events seem more accessible to secular Jews and students of other religions. Interfaith was not a new concept at Colgate. The Colgate Religious Association, comprised of representatives of the CHF, University Church, and the Newman Community, had sponsored speakers to unite all three groups.[108] Interfaith social events, however, were something new. In 1984, the CJU, Newman Community, and University Church co-sponsored an "Ecumenical Mixer" with dancing, a deejay, snacks, and conversation.[109] By not serving alcohol, this event attracted students who may not have been interested in attending fraternity parties. University Church member Debbie Powell went "because there was no beer. I can come here and go home without having had beer and drinks spilt on me."[110] According to CJU vice president Barry Solcoff, this event was a success: "These groups all have a religious orientation, and still can get together and have fun."[111] The fun continued. The year 1985 brought a "Wild Purim Celebration" to Colgate. Following a Megillah reading, students of all denominations could attend a carnival for local children and a "more intense" after-party. Given that the party was held in Judd Chapel, it could not have been too wild.[112] But the CJU had grown from its CHF days. Its members no longer had to invite students from neighboring colleges for mixers.

Serving as the "caregiver" for the students of the CJU, Ochs was able to boost morale through Israeli Café nights and bi-monthly Shabbat dinners and services. Or, if students desired a less Jewish-centric experience, through popcorn and movies.[113] Within his first year on campus, attendance at bi-monthly kosher dinners rose from ten to twenty students to over forty students.[114] Richard Sobelsohn '82, a transfer student and CJU leader, joined the CJU in his first semester and brought his friends to various CJU events. He cited his greatest challenge as a member of the CJU Executive Board as keeping people "motivated" to attend CJU events on a campus with more than enough to do.[115]

Strong Jewish programming has always required strong Jewish leadership and motivation. Dan Levin '91 felt the paucity of organized Jewish life when he came to Colgate in the interim between Peter Ochs and Moshe Gresser. During freshmen orientation in the Fall of 1987, he attended a CJU bagel brunch and was welcomed by an Executive Board Member of the CJU. In front of more than fifty Jewish freshmen, this student welcomed everyone to Colgate, introduced himself as the sole member of the CJU Executive Board, and immediately proceeded to resign. A shocked Levin decided to take over the CJU with David Purla, a friend from camp who transferred to the University of Pennsylvania. Levin, a rabbi in the making, became known as the leading Jew on campus—a title he did not have to fight too hard for. Yet Levin alone could not provide the leadership necessary to revive the CJU. That responsibility fell to Moshe Gresser—the next Counselor to Jewish Students—who Levin helped hire.[116]

Social Judaism thrived under Gresser. This success could be accredited at least in part to the creation of the Affiliation of Jewish Students (AJS) in 1989: "the established Colgate Jewish Union was not filling the social gap felt by Jewish students. . . the goal of the AJS is not to promote traditional Judaism, but rather to promote a social setting in which this sense of community can grow."[117] Comprised of an overlapping group of students, these two organizations were not in competition. All religious programming was under the domain of the CJU and all social programming was under the domain of the AJS.[118] The CJU and AJS shared the responsibility of upholding Jewish life at Colgate, and consequently both social and religious events prospered. The AJS adopted some traditional CJU events, including bagel brunches and movie nights.[119] It hosted a jazz band and barbeque to launch Spring Party Weekend respectively in 1989 and 1990.[120] A Jewish social club formally existed on campus for the first time, paving the way for the founding of the Blue Diamond Society a decade later.

As a result of the AJS, the CJU could dedicate its time and resources toward religious holidays. By strengthening its religious mission, the CJU became a "refuge" for observant students.[121] Future rabbi Matt Berkowitz '93 remembers that Shabbat dinner and services, once a burden, became the "highlight of our week."[122] Students were able to get to know each other while cooking brisket in the kosher kitchen, located then in the chapel basement. Shabbat created a Friday afternoon social outlet separate from the AJS for unaffiliated students like Berkowitz: "It was beautiful because people began to feel it was a home away from home. . . it didn't matter what they did afterwards. They ran to the fraternities, sororities. . . For those of us who were part of it, it was incredibly special."[123] Upon returning from a year abroad in Israel in 1990, Levin was surprised to encounter an active Jewish life. In just three years, the CJU had transformed from a single resigning member to a community of twenty-five regulars.[124]

While the AJS helped expedite this rapid growth, a separate social organization was not a permanent solution. Having two Jewish organizations would only work in the long run if they appealed to a vastly different audience, as seen later with the CJU and BDS. The CJU and AJS co-sponsored too many events, shared too many members, and overlapped on too many types of events, especially Purim parties, to merit this split.[125] The AJS provided the CJU with time to mature and find its core identity in Shabbat. But Jewish life had become a home without a house. The cooperation of the AJS and the CJU proved that

Jewish life was developed and expansive enough to qualify for its own space. The Saperstein Center was dedicated in 1993, the same year that the AJS dissolved and Moshe Gresser departed.

Neil Grabois, the first Jewish president of Colgate, recognized the importance of the Saperstein Center for Jewish social life: "Here was a separate building that was kind of the fraternity for people who couldn't be in fraternities."[126] Jewish life had always been volatile, and the Saperstein Center added stability. Since the dedication of the Saperstein Center, Jewish students, at least those who have elected to get involved with the CJU, have encountered similar experiences. Of course, some CJU events occur outside the Saperstein Center, but the building has provided a home base for a generation of students.[127]

From 1993 to the present, many CJU members have reserved their Fridays for Shabbat. Suzanne Brock '01, Caryn Fields '08, and Hillary Stiss '09 all planned their class schedules so that they would not have classes on Friday afternoons and could instead cook Shabbat dinner.[128] Groups of four to ten students, mainly underclassmen, cooked the Shabbat meal in the Saperstein Center's two kitchens. In accordance with kosher laws, one kitchen was used for the preparation of dairy dishes and the other for meat.[129] Cutting onions, Stiss joked, served as an initiation ritual for freshmen looking to get involved in the CJU.[130] Music drowned out the sounds of chopping, creating an atmosphere that was more about coming together at the end of the week than completing a chore. Students who wanted even more time to cook in the Saperstein Center could join Challah for Hunger, an organization founded by Rebecca Friedland in 2010 to bake and sell challah for charity. These students too helped prepare dinner, as Friedland and recent Challah for Hunger leaders donated the leftover challah to the CJU for Shabbat.[131] Weekly cooking and the accompanying Shabbat dinner and services provided a previously variable group of students with a sense of stability.

Jewish students sometimes extended common Friday plans beyond the Saperstein Center dinner table, hanging out in the apartments of

CJU members before or instead of going to fraternity parties.[132] Alex Willick '09 recalls a more unusual event: a bar mitzvah for the Colgate Raider. CJU members rented out the Old Stone Jug, a local bar, until ten p.m. to celebrate the coming of age of Colgate's mascot. The Raider was in attendance and was lifted up in a chair as if he were a real bar mitzvah boy.[133] A school that had discriminated against Jews now unknowingly has a Jewish mascot.

Holidays other than Shabbat also served as bonding experiences. Rabbi Joan Friedman embraced the costumes and rowdiness of Purim, allowing the CJU's "resident comedian" and future rabbi Joshua Strom '98 to read the megillah while dressed as Dr. Evil.[134] Friedman even permitted kegs in the Saperstein Center's kitchen for Purim in the mid-1990s, a surprise that still fascinates students today. Hanukkah too has been a celebratory affair. In 2001, the CJU held a "MatzoBall," or, as Jordie Slutsky Kattan referred to it, "a giant bar mitzvah for all of Colgate" at the Colgate Inn.[135] Prior to the event, CJU members gathered together to make giant matzoh balls out of paper mâché.[136] For more reflective holidays such as Passover and Yom Kippur, students have gathered to support each other. Passover has often been called the best time for Jewish community building.[137] The eight-day period of Passover is the only time when the majority of the CJU eats every meal together. Former CJU members have commented that, due to the Saperstein Center's vast array of kosher for Passover food, they ate better on Passover than any other time of year. In contrast, on Yom Kippur, CJU members congregated to not eat together, playing cards and board games to pass the time while fasting.[138]

The Saperstein Center has not only been active during religious services or scheduled events. Its location near academic buildings has made it the perfect spot for students to hang out during free time between classes.[139] Rebecca Blake '10 "basically lived there" her junior and senior year, an experience shared by Dana Laxer '15, who could have actually lived there if there had been a shower.[140] Walking into the Saperstein Center on a weekday, a student could expect to find a group of his or her friends napping, playing the Wii, studying, bouncing ideas off of each other, watching television, cooking, or just enjoying "couch time."[141] According to Frannie Kahan '14, she and her friends would form a "pile of humans" on one of the couches. The other couch was left empty, a testament to how close these students became through their time in the Saperstein Center. Laxer, a frequent participant in "couch time," described the CJU as a "strange dysfunctional family." The Saperstein Center has given these students a space to take a break and be "dysfunctional" together.[142]

The Colgate Jewish Union, especially since 1993, has helped forge lasting friendships among students. Students have gotten involved with the CJU in various ways: visiting the Saperstein Center as prospective students, attending the first Shabbat with a friend, or, in the case of Chelsea Mohr '17 and Arielle Pearlman '17, through a community service pre-orientation program. While cleaning, Pearlman went up to Mohr to say, "Are you Jewish?"[143] After this first awkward interaction, the women started to attend CJU events together, eventually becoming close friends and co-presidents. Together they were able to join a diverse group of Jewish students. Here fraternity and sorority men and women, athletes, and academics can gather "where the land of milk and honey met the land of beer and snow."[144]

The Blue Diamond Society (2005–Present)

Growing up, Sean Altman '08 had limited social involvement with Judaism, but he wanted to engage with the Jewish community when he came to Colgate. In 2004, when Altman arrived on campus, the CJU was struggling with attendance and could not fulfill its social role as a quasi-fraternity. When he attended a CJU Shabbat service in an attempt to meet other Jewish students, less than half a dozen students were there, and disappointed by his initial experience, he found friends in other social circles. But by the conclusion of his freshman year, Altman was not satisfied socially. He tried to join a Greek organization during his sophomore year but did not receive a bid. Altman was not devastated by this outcome. He had been turned off by what he saw as the Greek organizations' lack of emphasis on philanthropy and their attitude toward his Jewish identity: "I wouldn't say I experienced outright anti-Semitism, but I will say when I looked into Beta and DKE, when they found out I was Jewish, it felt like there was a little bit of friction."[145] He needed to find a group where friction would not be a concern. Thus Altman, with the help of Matthew Guber and Ivan Karaivanov, created the Blue Diamond Society (BDS) in 2005. He unified a group of Jewish men who also sought an alternative to what the CJU or Greek life could offer.[146]

Founded as an all men's Jewish social and philanthropic organization, BDS serves a different demographic than any other organization in Colgate's history. The CJU and AJS have supported Jewish life for men and women, and the CCC had Jewish members, but BDS is predominantly Jewish. Given that Altman had never heard of the CCC when starting BDS, the two organizations share striking similarities.[147] They both have a diamond as their logo, have mirrored Greek fraternities, have been dependent on housing for survival, and have served as a social home for Colgate's expanding Jewish population. The unintentional similarities between the Colgate Commons Club and the Blue Diamond Society, present on campus nearly fifty years apart, demonstrate the continual need for Jews to have a Greek-like social outlet that is not actually a fraternity. In a way, BDS is a combination of all the quasi-fraternities that came before it, emphasizing the CCC's brotherhood, AJS's social events, and the CJU's Jewish identity.

The concept of BDS goes back to the kind of social and service group that has long been a feature of American Jewish life for adults, frequently self-separated by gender. The Jewish Federations of North America (JFNA) serves as the religiously unaffiliated umbrella organization for these groups, which focus on philanthropy and cultural programming. While the JFNA focuses on creating bonds among Jews of all generations across the United States, BDS sets its sights locally, on

Colgate men. BDS is not associated with the JFNA and some members may be altogether unaware of it. But the resemblance is strong enough that it can look to an outsider like a collegiate version of the organization, preparing young Jewish men to join their relatives in federation activities after they graduate.[148]

Colgate's BDS is also not associated with the other BDS sometimes seen on college campuses: the Boycott, Divestment, and Sanctions Movement. That particular BDS, founded less than a year before the Blue Diamond Society, is an anti-Israel organization that protests the occupation of the West Bank (and, according to Rabbi Dena Bodian, has never been present at Colgate).[149] BDS at Colgate often advocates for Israel through fundraisers and celebrations of Israeli culture.[150] Many BDS men display Israeli flags in their rooms and the revived Israel Club even operated out of BDS for a semester in 2013.[151] The society's name comes from its logo, an abstract representation of the Star of David that, like a diamond, is constructed from two triangles. Altman was not aware of the other possible connotation, nor did he, at first, take it seriously: "After we had started the organization we found out that there was a BDS which was anti-Semitic, and at the time we thought it was funny."[152] Some current members no longer find the coincidence funny and are discussing changing the organization's name. Until this change happens the irony will remain: at Colgate, a school that historically marginalized Jews, BDS is collectively understood to mean a small Jewish social organization rather than a well-known anti-Israel movement.

BDS was unable to attract a substantial founding class. In 2005, it pledged only ten founding fathers, including Altman, Guber, and Karaivanov.[153] Many of these men, representing all class years, were strangers or acquaintances at the time. Even Altman only knew half of the founding class. As a result of their shared Jewish identity, these men "all quickly became very close."[154] Members were found through various platforms: mutual friends, a BDS pamphlet that was distributed around campus, and CJU events.[155]

The organization has always held one advantage in recruitment over Greek fraternities: its ability to accept freshmen. Since BDS is a club under the Center for Leadership and Student Involvement rather than a Greek organization, it is not subject to the university policy that prohibits students from joining Greek life until their sophomore fall. Freshmen who join BDS can immediately find a social home—an experience in stark contrast to that of many Jewish alumni who spent all four years struggling to find a social community. Freshmen men, Jewish and non-Jewish alike, often feel isolated from the Colgate social scene. In both the present and past, Colgate has sponsored few open parties and freshmen men have rarely been able to attend fraternity events. Thus the social life of freshmen men has often been confined to the dormitories. By joining BDS, a freshman can attend parties. More importantly, he can expand his social network by meeting other freshmen that do not live in his dormitory and upperclassmen, especially his "student-parent."[156] Furthermore, in BDS, freshmen can take on leadership roles before they are even allowed to rush a Greek fraternity.[157] In October of 2007, BDS Vice President Matthew Guber told the *Maroon-News* that BDS had attracted ten freshmen—an accomplishment especially impressive considering BDS had only ten founders.[158]

Yet given the fledgling nature of the organization and its uncertain future, some BDS members decided to rush a fraternity to have a more secure social life. There have never been any BDS rules prohibiting members from joining a Greek organization and, early in the organization's history, one or two men per class year joined a fraternity.[159] For most men who were able to do this, BDS became a secondary commitment, and they later dropped out of it entirely.[160] However, at least prior to 2012, most BDS men did not get bids from fraternities, likely due to fraternities' frustration at the organization's policy of accepting freshmen.[161] Some BDS men who were successful in getting bids chose not to affiliate with a fraternity. This was the case with Alex Djaha '14, who was offered admission to every fraternity but Sigma Chi. Djaha and four of his closest BDS friends, who also rushed, decided together not to join a fraternity, believing that they could have a "more memorable" experience at BDS.[162] Jordan Sheiner '12 described this collective understanding as a "turning point." BDS men, both those who received bids and those who did not, realized that BDS could offer them an experience "equal to" or "better" than that of a Greek fraternity. These men shared this enthusiasm with future BDS members, allowing the organization to grow in size and strength.[163]

BDS's connection to the CJU and then Colgate Chaplain Rabbi David Levy helped distinguish it from Greek fraternities and create a different experience for its members. While the CJU and BDS have formally never been affiliated, they have always worked together. Levy served as BDS's unofficial advisor, advertising and advocating for it. He had a vested interest in this Jewish social club or, as he called it, "secret Jewish fraternity," which reminded him of his undergraduate days at Columbia University, where he was a member of Alpha Epsilon Pi (AEPi), a traditionally Jewish fraternity.[164] BDS "wanted to have a different DNA" than the CJU but also wanted to support as many Jewish events as possible.[165] Altman, who served as a "Sap Monitor," invited his BDS brothers to utilize the Saperstein Center while he was on duty there and held BDS's weekly meeting in that space.[166] He also increased attendance for Shabbat among cultural Jews:

> At this point in time, less than half of us regularly attend Jewish services or Friday night dinners at Colgate. Yet every time we have agreed to meet in a group ahead of time and attend services and dinner together, every member of the club showed up. The reason for this increased attendance when we go as a group is that most of the members of our club are apprehensive about attending services on their own, but when they are with a group of their friends, they feel much more comfortable.[167]

Marc Frankel ' 06 did not frequently attend CJU events during his first three years on campus but started to attend Shabbat once BDS was founded during his senior year.[168] By 2010, BDS had begun hosting and leading a Shabbat service every semester, a tradition that remains today.[169] Attendance at CJU events grew as BDS increased its member base. BDS attracted Jews who wanted to explore their religion while still fitting in with the social scene to the Saperstein Center. When Sheiner was at Colgate, BDS held once-a-semester dinners with the rabbi to discuss topics such as "male leadership" and "what it means to be a Jewish man."[170] BDS members were and continue to be on the Executive Board of the CJU.

One goal of BDS has yet to be fulfilled—its desire to go Greek. Its members have wanted access to resources allotted to fraternities such as housing, funding, and a national alumni network.[171] Socially, BDS has always functioned similarly to fraternities, albeit on a smaller scale. Its members participate in intramural sports with Greek organizations and independent teams (although their main athletic achievements can be seen on the club baseball team).[172] They host parties and formals, some of which have been Jewish-themed, including a "MatzoBall."[173] Its similarities to official fraternities have not gone unrecognized by the student body. In a *Maroon-News* article from 2010, Josh Glick of Phi Kappa Tau commented on a possible connection between BDS and AEPi: "AEPi at Harvard reminds me of Blue Diamond Society. Do what you want with that . . ."[174] Glick's speculations were not unfounded. The Jewish fraternities AEPi and Zeta Beta Tau (ZBT) have approached BDS multiple times. Both of these organizations were (and possibly still are) looking to add BDS as a national chapter. Despite BDS's desires to affiliate with a national fraternity, not necessarily AEPi or ZBT, it has been unable to do so due to pushback from the administration and the Board of Trustees.[175]

This opposition does not mean that the administration or the Board of Trustees is anti-BDS, although there have been misunderstandings. Initially, the administration was unsure of the organization's role, mistakenly believing it to be either an offshoot of the CJU or "unauthorized Greek activity."[176] At present, the administration and

Board have been cautious about expanding Greek life because of incidents of sexual assault, hazing, and underage alcohol consumption. The year before BDS was founded, Colgate's chapter of Delta Kappa Epsilon was expelled, and while BDS has been on campus, the same happened to both the Kappa Alpha Theta sorority and the Sigma Chi fraternity.[177] Then in 2005, the year when BDS began, the university acquired ownership of all the fraternity and sorority houses to increase control over the Greek system.[178] This timing put BDS at a disadvantage for affiliating with a national Greek organization. Representatives of BDS have met with the administration and Board of Trustees almost every year since 2005 seeking fraternity status.[179] Every year this request has been denied. The men of BDS may want to affiliate and the IFC may not be opposed to this idea, but until Greek life becomes less problematic, BDS will remain a club.[180]

Some BDS members have questioned whether Colgate does not want any more fraternities or specifically not a Jewish fraternity. Former BDS president Adam Basciano '16 believes it is a "matter of perspective . . . [there's] something to be said that there's never been a Jewish fraternity in the nearly 200–year [history] (although Basciano 'heard in passing' that there were efforts in the 1980s to organize one at Colgate) ."[181]

While BDS was founded on Jewish values, it has never restricted its membership to only an "insular group of Jewish guys."[182] Djaha believes these Jewish principles have made BDS more inclusive: "Part of being a Jew is embracing others who might not be Jewish but share your values, share your beliefs, share your goals."[183] Most men who have expressed interest in the organization have been admitted. Djaha recalls only one man getting rejected from BDS in his four years on campus, citing a "bad reputation" and lack of philanthropic interest as the reasons.[184] Beyond supporting diversity, there may be another reason for BDS's high admission rate: struggles with membership. BDS grew from ten members in 2005 to fifty members in 2012 at least in part because of its decision to accept non-Jewish members.[185] Altman welcomes the admission of non-Jewish students, as it has allowed BDS to educate members of varied race, religion, and socioeconomic status about Jewish culture and beliefs.[186]

If BDS men could not go Greek, then they wanted to at least have a house. Housing for upperclassmen has been an ongoing challenge throughout Colgate's history. Altman wanted a space for Jews similar to the Harlem Renaissance Center for African American students or La Casa for Latino students. He wanted a "place at Colgate for Jewish students to live together and publicly display their religion and heritage comfortably without feeling like an outsider."[187] Altman ended up placing his group in multiple Parker apartments.[188] The arrangement provided BDS with enough communal space to host "hookah and hummus" or "Booze for Jews" events but not enough to throw large open parties that could compete with Greek nightlife.[189] They proceeded to rent off-campus houses, echoing the experiences of Colgate Jews in the middle of the twentieth century who also could not live together on campus.

Off-campus housing at Colgate is unreliable and hinges on a lottery system. BDS men needed to ensure that they would have a place to live and host events. For five consecutive years, they tried to get an Interest House on Broad Street from the Office of Residential Life. (Broad Street has always been the elusive goal for Colgate Jews.)[190] The CCC had never been successful in completing this goal. BDS was. In 2013, BDS president Alex Djaha transformed 110 Broad Street, formerly the Delta Kappa Epsilon house, into Philanthropists at Colgate (PAC).

While PAC was neither the all-BDS nor all-Jewish house that Altman had envisioned, it was still more than Jews had previously been offered. The core of the house consisted of BDS juniors. PAC has never been marketed as the BDS house, although some Colgate students continue to refer to it that way.[191] Demand to live in PAC was in high demand before its inaugural semester. Thirty-five people, including two BDS juniors, were on the waitlist to live in a house which could sleep forty-four.[192] As a place for "responsible leaders with charitable global goals," PAC in its first year attracted students from the Colgate Dischords, Amnesty International, LGBTQ Initiatives, The Colgate Thirteen, Challah for Hunger, Gamma Phi Beta, Delta Delta Delta, and Theta Chi.[193]

Inspired by the Jewish idea of "tzedakah" or charitable giving, BDS has always encouraged philanthropy at Colgate.[194] Its annual Gate-Town Connection was organized by Sheiner in 2011 to bridge the divide between the Colgate and Hamilton communities. Assisted by other organizations, BDS hosted a carnival on Whitnall Field for over 1000 students and town members—an event instrumental in the administration's decision to create PAC.

The appearance of PAC has elevated the status of BDS and other non-Greek student groups, in part by giving them a party venue on Broad Street. Open events at PAC, all charity-related, have included March Madness tournaments, Halloween parties, and a Passover Seder. The philanthropic nature of these events hosted in a house led by nice Jewish boys has caused PAC parties to be seen as safe alternatives to fraternity parties. Rabbi Bodian has never heard of women on campus feeling uncomfortable at a BDS party.[195] PAC's successes have therefore been threefold: it has allotted Jews a space on Broad Street, encouraged charitable giving, and provided non-Greek students the ability to have more social options.

Some of BDS's more than one hundred alumni, including Djaha and Sheiner, are satisfied with PAC and the growth of the organization:[196]

> Today the group is not affiliated with any Greek organization whatsoever. They're a group on campus. A sponsored club. They have some locations. They can host events. And that's what we were looking for. We wanted a place where we could do these things so that we could provide a social aspect to Jewish life that wasn't just the CJU.[197]

As evidenced by the organization's attempt to go Greek in 2015 and its renting of off-campus houses in addition to PAC, some members desire more. Yet if BDS continues to become more like Greek fraternities, it could move farther away from the Jewish values on which it was founded. Sammi Steinfeld '13, former CJU co-president and attendee of BDS events, commented, "When I was in college, BDS was less of the institutional pseudo-frat than it is now."[198] Rabbi Bodian shares a similar fear. She feels that the departure of Rabbi Levy and BDS's increased independence through PAC has diminished the group's connection with the CJU. Fewer Jewish men have been attending Shabbat services or other CJU events. Basciano, Djaha, and Sheiner all said that they were not particularly involved in the CJU because they felt they were getting their Jewish fix through BDS. As a result, and despite the addition of a BDS liaison on the CJU Executive Board, the CJU leadership remains predominantly female. The two organizations now seem to be at odds, as BDS moves more toward the dominant "fraternity culture" and the CJU regresses to serving as more of a religious than a social home for Jews.[199]

A criticism of BDS is its decision to remain a men's organization. No woman has ever asked to join.[200] Jewish women may not feel they can rush a quasi-fraternity that has gender restrictions while BDS men feel the admission of women would change the nature of the group which was founded as a brotherhood.[201] An alternative has been suggested: the creation of a female version of BDS. According to Djaha, BDS for women or, as his female Jewish friends called it, the Pink Diamond Society, has been a running joke for years. If recent alumnus Basciano could change one thing about Jewish life at Colgate, he would turn this joke into a reality: "[For] Jews who really love their Jewish identity and their experience at college . . . often it's tied to their social experience, and right now male Jews have that and female Jews don't."[202] Rabbi Bodian worries about the creation of a sister organization to BDS. She is not certain if it would decimate Jewish life by further decreasing attendance at the CJU or if it would make BDS accountable for upholding Jewish life.[203] These worries may be unfounded: just as many Jewish men at Colgate choose not to join BDS, not all Jewish women would be interested in a Pink Diamond Society. The nature of the social scene is that women have more opportunities than men, and some women believe Delta Delta Delta's high proportion of Jews already satisfies Jewish women who would have been interested in a Pink Diamond Society. To further complicate matters, the administration has recently created a policy that new clubs must be all-inclusive and cannot restrict admission on the basis of gender or sex. Only time will tell whether or not a Pink Diamond Society will materialize at Colgate. Nevertheless, social Judaism has secured a malleable space at Colgate, constantly adapting to the changing needs of the student body. It is now "cool to be a Jew and attend Jewish events" on a campus where being Jewish formerly meant forfeiting a social life.[204]

Endnotes

1. James Parsons, "DU Responds to Allegations," *Colgate Maroon,* April 26, 1988.

2. Gilbert Simon, interview by Emily Kahn, February 16, 2017, recording in possession of the author.

3. Al Pasternak, Steve Greenleigh, Peter Greenwald, interview with Rachel Cohen, Winter 2016, recording in possession of the author.

4. Marvin Forland, "Recognizing the 'Others': A College's Progression," 2004, unpublished memoir in possession of Rabbi Dena Bodian.

5. Jim Oestreich, interview by Rabbi Dena Bodian, January 10, 2017, recording in possession of the author.

6. Pasternak, Greenleigh, Greenwald, interview.

7. Pasternak, Greenleigh, Greenwald, interview.

8. Bernie Siegel, interview by Rachel Cohen, Winter 2016, recording in possession of the author.

9. Pasternak, Greenleigh, Greenwald interview.

10. Marvin Forland, interview by Emily Kahn, April 11, 2017, recording in possession of the author.

11. "Statement by Forty Faculty Members Who Actively Supported the Asso-

ciation of Black Collegians," April 14, 1968, CU Protest and Activism Collection, Colgate University Special Collections and University Archives, A1021.1.3, Colgate University Library.

12. "Statement by Forty Faculty Members Who Actively Supported the Association of Black Collegians."

13. "Statement by Forty Faculty Members Who Actively Supported the Association of Black Collegian"; "Discriminatory Regulations Specify Rush Restrictions," *Colgate Maroon,* November 5, 1958.

14. Jerry Weigler, "IFC Okays TKE as Local Chapter," *Colgate Maroon,* March 19, 1952; Marc Rosenbaum, "Senate Votes to Suspend Phi Delt," *Colgate Maroon,* March 14, 1968.

15. "TKE to Petition National for Full Chapter Status," *Colgate Maroon,* December 7, 1955.

16. Weigler, "IFC Okays TKE as Local Chapter."

17. Mark Krinsky, interview by Emily Kahn, December 27, 2016, recording in possession of author.

18. Krinsky, interview.

19. "No Pledging for TKE: Frosh Already Initiated," *Colgate Maroon,* February 16, 1967.

20. "Tekes Plan to Go Local,"*Colgate News,* October 31, 1968.

21. Tim Parshall, "Alpha Delt," *Colgate News,* March 9, 1975.

22. Ralph K. Arlyck, "AXE Policies Questioned," *Colgate Maroon,* November 2, 1960.

23. Arlyck, "AXE Policies Questioned."

24. Parshall, "Alpha Delt."

25. Neal Rosenberg, interview by Emily Kahn, February 2017, recording in possession of the author.

26. Robert Kahn, "Hillel Replaced by Hebrew Union. Rabbi is Sought," *Colgate Maroon,* April 29, 1970.

27. Simon, interview.

28. Simon, interview.

29. Simon, interview.

30. Eric Cochran, "The Administration Building Sit-In, April 1968," January 26, 1978, CU Protest and Activism Collection, Colgate University Special Collections and University Archives, A1021.1.3, Colgate University Library.

31. Cochran, "The Administration Building Sit-In, April 1968."

32. "Fraternity Discrimination Policies," *Colgate Maroon,* October 17, 1956.

33. "Fraternity Membership Policies," *Colgate Maroon,* November 9, 1960.

34. Cochran, "The Administration Building Sit-In, April 1968."

35. SMS, "Colgate's 100 ½ Hours," April 18, 1968, CU Protest and Activism Collection, Colgate University Special Collections and University Archives, A1021.1.3, Colgate University Library.

36. Dan Levin, "DU Shows Film on Holocaust," *Colgate News,* November 11, 1988.

37. Rebekah Ward, "The History of Greek Life," *Colgate Maroon News,* October 29, 2010, http://www.thecolgatemaroonnews.com/arts/article_a02b8fc0–a729-59f4-ab3f-dfc4d3569cdb.html/.

38. Suzanne Brock, interview by Chelsea Mohr, Spring 2016, recording in possession of the author.

39. Young Alumni Interview (Jessica Benman, Dylan Pulver, Jake Pulver, Dana Laxer, Lindsey Skerker, Frannie Kahan, Jessica Friedberg), interview by Emily Kahn, February 12, 2017, recording in possession of the author.

40. Brock, interview

41. Young Alumni interview.

42. Pasternak, Greenleigh, Greenwald, interview.

43. "Formal Initiation Ceremony," 1932, Colgate Commons Club Records, Colgate University Special Collections and University Archives, A1301.1.3, Colgate University Library.

44. Association of Commons Club, "Chapter Roll," http://commonsclub.org/7501/6106.html, accessed May 13, 2017.

45. "Non-Fraternity Meeting," *Madisonesis*, December 12, 1908.

46. Al Aylor (Assistant National Extension Secretary of ACC), "Report of Extension Trip to Colgate Commons Club," December 1930, Colgate Commons Club Records, Colgate University Special Collections and University Archives, A1301.1.7, Colgate University Library.

47. Bruce Evgood (former CCC Member), "Happy Thirtieth Birthday Card," April 18, 1957, Colgate Commons Club Records, Colgate University Special Collections and University Archives, A1301.1.7, Colgate University Library.

48. "Formal Initiation Ceremony," 1932.

49.Aylor, "Report of Extension Trip to Colgate Commons Club," 1930; Kenneth Howard (CCC President), letter to Professor Howard D. Williams (CCC Advisor), May 15, 1959, Colgate Commons Club Records, Colgate University Special Collections and University Archives, A1301.1.5, Colgate University Library; Roll Book Used at Meetings (Alumni and Membership, The Colgate Commons Club),

1927–1954, Colgate Commons Club Records, Colgate University Special Collections and University Archives, A1301.1, Colgate University Library.

50. Philip Seymour, letter to Kent Kehr, Howard Williams, Michael Levine, George Schott, and Charles Rider, May 2, 1952, Colgate Commons Club Record, Colgate University Special Collections and University Archives, A1301.1.5, Colgate University Library.

51. Bruce Evgood, "Happy Thirtieth Birthday Card," 1957.

52. Aylor, "Report of Extension Trip to Colgate Commons Club," 1930. This was the same room that was used by the Neutral Club, Non-Affiliated Club, and first Commons Club.

53. "The Student Senate on Physical Living Conditions," June 1951, Colgate Commons Club Records, Colgate University Special Collections and University Archives, A1301.1.4, Colgate University Library.

54. Pasternak, Greenleigh, Greenwald, interview; "The Student Senate on Physical Living Conditions," 1951.

55. Noel Rubinton, Jr., e-mail message to Alice Nakhimovsky, April 16, 2017.

56. The CCC chose not to affiliate with the American Association of Commons Clubs. They did not want to comply with the ACC's policy to eliminate all selective admissions policies, fearing a similar fate as the Neutral Club, Non-Affiliated Club, and original Commons Club.

57. Roland J. Brown (Assistant Extension Secretary of ACC), letter to Howard D. Williams (CCC Advisor), July 8, 1953, Colgate Commons Club Records, Colgate University Special Collections and University Archives, A1301.1.4, Colgate University Library.

58. "The Colgate Commons Club Alumni News," March 24, 1949, Colgate Commons Club Records, Colgate University Special Collections and University Archives, A1301.1.5, Colgate University Library.

59. Rubinton, Jr., e-mail.

60. Jerry Balmuth, interview by Alice Nakhimovsky and Rich April, 2009, video recording in possession of the author.

61. Jerry Berkson '58, interview by Rachel Cohen, January 12, 2017, recording in possession of the author.

62. "The Colgate Commons Club (Its History and Achievements)," June 7, 1958, Colgate Commons Club Records, Colgate University Special Collections and University Archives, A1301.1.5, Colgate University Library.

63. "Dekes, D.U.'s Lead in Touch Football Tourney," *Colgate Maroon,* October 10, 1939; "Fraternity Standings," *Colgate Maroon*, May 12, 1948.

64. Balmuth, interview.

65. "The Student Senate on Physical Living Conditions," 1951.

66. "Neutral Dance to be Held by Commons Club," *Colgate Maroon,* October 15, 1954. "The Student Senate on Physical Living Conditions," 1951.

67. Seymour, letter to Kent Kehr, Howard Williams, Michael Levine, George Schott, and Charles Rider, 1952.

68. Forland, interview.

69. "Notes for a Statement re Colgate Commons Club and Kendrick House," October 8, 1957, Colgate Commons Club Records, Colgate University Special Collections and University Archives, A1301.1.4, Colgate University Library.

70. Charles Arno Reincke, Jr. (Final CCC President), letter to Alumni Brothers, May 10, 1959, Colgate Commons Club Record, Colgate University Special Collections and University Archives, A1301.1.5, Colgate University Library.

71. Sidney J. French, letter to members of the Colgate Commons Club on the occasion of its 25th reunion, April 11, 1952, Colgate Commons Club Record, Colgate University Special Collections and University Archives CCC on 25th anniversary, A1301.1.7, Colgate University Library.

72. Salmagundi (Hamilton: Colgate University, 1950), 130.

73. Siegel, interview.

74. "Bekoff Named Head of Hillel Foundation," *Colgate Maroon,* December 1, 1948.

75. "Hartshorne is First of CRA Speakers," *Colgate Maroon,* September 28, 1949; R.V. Smith (University Chaplain), letter to Noel Hudson, May 27, 1965, History of Jewish Life at Colgate, manuscript in possession of Rabbi Dena Bodian.

76. Sean Altman (BDS Founder), interview by Emily Kahn, December 22, 2016, recording in possession of the author.

77. "Notices," *Colgate Maroon,* March 16, 1949.

78. "Notices," *Colgate Maroon,* April 13, 1949; Barbara Brooks, "Colgate Celebrates 60 Years of Jewish Life." Colgate University, November 28, 2008, http://news.colgate.edu/2008/11/colgate-celebrates-60–years-of.html/.

79. "Notices," *Colgate Maroon,* October 14, 1953; "Hillel Plans Passover Activities Tomorrow," *Colgate Maroon,* April 4, 1951.

80. "Hillel Foundation Begins Activity: Sunday Party Fetes Cazenovia Girls," *Colgate Maroon,* October 24, 1951.

81. Pasternak, Greenleigh, Greenwald, interview.

82. "Hillel Foundation Begins Activity: Sunday Party Fetes Cazenovia Girls."

83. "Hillel Will Observe 'Festival of Lights,'" *Colgate Maroon,* December 10, 1952.

84. "Hillel Predicts Eventful Year," *Colgate Maroon,* October 4, 1961.

85. "Notices," *Colgate Maroon,* October 8, 1958; "Hillel Predicts Eventful Year."

86. Oestreich, interview.

87. "Hillel Has Active Year: Stronger Program Increases Interest," 1958, History of Jewish Life at Colgate, manuscript in possession of Rabbi Dena Bodian.

88. "Hillel Has Active Year: Stronger Program Increases Interest"; Krinsky, interview.

89. Krinsky, interview.

90. "Hillel Offers High Holiday Services," *Colgate Maroon,* September 15, 1966.

91. Krinsky, interview.

92. "Hillel to Hold Passover Seder April 4 at Inn," *Colgate Maroon,* March 10, 1966.

93. Krinsky, interview.

94. "Student's Father Donates a 250-Year-Old Torah," *Colgate Maroon,* October 28, 1964.

95. "Hillel Voters Pick Slate of Officers," *Colgate Maroon,* February 17, 1965.

96. CHU Founders, "Death of Hillel," *Colgate News,* April 30, 1970.

97. CHU Founders, "Death of Hillel."

98. Joanne Rogan, "Knish-In Introduces CJU to Frosh,"*Colgate News,* September 21, 1971; Brian Rooney, "CJU Fosters Search for Jewish Identity," *Colgate Maroon,* February 29, 1972.

99. "CJU Discusses D.C. Protest, Future Program Schedule," *Colgate Maroon,* April 15, 1972.

100. "CJU Discusses D.C. Protest, Future Program Schedule."

101. Esther Bless, "C.J.U. Strives Towards Greater Participation; Sees Awakening of Jewish Consciousness," *Colgate Maroon,* November 7, 1971.

102. Peter Ochs, interview by Alice Nakhimovsky, January 6, 2017.

103. Ochs, interview.

104. Ochs, interview.

105. Ochs, interview.

106. Richard Sobelsohn, interview by Robert Sobelsohn, January 15, 2017, recording in possession of the author.

107. Claudia Zayfert, "Jewish Union Promotes Heritage," *Colgate Maroon,* March 10, 1981.

108. "CRA Coffee Hour to Feature Avirett," *Colgate Maroon,* April 11, 1951.

109. "Ecumenical Mixer," *Colgate Maroon,* October 16, 1984.

110. Jeanne Vezina, "Students of All Faiths on Common Ground," *Colgate Maroon,* October 23, 1984.

111. Vezina, "Students of All Faiths on Common Ground."

112. "CJU Presents a Wild Purim Celebration," *Colgate Maroon*, March 5, 1985.

113. Ochs, interview; Zayfert, "Jewish Union Promotes Heritage."

114. Zayfert, "Jewish Union Promotes Heritage."

115. Sobelsohn, interview.

116. Dan Levin, interview by Abe Benghiat, Winter 2016, recording in possession of the author.

117. Karen Weiss, "Jewish Students Found New Organization," *Colgate Maroon*, February 28, 1989.

118. Mary Pasciak, "CJU Funding Question Resolved at Senate," *Colgate News*, November 10, 1989.

119. David Griff, "AJS Announces Plans," *Colgate Maroon*, February 13, 1990; Mark Freedman, "Purim: "Have Fun, Take Care, and Take Pride," *Colgate Maroon*, March 6, 1990.

120. Griff, "AJS Announces Plans"; Sandy Harding, "Spring Party Schedule Takes Shape," *Colgate News*, March 17, 1989.

121. Matt Berkowitz, interview by Anat Guez, January 9, 2017, recording in possession of the author.

122. Berkowitz, interview.

123. Berkowitz, interview.

124. Berkowitz, interview.

125. Freedman, "Purim: "Have Fun, Take Care, and Take Pride."

126. Neil Grabois (former President of Colgate), interview by Alice Nakhimovsky, January 10, 2017, recording in possession of the author.

127. Jess Dodge, Recent Alumni Interview (Allie Kashkash, Benjamin Suarato, Hillary Stiss, Jess Dodge, Alex Willick, Carly Ackerman, Ceci Cibony, Caryn Fields), interview by Dena Bodian, 2017, recording in possession of the author.

128. Stiss, Recent Alumni Interview; Brock, interview.

129. Brock, interview.

130. Stiss, Recent Alumni Interview.

131. Rebecca Friedland, interview by Emily Kahn, December 22, 2016, recording in possession of the author.

132. Recent Alumni Interview.

133. Willick, Recent Alumni Interview.

134. Jordie Slutsky Kattan, interview with Alice Nakhimovsky, January, 2017, recording in possession of the author.

135. Kattan, interview.

136. Kattan, interview.

137. Laxer, Young Alumni Interview.

138. J. Pulver, Young Alumni Interview.

139. Rebecca Blake, interview by Emily Kahn, January 22, 2017, recording in possession of the author.

140. Laxer, Young Alumni Interview.

141. Lindsey Skerker, Young Alumni interview; Blake, interview; Caryn Fields, interview by Dena Bodian, 2017, recording in possession of the author; Laxer, Young Alumni Interview.

142. Laxer, Young Alumni Interview.

143. Brock, interview.

144. Recent Alumni Interview. This phrase was printed on a t-shirt the CJU sold for charity.

145. Altman, interview.

146. Altman, interview.

147. Sean Altman, e-mail message to Emily Kahn, March 27, 2017.

148. "The Jewish Federations of North America Homepage," https://jewishfederations.org/jewish-life, accessed May 27, 2017.

149. BDS Movement, "BDS," https://bdsmovement.net/what-is-bds, accessed May 14, 2017. Within this paper, "BDS" will *always* stand for the Blue Diamond Society.

150. Adam Basciano (former BDS president), interview by Emily Kahn, January 25, 2017, recording in possession of the author.

151. Sean Altman, "BDS CLSI Proposal," 2005; Basciano, interview.

152. Altman, interview.

153. "BDS Roster," email attachment from BDS Secretary, April 13, 2017.

154. Altman, interview.

155. Altman, interview; Amanda Fox and Laura Blau, "In the Light Matthew Guber," *Colgate* Maroon, October 25, 2007.

156. Alexander Djaha (founder of PAC House and former BDS president), interview by Emily Kahn, April 28, 2017, recording in possession of the author.

157. Djaha, interview.

158. Fox and Blau, "In the Light Matthew Guber."

159. Djaha, interview.

160. Jordan Sheiner (BDS Leader and Gate-Town Connection Founder), interview by Emily Kahn, January 4, 2017, recording in possession of the author.

161. Altman, interview; Djaha, interview.

162. Djaha, interview.

163. Sheiner, interview.

164. Rebecca Blake (CJU member), interview by Emily Kahn, January 22, 2017, recording in possession of the author.

165. Sheiner, interview.

166. Altman, interview.

167. Altman, interview.

168. Marc Frankel (former BDS president), interview by Cameron Pauly, Spring 2017, interview in possession of the author.

169. Sheiner, interview.

170. Sheiner, interview.

171. Djaha, interview.

172. Max Troper and Paul Kasabian, "IM Flag Football Update and Playoff Preview," *Colgate Maroon News,* September 27, 1907.

173. Altman, "BDS CLSI Proposal."

174. Josh Glick, "Hollywood on the Hill: My Diary of the Social Network," *Colgate Maroon News,* October 10, 2014.

175. Altman, interview; Sheiner, interview; Djaha, interview; Basciano, interview.

176. Frankel, interview.

177. Caitlin Gilligan, "Conduct Board Revokes Sigma Chi Fraternity's Charter," *Colgate Maroon News*, October 23, 2014, http://www.thecolgatemaroonnews.com/news/article_754406e8–abed-11e4–9271–1b60a16cdb4b.html.

178. Chris Nickels, "Voting into Escrow," *Colgate Maroon News,* April 22, 2005.

179. Sheiner, interview.

180. Djaha, interview.

181. Basciano, interview.

182. Djaha, interview.

183. Djaha, interview.

184. Djaha, interview.

185. Sheiner, interview.

186. Altman, interview; Altman, "BDS CLSI Proposal."

187. Sean Altman, "BDS Housing Proposal," 2007.

188. Altman, "BDS Housing Proposal"; Altman, "BDS CLSI Proposal."

189. Altman, interview; A.J. Farkas and Sammi Steinfeld (CJU members), interview by Rachel Cohen, Winter 2016, recording in possession of the author.

190. Alexander Djaha, "PAC Constitution and Accepted Proposal," July 15, 2012.

191. Djaha, interview; Djaha, "PAC Constitution and Accepted Proposal."

192. Djaha, interview.

193. Djaha, "PAC Constitution and Accepted Proposal."

194. Djaha, "PAC Constitution and Accepted Proposal."

195. Rabbi Dena Bodian, interview by Emily Kahn, May 6, 2017, recording in possession of the author.

196. "BDS Roster."

197. Sheiner, interview.

198. Farkas and Steinfeld, interview.

199. Bodian, interview.

200. Djaha, interview.

201. Basciano, interview.

202. Basciano, interview; Djaha, interview.

203. Bodian, interview.

204. Altman, interview.

5

Standing Up and Sitting In

| Resistance to Discrimination at Colgate University |

Cameron J. Pauly

> *I think that how you overcome a lot of the prejudices that exist is not so much by sitting out but by getting involved and really shaping the future.*
>
> —Adam Basciano '16[1]

The many acts of resistance that have occurred on campus against anti-Semitism and other forms of discrimination form a crucial part of Colgate University's Jewish history.[2] While the most insidious and overt anti-Semitism at the University took place under the direction of President George Barton Cutten beginning in 1922 and continuing through the end of his tenure in 1942, there was very little in terms of public resistance to his regime from within the institution. The sheer absence of Jewish students and faculty, a direct result of his anti-Semitic policies, undoubtedly played a role in this, but so did societal apathy toward anti-Semitism.[3] Under Cutten's successor Everett Needham Case (1942 to 1962), more and more instances of resistance began to occur.

Though President Case discreetly continued to uphold the policies of the Cutten era, in the aftermath of World War II more and more Jews, many of them veterans, began to appear at Colgate. In turn, Jewish life at Colgate began to advance at a rapid pace: in late 1948, merely three years after G.I.s returned home from the war, a campus Hillel was organized for the first time.[4] Even before this historic event, Case's policies had come under fire from the student body. On November 3, 1946, Gilbert Geis '47 of the *Colgate Maroon* wrote to President Case demanding the President's clarification regarding "the University's official position on discrimination and quotas."[5] Geis posed seven questions:

> 1. Official statement of Colgate's policy on discrimination.
> 2. Would you favor the removal of tax exemption rights from any educational institution which discriminated against applicants on the ground of race, color, or creed?
> 3. What is the explanation of the completely non-Negro student body?
> 4. Would you favor a statewide investigation of discrimination in the colleges?
> 5. Have Colgate graduates encountered difficulty in gaining admittance to professional schools because of quota systems?
> 6. Does Colgate still ask religion, mother's maiden name and nationality and color on entrance applicants [sic]? If so, do you favor it?
> 7. What would you emphasize as selection bases of new students (scholarship, social, "pull," athletic)? Do you feel that any of these are overemphasized—either here or in general?[6]

That a student reporter had the nerve to directly confront the university's sitting president is remarkable, though no less remarkable than Geis himself.

Gilbert Geis is a fascinating alumnus: a Navy veteran able to attend Colgate due to the G.I. Bill, he went on to earn a master's degree from Brigham Young University and a doctorate from the University of Wisconsin-Madison on his way to becoming a "giant" in the field of criminology.[7] One of Geis's criminology colleagues, Dr. John Gill, recalls how "virtually every academic article he saw on behaviors of white-collar criminals was either written by Dr. Geis or quoted him extensively."[8] Geis's strong sense of justice and ethics is reflected in his chosen field and his master's thesis at BYU on race and education.[9]

The seeds of his penetrating moral drive can be seen in his time as an undergraduate at Colgate. Like many returning veterans, Geis was more vocal and less deferential than other college students.[10] As we can see from his letter to the President, Geis was interested in social justice as early as his time at Colgate. He did not plead in his letter, he was polite but not at all submissive; he was acting like the scholar and advocate he would become. Maurice Hindus, in *A Traveler in Two Worlds*, describes his fellow Colgate students as rather adolescent and immature.[11] Gilbert Geis does not fit this mold. He is a man, and a dissenter, as an undergraduate. Quite simply, he took Everett Case to task.

The questions Geis posed to President Case, along with the act of Jewish students voluntarily self-identifying and rendering themselves visible by organizing as a Hillel, demonstrate that, as early as the 1940s, at least some Colgate students refused to stand for discrimination on their campus and would proudly resist it when they could. Many other students and other members of the Colgate community would follow suit in the years to come. In an atmosphere characterized by non-Semitism, these acts of resistance stand out.

Allies have played a large part in the narrative. Specific moments of defiance have occurred in response to discrimination by fraternities, such as the 1968 sit-in organized largely by the Association of Black Collegians where more than 450 Colgate students and faculty protested a Jewish student being "blackballed" by the Phi Delta Theta fraternity.[12] Fraternities themselves have sometimes taken stands against discrimination, as when the Colgate chapter of Alpha Tau Omega attempted to admit a Jewish student in 1956, in opposition to the national organization's bylaws.[13] Alpha Tau Omega's defiance of the national organization's racist and anti-Semitic exclusion policies was led by mostly white fraternity members.

Resistance to discrimination at Colgate was not exclusively overt, either: a quieter battle took place among the faculty involving the position of the Hebrew language and Jewish literature in the curriculum, ultimately culminating in the creation of a separate program in Jewish Studies in 1993. Non-Jewish professors like Marilyn Thie and Terrence Des Pres helped to lay the groundwork for the effort to establish a Jewish space on campus. Then, as Colgate continued to move through the 1990s and the new century, the struggle against discrimination changed from a fight for access to a fight for private spaces, places to call one's own. The Saperstein Center, the first permanent Jewish space at Colgate, was formed in 1993 in part as a reaction to multiple anti-Semitic acts on campus. In 2006, the Blue Diamond Society, a Jewish men's organization which functions as a quasi-fraternity, was established for Jewish men to have a place of their own in opposition to a fraternity system still perceived as hostile.[14]

Colgate's Jewish community, other minority communities, and allies have stood against discrimination time and again in the years since Gilbert Geis challenged Everett Case to provide a justification for discriminatory policies. Indeed, resistance to discrimination has always been a common thread of Jewish existence at Colgate.

Early Struggles: Administrative Racism and Fraternal Hate

George Barton Cutten may have been the first, most overt discriminatory president of Colgate University, but his chosen successor, Everett Case, was cut from the same cloth. When the *Maroon* in 1946 confronted President Case with the discriminatory policies of his administration and that of his predecessor, the climate of the American university was rapidly changing. Before World War II, American private colleges catered almost exclusively to the elite.[15] Colgate, as a former Baptist seminary, is somewhat of an exception to this rule, as it continued to educate young men of Central New York who were not from wealthy backgrounds—so long as they were Protestants, and preferably Baptist. This privilege was not extended to Jews and was taken away from African Americans under President Cutten.

On many occasions before and during the war, Cutten and Case would fight accusations of discriminatory admissions practices by claiming that the campus's rural location was not of interest to urban applicants, a label often used as a code for African Americans and Jews.[16] Regarding African American students, this was clearly false, as Colgate was a leading educator of African Americans until Cutten stopped admitting African American students.[17] There is also strong evidence for a quota system for Jews from two exterior sources citing Colgate informants, both of whom were quoted as saying that there would never be more than six or seven Jews on campus at one time.[18] In fact, the number of Jewish students at Colgate remained rooted at two students per incoming class until after World War II.[19]

Though Case was much less vocal than his predecessor, one letter in Colgate's archives indicates his distaste for being in the same social space as Jews. In June 1945, with the war at its end, Case writes that he has cancelled his vacation reservations due to the club "opening their doors to a large number of Jews."[20] Case may have been able to keep his anti-Semitism under wraps, but private conversation revealed his true feelings; the university's policies at the time certainly reflect this side of Case.

After the war ended, waves of veterans returned to America looking for an education. Among them were a large number of Jews: fifty percent of American Jewish men aged 18 to 44 served in the war, and many of them had put their education on hold to do so.[21] Bolstered by the G.I. Bill and their experiences in the military, many found it at universities such as Colgate. The G.I. Bill provided numerous Jewish veterans with opportunities that would never have been provided to them in years past, but fighting in World War II emboldened them to oppose anti-Semitic quotas.[22] Many Jewish veterans found a "renewed respect for Judaism" through their time in the military; likewise, many "felt empowered to undercut" anti-Semitism and found that they emerged from the war with a "strengthened identity as Jews."[23] One soldier, Albert Eisen, reminisced that "as a minority, it became necessary for us to declare ourselves to those who, unfortunately, are imbued with anti-Semitic sentiments."[24]

Jewish students, mostly veterans, came to Colgate and other universities in the late 1940s in increasing numbers. This was a crucial shift in the story of Jews at Colgate, as the Colgate administration was no longer able to hide behind its location as a front for a quota-based admission system. The Colgate Hillel Foundation (CHF) appeared on campus for the first time in 1948, the first evidence of organized Jewish life at the university.[25] As noted in Chapter 1, the passage of the Austin-Mahoney Bill that same year prevented overt discriminatory admissions practices by non-sectarian private colleges in New York State. When combined with the G.I. Bill, these two pieces of legislation resulted in increased enrollment and visibility of Jewish students at Colgate.

As the calendar turned to the 1950s, the sphere of Jewish life on campus continued to expand. The CHF held its first "Friday Eve [Shabbat] services" in April 1951, hosted talks by Colgate professors, and—according to an article in the *Maroon*—"frequently" invited rabbis to speak on campus.[26] One such visitor, Rabbi Jerome Malino, gave a talk on cultural pluralism to students in 1951.[27] Rabbi Malino's talk reflected a position in opposition to the Colgate administration's ideals, and eager participation by Philosophy and Religion professors in CHF events indicate that some of the institution's faculty willingly associated with Jewish students in an academic fashion.[28] This does not seem to have included Jewish faculty. Despite the acceptance of a detached academic relationship with Judaism, Colgate was, as seen in Chapter 2, deeply rooted in non-Semitism: none of Colgate's Jewish professors at the time, according to Marvin Forland '54 and Jerry Balmuth, acknowledged their Jewish background or identified as Jewish.[29] Still, the

Colgate Religious Association, which hosted a lecture series on issues deemed "pertinent, often quite controversial, [and] of concern to students," included Jewish topics in their roster.[30] The disjunction between these talks and the admissions policies President Case pursued behind the scenes indicates either that he did not have a very strong influence on faculty and student life, or that he didn't pay much attention to it. Despite a strong program of events, the CHF would struggle to provide adequate services, as it did not receive any funding from the university until it evolved into the Colgate Jewish Union in 1970.[31]

During the 1950s, the first arguments for a separate prayer space for Jews appear in the record. A letter in the *Colgate Maroon* signed by the initials B.H.B. notes that Jews at Colgate "have often met for worship services in seminar rooms . . . one of the weakest features of the common experience shared by this community."[32] As Colgate's Chapel had "physical limitations" to worship by multiple faiths, the author asked for a "concerted drive to supply Colgate with adequate facilities for religious worship" by minority groups.[33] While this request would not be satisfied for more than three decades, the fact that it was aired at all indicates that by 1954, Jews who sought to hold services constituted a large enough group to think about a dedicated space. At least one student—"B.H.B."—was bold enough to publicly request one, though not bold enough to sign his name. In the interim, contemporary Jewish artist Elbert Weinberg was commissioned to supply Chapel House with an original bronze bas relief sculpture to "express the religious insight and aspirations of Judaism," an order that nominally acknowledged the Jewish presence on campus in the context of Chapel House's deliberately pluralistic space.[34]

Alongside the administration, the main antagonistic force in the history of Jews at Colgate has been the fraternity system. In 1951, six of the fourteen fraternities on campus stated publicly that they had discriminatory constitutions or policies against Jews, blacks, Asians, and other non-white groups, with many of these policies coming from the national organizations.[35] Alpha Tau Omega accepted "all white students"; Lambda Chi Alpha accepted "all white gentiles"; Phi Delta Theta acknowledged that "restrictions are in existence on the national level, but because the constitution and statutes of the fraternity are secretive, we are not at liberty to reveal what these restrictions are"; Sigma Chi allowed "bona-fide white male college students" to apply; Sigma Nu stated that "any man is eligible to become a brother . . . except those of Oriental descent"; and Theta Chi accepted "all white males."[36] It is interesting to note that, contrary to common perceptions of this era, Jews in America until the 1960s were often not considered "white": physical anthropologists of the early twentieth century often associated "Jewish" racial types with a "Negroid" classification, and public discourse continuing into the 1960s spoke of three races in the United States—white, black, and Jew.[37] Even today, the whiteness of Jews is a contested classification; the American presidential election of 2016 has been cited as "reopening" debate about the relationship between these categories.[38]

One very prominent Colgate Jew who was on campus when many of the fraternities declared their discriminatory practices was Marvin Forland '54. Forland was very active as a student: he was president of the CHF, a member of Alpha Tau Omega, and editor of the *Colgate Maroon*.[39] As shown in Chapter 4, Forland recalls pledging to Alpha Tau Omega as a freshman, and at that time no mention of his ethnicity or religion was made to him by any of his new brothers.[40] When he was a senior, however, Alpha Tau Omega's leaders—many of his good friends—revealed to him that he was listed as "of Jewish origin but not practicing" in the fraternity's official records.[41] As he was in fact a practicing Jew, Forland asked why this was how he had been classified. His fraternity had given him this designation without his knowledge in order to protect him from the national organization's discriminatory policies.[42] Disgusted by the situation, Forland resigned from Alpha Tau Omega in his senior year; two non-Jewish (and very prominent) members of the fraternity resigned in solidarity.[43] As the newly unaffiliated editor of the *Maroon*, who had been fighting fraternity discrimination since before he left Alpha Tau Omega, Forland sustained his attempts to use his position to make the discrimination of the fraternity system a well-known issue on campus.[44] The discussion eventually reached the desk of President Case (who was, surprisingly, not off-campus at the time).[45] Case, appearing perfectly content with the inequitable state of affairs, declared fraternity discrimination to be a "student problem" and continued to ignore the issue.[46]

In the mold of his *Maroon* predecessor Gilbert Geis, Marvin Forland was one of the first well-known figures on campus to challenge the longstanding system of fraternal discrimination. Other critics, both within the fraternities and outside the system, would continue to confront the racist system throughout the 1950s. The Student Senate passed a resolution which "called for the elimination of discrimination in fraternities" in 1954.[47] In 1960, they delivered an ultimatum: "Fraternities must either accept or reject [a Senate] committee's report for discrimination [within the week]. . . Other portions of the report must be complied with, including the pledge to sincerely support a movement at the conventions for elimination of the clauses and for local autonomy."[48] In just ten years, amid national, and frequently collegiate, struggles for school integration and civil rights, a sea change had occurred in attitudes toward discriminatory practices in Colgate's Greek life.

While valiant resistance continued through the 1950s and beyond, the fraternities—on both the national and collegiate levels—often did not comply with civil rights demands. Some fraternities, however, did join the fight for inclusion. Two specific incidents at Alpha Tau Omega and Phi Delta Theta demonstrate the diverging responses of Colgate's fraternity system quite well.

In 1956, five years after publicly stating the organization's restrictive acceptance policy and two years after Marvin Forland resigned in protest, his old fraternity Alpha Tau Omega once again had a decision to make about Jewish members of the organization. While in 1951 the members "protected" Forland by labeling him as "non-practicing," here they made no excuses. John Glynn '58 recalled that despite the national fraternity's rules requiring that all members of the fraternity be Christian, Colgate's chapter decided to accept multiple Jewish students and made no attempt to hide it: "we took them in; we defied the national."[49] The chapter even sent member John G. Stewart '57 to the fraternity's National Congress to argue that they should change their religious discrimination policy.[50] The national leadership was able to retaliate, though, as they held the mortgage on the fraternity house.[51] The Colgate chapter was slapped with a "social suspension" preventing them from holding parties on fraternity property for a year.[52] Glynn noted that the decision to accept the Jewish students and to stand up to the national fraternity was a consensus decision reached by every member of the fraternity and credited the maturity of the fraternity to the presence of veterans on the G.I. Bill in the house.[53] The brothers refused to back down.

In 1968, merely a decade after the brothers of Colgate's Alpha Tau Omega chapter fought for the rights of Jewish students, a different fraternity refused to allow the enrollment of a Jewish student. That student, Bruce Hunter, requested membership in Phi Delta Theta and was denied a place on the grounds that he was Jewish.[54] This incident occurred despite the vote of Phi Delta Theta's national organization to remove restrictions for entry just two years earlier, in August 1966.[55] Colgate's local chapter of Phi Delta Theta claimed that it had never "refused membership to anyone because of race or creed," with chapter President Charles Thomas declaring in 1966 that "no person who would've been restricted under the national's present constitution has shown a serious interest in joining Phi Delta Theta at Colgate."[56] While we don't know for certain if there is any truth in Thomas's statement, one which is reminiscent of President Case's geographical explaining-away of the university's demographics regarding application and acceptance rates, the fact that only two years later the fraternity would be implicated in a racially- or religiously-motivated denial of membership makes it appear that Phi Delta Theta and other fraternities at Colgate

Students and faculty protesting the discriminatory policies of Phi Delta Theta fraternity following the blackballing of a Jewish student, 1968. Courtesy of Colgate University Special Collections and University Archives.

had a long history of discriminatory practices leading up to what would become known as the 1968 sit-in.

After public backlash to Hunter's blackballing, the Student Senate suspended Phi Delta Theta's representatives by a vote of 18 to 12.[57] Roughly 150 spectators were present for the meeting and heard a senator declare that "unless Phi Delt makes some important changes, the fraternity won't be here [in the Senate, and eventually on campus at all]."[58] Through the Senate's actions against Phi Delta Theta, the resolution from 1954 calling for an end to discrimination in fraternities was finally acknowledged by the Senate after gathering dust for 14 years.[59] The strong words from the student body were accompanied by doubts, however, that the Board of Trustees would kick Phi Delta Theta off campus because of the financial clout of the fraternity's alumni.[60]

Some time passed, and the issue was reignited in the form of a protest and sit-in that drew more than 450 students and faculty.[61] Thomas Baker '69 remembers that the Jewish community, for one reason or another, did not pursue justice against the fraternity until African American students, already angry about an incident of anti-black racism (a student fired a starting pistol at a group of African American students as they walked past his fraternity, Sigma Nu), decided to protest Hunter's blackballing.[62] This is very interesting to note: while the main catalyst for the sit-in was discrimination faced by a *Jewish* student, the protest was led by and large by *African American* students. It was not uncommon at this time for Jews and African Americans, including college students, to work together to combat discrimination.[63] While this inter-group relationship was not always perfect (the fallout from a talk by Kwame Ture, discussed further on, is a good example), African Americans and American Jews have both consistently fought for civil rights.[64] At Colgate, the 1968 sit-in was the strongest and most visible example of this cooperation.

The sit-in at the Admissions Building lasted for 100 hours. After that time had passed and the dust had cleared, the protesters and the administration had signed an agreement that would result in the suspension of Phi Delta Theta from campus.[65] The Phi Delta Theta sit-in was a pivotal moment in Colgate's history, the first time the Colgate community publicly came together and demanded change.

The struggle to gain access to fraternities was analogous to the struggle to get through the admissions process of an elite school: the university acceptance letter and the fraternal pledge opened the door to spaces and opportunities that had long been denied. The white male gatekeepers—those already inside each private club—selected the kind of recruits with whom they felt most comfortable, and resisted change for a long period. Still, with the national fight for civil rights as the backdrop, many other barriers eventually fell at Colgate as well. The transformation was hardly complete: as we see throughout this book, institutional and societal discrimination remained a dominant force on campus for many decades. The agency of individuals and small groups was limited. Even events like the stunningly successful and vibrant 1968 sit-in were episodic and confined in scope. The climate of apathy that often haunts Colgate did not make it easy to create permanent change.[66] The need to fight remained.

Hebrew, Lost and Found: Jewish Language and Texts in the Colgate Curriculum[67]

In addition to the struggle for acceptance, Colgate's Jews have fought for their own spaces on campus. A major part of the effort to carve out a Jewish space at Colgate was establishing Hebrew and Jewish Studies in the modern academic curriculum. Colgate's fraught relationship with Hebrew and Judaism is as old as the university itself.[68] Founded in 1819 as a Baptist seminary, the institution that would become Colgate University had as its academic mission the education of Christian young men, especially those who would become ministers.[69] The seminary's education naturally focused on a practical theology of the Bible, including the Old Testament. Hebrew, the language of that fundamental Christian text, was taught as a part of the very early Baptist curriculum.[70] The language had to be learned, because, like Greek, it was a language of Christian religious texts—Howard Williams noted that Hebrew had a "prominent place" in the early curriculum due to its "special value" for future ministers.[71] While foundational texts of Judaism formed a core part of the seminary's religious education, the way these texts were taught made it clear that Judaism as a body of religious and spiritual knowledge did not have a claim to the teaching of those texts in the seminary—students were not studying the Torah or Tanakh (the Hebrew Bible), they were studying the Old Testament through a Christian reading that connected it seamlessly to the New Testament. The study of exegetic works for these Baptists included no examination of Talmud or Midrash. Tellingly, Peter Ochs recalled that during his first year at Colgate in 1979, a colleague in Philosophy and Religion mocked the Midrash by calling it "mish-mash"—to many Christians studying religion, Judaism still had no merit whatsoever.[72]

Leading up to the first acceptance of non-ministerial students to the institution in 1839, the course of study slowly started to take on a more secular quality.[73] Eventually, the institution's primary focus became lay education—the goal of the university was no longer to produce Baptist ministers, but to educate America's youth. The study of religion at the university was still dominated by its seminary division, but as time went on the department diversified its offerings to accommodate the idea of religion as an object of non-sectarian, even secular examination. Universities across the United States underwent a similar shift, from the study of theology and dogma, to a critical and scientific study of religion, to a comparative discipline grounded in the study of society.[74] By the 1920s, Colgate had separated completely from the seminary, which relocated to Rochester.[75] In Hamilton, the study of the Old Testament became the purview of the Philosophy and Religion department.[76] Teaching the language of that text was no longer a priority, the seminary professors who claimed dominion over its instruction moved away, and Hebrew fell out of the Colgate curriculum.[77]

Even after the university began to operate as a fully secular institution, Baptist conceptions of religion continued to hold sway over the Philosophy and Religion department. Educational historian Julie Reuben wrote that, even as the study of religion in American universities evolved into that of a social science, professors and universities believed that their courses would "stimulate students to be religious" and lead to a "religious awakening."[78] To this end, there was a pervasive Christianizing of Hebrew and the Hebrew Bible in the Colgate education: for most of the university's history these subjects were exclusively taught by Christian ministers through a Christian lens.[79] Even the Reverend R.V. Smith, who taught Jerry Berkson '58 about Judaism, lectured on the Old Testament, not the Hebrew Bible, and Rev. Smith's "Jews" were essentially Old Testament Hebrews, a people of the past.

Eventually, however, classes would come to be taught at Colgate about Jews and Judaism, and not just as proto-Christians. One of the classes with the most impact on a Jewish theme ever taught at Colgate was Terrence Des Pres's "Literature of the Holocaust," first taught in the 1970s.[80] Des Pres's class regularly enrolled between 100 and 200 students, unprecedented for an English course that was not required.[81] The professor—and also the subject matter, entirely new for Colgate—had a profound effect on his students. One of them wrote

> Sometimes I walk out of class totally silent. . . On other days, I turn to a friend as soon as the film or lecture is over, wanting to discuss my reactions, to "talk it out." The course inspires both silence and discussion. It provokes hatred, and hope. But, the consensus of the students I spoke to was that "it is the most *important* course they have ever taken."[82]

Des Pres himself noted that his class was "more emotional than intellectual" and tapped into his students' psyche to create a strong reaction to the material.[83] The course was covered in student newspapers many times, and each time the writer of the article was struck by the strength of student reactions.[84] "Literature and the Holocaust" became an influential predecessor to a formal Jewish Studies department.

The Jewish experience took on a larger role on campus in other ways as well. An "art and literary magazine" called *Face of the Sage,* initially printed by the Colgate Jewish Union (CJU) though an independent publication by 1982, prominently featured works on Jewish themes and experiences.[85] In addition, the CJU conducted a program of Holocaust remembrance during the 1980s.[86] In 1980, the importance of Holocaust commemoration was discussed in the *Maroon*, and, one year later, the two most prominent Christian student organizations on campus, University Church and the Newman Community, joined the CJU's Holocaust Memorial Week.[87] Later, in 1987, some students began to push for a more active program to remember the Holocaust.[88] Claiming that the CJU's program at that time was inadequate, they asked for a more powerful program of events, since stopping future horrors like the Holocaust required a form of remembrance that would truly stick in the brain and prevent the complacency that had such tragic results.[89] On the curricular side, "Faith after the Holocaust" was first taught by Steven Kepnes in 1988 and has been taught ever since, now by Ben Stahlberg.[90]

The campus also played host to a long-running series of lectures on Jewish topics throughout the decade, including some in conjunction with Holocaust remembrance.[91] Nobel Laureate and Holocaust survivor Elie Wiesel gave the baccalaureate address to the class of 1984.[92] Wiesel returned to campus in 1998, as the incoming class had all read his *Night* that summer, and Jordie Slutsky Kattan '02 recalled the powerful effect meeting him had on her.[93] Another Holocaust survivor, the great Israeli writer Aharon Appelfeld, came to Colgate in 1998 as the first visiting scholar funded by the Finard Chair in Jewish Studies to co-teach a course in modern Jewish literature.[94] The course is still given, and many generations of students have read *Katerina* and other books by Appelfeld. The Finard Chair brought a few other prominent scholars to campus before eventually becoming a faculty position, first held by Steven Kepnes and now by Lesleigh Cushing.

Parallel to the expanding role for Judaism and the study of the Jewish experience on Colgate's campus, a formal curriculum of Jewish Studies spanning the humanities and social sciences slowly began to take shape. The Colgate Jewish Union started pressing for a non-credit Talmud course and advanced Hebrew classes in 1981.[95] Hebrew language courses returned to Colgate in 1986 and have been continuous ever since.[96] The pace of this effort increased greatly in the last years of the decade: by 1989 a "minor in the Jewish Tradition" had been established within the Philosophy and Religion department.[97] In 1990, the first full-time tenure stream appointment in Jewish studies was created; the position was filled by Steven Kepnes.[98] The final impetus for a full

Jewish Studies program, however, was provided in the aftermath of an anti-Semitic talk given on campus in 1991.

As discussed in Chapter 3, Kwame Ture (né Stokely Carmichael) was a prominent civil rights leader with a penchant for anti-Semitism and a desire to publicly share it. In 1991, Ture was invited to campus to give a lecture. Colgate's Jewish student leadership, well aware of the likelihood for the event to take a sharp turn toward anti-Semitism, prepared to stand up to Ture at his lecture. Ture's monologue began innocently enough, but about 30 minutes into a 75–minute speech, he began to make unusual claims about Judaism. Ture claimed that the first Jews were Africans—Moses, he claimed, was Egyptian—and that anyone who claimed a different origin for Judaism was a "racist pig."[99] Since most Jews (and nearly all biblical historians) place the religion's origin in the Levant, the implication was that Ture was saying that modern Jews were "racist pigs." The final third of Ture's lecture consisted predominantly of anti-Semitic rhetoric camouflaged as extreme anti-Zionism, going so far as to call Zionism a satanic movement.[100] While anti-Zionism is not necessarily an expression of anti-Semitism, particularly insidious forms of anti-Zionism such as the views of Kwame Ture are widely considered to fall into the category of anti-Semitism.[101] With the justification that his criticism was being levied against "Zionists" and "Israel," and not against Jews as a larger group, the esteemed champion of civil rights proceeded to spout vile and clearly anti-Semitic rhetoric for more than 30 minutes.

Ture started his attack by implicating Zionism in the destruction of the African continent. Despite the fact that Israel had provided, according to journalists Anthony Weiss and Rebecca Spence, "massive" amounts of foreign aid to Africa in the 1960s and early 1970s through its international cooperation agency Mashav—aid which ended after many African nations cut ties with Israel after 1973's Yom Kippur War and had not yet resumed by the time of Ture's speech—Ture labeled "capitalism and Zionism" as the two primary forces fighting against African unity.[102] Having spent most of the first half of his speech bashing capitalism as a "corrupt system," lumping Zionism into the same category was a severe insult setting the tone for what was to come.[103] In an attempt to distance Zionism from Judaism, and thus to legitimize his vitriol, Ture then stated that Zionism was a European creation and reaffirmed his statement that Judaism was an African religion.[104] Prying Zionism away from the religion it is grounded in was a rhetorical move, which Ture set up to give weight to his critique: if Zionism is European and Judaism is African, then Zionism is a corruption of African ideas, and thus deserves to be destroyed. Unfortunately for Ture, history fails to support him: Judaism does not have an African origin, and Zionism only originated in Europe because a large portion of the (forcibly displaced) diaspora Jews happened to settle on that continent.

Nevertheless, Ture continued. He attacked Theodor Herzl, one of the most prominent early Zionist thinkers, and claimed that because Herzl was an atheist, Zionism has no roots in Judaism.[105] Later, he repeated this sentiment, noting that he was "against this Zionist community who calls itself 'Jewish.'"[106] Ture followed his attacks on Herzl with a series of truly despicable statements: he mumbled into the microphone that Zionism is "a diabolical movement" that's "got to be satanic"; stated that the Jews are not a people; mocked the Colgate Jewish Union's mission statement; parroted the classic anti-Semitic canard that "all of our politicians bow down before the state of Israel"; proclaimed that $50 billion were sent from America to Israel to "shoot Palestinians"; said that Zionism is "an enemy of the people"; and asserted that Zionists "colluded with Hitler."[107] Near the end of his talk, he mocked the CJU mission statement for a second time.[108]

After Ture finished his speech, there was a question and answer period. The CJU members who were in attendance and prepared to defend their religion and their people asked the second question. One stood up and said, "to be against Zionism is to be against Jews who want to liberate themselves from oppression. That is anti-Semitism. . . . And if you're not part of our Jewish struggle, how dare you tell us how you think about it?"[109] In his response, Ture stated, "I cannot accept the assumptions that you gave"; specifically, he questioned the basis of Jewish peoplehood, asking "what imperialism did your national movement fight against, or what imperialism did you collude with to get your land?" and directly insulted Judaism and Christianity by saying that in Mesopotamia people were "worshipping idols until the prophet Muhammed came."[110] Many of the non-Jewish audience members came to Ture's defense during the questioning: the room burst into laughter on multiple occasions, including when he responded "I gave it to you" to the question "who are you to tell us what we are?" and one African American student defended him from charges of anti-Semitism by noting that Ture was "friends with the PLO," and that since "Palestinians are also Semitic" it was impossible for Ture to be "anti-Semitic."[111]

To reiterate: anti-Zionist and anti-Israel rhetoric are not necessarily anti-Semitic. However, when one looks at what Kwame Ture said at Colgate in 1991, it is very difficult to conclude that his "anti-Zionism" was not in fact anti-Semitism. Ture implied that most Jews are "racist pigs"; claimed Zionists were colluding to prevent African unity; termed Zionism "diabolical" and "satanic"; stated that Jews are not a people and that Zionism is not a Jewish movement; mocked the CJU mission statement twice; repeated well-known anti-Semitic catchphrases; claimed Zionists colluded with Hitler; and insinuated that Judaism is a form of idol worship. Ture may have claimed that "these are facts," but none of his statements were anything more than blatant anti-Semitism.[112]

In the aftermath of Ture's appearance at Colgate, the atmosphere on campus was tense, to say the least. The shockwaves of the event reached across the nation: a binder distributed by B'nai B'rith and the Anti-Defamation League entitled "Countering Anti-Semitism, Racism and Extremist Propaganda: A Campus Kit," a copy of which can be found in Colgate's library, cites his talk at Colgate three times.[113] In the next few weeks, Colgate's Jewish community made its anger and concerns known. A faculty panel was held to start a conversation on African-American and Jewish-American relations in response to the talk.[114] Then, led by President Neil Grabois, Jewish students and faculty began to implement a plan to make Colgate a more welcoming place for Jews. Earlier, Marilyn Thie of the Philosophy and Religion department had approached Grabois and expressed her concern that there was no Jewish Studies program at Colgate.[115] As Colgate's first Jewish president, Grabois had every incentive *not* to focus on Jewish needs. The trustees who appointed him had made no reference to his background, and (while he doesn't say this), he might have been expected to distance himself from Jewish concerns.[116] He did not take this path. Grabois discussed the possibility of creating a Jewish Studies program with a group of Jewish alumni, but they were hesitant—they "did not wish to be prominent."[117] Grabois decided that, to make the argument for a Jewish Studies program, the "best thing to do was to start with a place."[118]

After the launch of a Jewish space on campus, the Saperstein Center (discussed in the next section), President Grabois turned back to the curriculum. By the 1992–1993 school year, 214 students were enrolled in Jewish studies courses in the Department of Philosophy and Religion and 3 seniors would be graduating with a minor in Religion in the Jewish Tradition.[119] Armed with these enrollment numbers and the spark provided by Kwame Ture's speech, Grabois and Professor Steven Kepnes led a successful effort to spin the new Jewish Studies Program out from under the Department of Philosophy and Religion's umbrella the following year as an independent interdisciplinary program.[120] For the first time, Jewish Studies had its own academic space at Colgate. By emphasizing what Professor Lesleigh Cushing, who became the first faculty member hired specifically for the Jewish Studies Program in 2001, called an examination of "lived Judaism," the program completed the transformation of Colgate's traditional seminary model, which viewed Jews as an antiquated, proto-Christian people, into a system tailored for a modern, multifaceted university, where "the complex interaction between religion and culture in Jewish life and the diversity of Jewish historical experience" are valued parts of the course of study.[121]

Nevertheless, there are still problems in how the Colgate curriculum treats Judaism. Lesleigh Cushing noted that the university's Baptist legacy was still very strong when she was hired in 2001.[122] One of the courses in the Core Curriculum that every Colgate student takes before graduating, Legacies of the Ancient World, is based primarily on de-Judaized texts from the Old Testament, perpetuating conceptions that Christianity has more of a claim to the text than Judaism. The huge difference in age between the Hebrew Bible and the Gospels can lead to the sense that the older text is more primitive (later Jewish commentaries are not read). Campus Rabbi Dena Bodian sees the particular presentation of the Jewish text as fostering an "identity crisis" for many first- and second-year Jewish students.[123] The same, of course, might be said of practicing Muslim students who encounter these texts in a strictly academic setting.

"Have Fun, Take Care, and Take Pride": An Expanding Jewish Presence at Colgate[124]

At around the same time that a curricular role was being carved out for Judaism, a more vibrant Jewish social and cultural life at Colgate was also coming out of the woodwork. As discussed in Chapter 2, non-Semitism was the major theme of Colgate Jewish life in the 1950s. Jerry Balmuth, who coined the phrase, noted that many non-Jews were simply not aware of Jews on campus and that Jews "never identified themselves" as such.[125] Many Jews felt left out during their time on campus, and many alumni from this period recalled that "their Jewishness was a problem for them."[126] During the late 1960s and 1970s, however, Jewish college students across the country were becoming more active in claiming a Jewish identity on campus. Scholar David Glanz has posited that the development of a Jewish counterculture on college campuses led to an increase in Jewish campus activities; sociologist Marshall Sklare has credited the growth of Jewish summer camps, along with a burgeoning Jewish counterculture, with sparking the claiming of Jewish identity by Jewish college students.[127] At Colgate specifically, this change occurred at around the same time. During this transitional period, many students struggled with being Jewish, but others embraced their Jewishness to varying extents. As illustrated in Chapter 2, Thomas Baker '69 felt a paucity of Jewish life on campus until the Six-Day War, which accelerated the embrace of Jewish identity, while Mark Krinsky '67 recalled working toward a "revival of Jewish religion and culture" while leading the Colgate Hillel Foundation.[128]

After Krinsky and Baker graduated, a wave of dissent hit Colgate's Jewish life. In 1970, the CHF board members opted to join a sit-in against anti-Black racism in Hamilton; many Jews on campus did not approve of their decision.[129] Many politically active Jews, in turn, criticized the CHF for providing "sterile, sporadic and half-hearted religious efforts" and nothing more.[130] With board members recognizing that a "hard core stand was needed," they dissolved the CHF and established the Colgate Hebrew Union (soon renamed the Colgate Jewish Union).[131] In order to more effectively take political action, the new organization "did not pretend to speak for" all Jews, "it represented only its members."[132] In various places, the Colgate Jewish Union's mission was described as "emphasizing action"; adding "political and cultural programs" so that Jewish students could "express their Jewishness" in different ways; stimulating "an awakening of the Jewish consciousness" and respect for Jews; establishing a "closer link between Jews and their unique Jewish identity through political, cultural, and religious action"; eradicating injustice; and fighting "fear and complacency."[133] The new CJU's early political activities, including a protest rally that was both for Israel and against "appalling quietude" on campus, had it labeled by the *Colgate Maroon* as a "radical organization."[134]

By 1975, the CJU had evolved into a vibrant cultural and political organization.[135] Even so, as discussed in Chapter 3, Jewish identity in the 1970s was often kept under the radar, as Jews avoided public markers of their origins like frequenting the university's kosher kitchen. By the late 1970s, however, the Jewish community was becoming more and more visible. In 1979, Colgate's Jewish students were very outspoken about the lack of respect paid to their needs by the administration: two *Maroon* articles in April 1979 lamented the absence of recognition for the Jewish religion. One article requested "a Jewish Chapel . . . kosher dining room facility . . . full-time salaried Rabbi . . . suspension of classes on Jewish holidays, [and] a weekly [newspaper] column concerning the Jewish scene"; a second observed that "last year [1978], Spring Party Weekend inadvertently fell on the same weekend that Passover began."[136] The request for a kosher kitchen is curious, considering that just a few years before, a kosher kitchen on campus was largely unused: as we have often seen, reinvention is a constant feature of campus life. The second article went on to comment that after the issue of scheduling Spring Party Weekend was brought to the administration, "there have been no such problems [in 1979] . . . When we speak up, we are eventually heard."[137] Despite this small victory, the requests of the article's author were largely forgotten; Spring Party Weekend was again scheduled for Passover in 1986.[138]

In 1981, the issue of Jewish cultural presence on campus became an integral part of public discussion by Colgate's Jews. Claudia Zayfert of the Colgate Jewish Union wrote that the CJU's mission included a desire to "bring Jewish culture to Colgate" and enhance its acceptance and appreciation by the campus at large.[139] By publishing their intentions, Zayfert and the CJU were publicly advertising their Jewishness and staking a claim that their culture was a valuable addition to the university. In the same article, Zayfert also declared that 90 percent of Colgate's Jewish students were "afraid to be affiliated with Jews."[140] This assertion sparked a minor controversy among Colgate's unaffiliated Jewish students, leading to a response in the next week's edition of the newspaper, in which authors Gwen Tutun and Jennifer Mayer stated that "the article was offensive to those who see Judaism as a valuable, albeit private, part of their lives."[141] At this time, Colgate's Jews were opening up an internal dialogue of how to approach Judaism, Jewish culture, and alternative Jewish identities on campus. Even those Jews who preferred to have Judaism be a private matter were comfortable enough to embrace their self-proclaimed identity as Jews in public discourse.

The 1980s also featured multiple startlingly racist and anti-Semitic events on campus. In Spring 1982, a professor's research carrel in Case Library was vandalized with Nazi imagery and graffiti declaring "Death to the Jews" and "Fuck the Kikes for Nazi Power."[142] There had been a number of other similar incidents that year, and the vandalism was discovered during the CJU's Commemoration Week for the Holocaust.[143] In response to the incident and in recognition of the timing of the discovery, the chapel bells were rung for 60 seconds to commemorate Holocaust victims.[144] Six years later, in 1988, two racist events were perpetrated by Greek organizations at roughly the same time. Theta Chi hosted a "Jungle Safari Party" where partygoers dressed in blackface, and Delta Upsilon used Nazi imagery in the course of pledging.[145] According to the account published in the *Maroon*, Delta Upsilon students "spray painted a swastika on the shirt of one of the pledges and questioned pledges in a room in the fraternity designated as the World War II room which was decorated with flags from America, Great Britain, Japan, and Nazi Germany. . . One of the students represented Adolf Hitler by wetting his hair and creating a Hitler-like mustache with a ball point pen."[146] In the aftermath, Delta Upsilon received a year of university sanction and Theta Chi were suspended from all campus activities for six weeks.[147]

While African American and Jewish students reacted strongly to the two fraternities' offenses and the university administration disciplined the wrongdoers, the general student population largely remained indifferent. When the *Maroon* asked five students for their opinion on the controversy, four of them were extraordinarily apathetic: "If it is true it is an unfortunate incident, but I don't see racism as a problem on this campus"; "I think that the administration should let fraternities be fraternities"; "I think it was a little over-exaggerated"; "I think it was probably just the typical Colgate rumor mill blowing things out of proportion."[148] Only one of the five students surveyed considered Delta Upsilon's actions to be reprehensible: "I think it's appalling that Colgate students have no comprehension of the possible repercussions of their actions. The swastika is still a symbol of anti-Semitism to this day and is offensive to everybody."[149]

The disinterested responses of Colgate students to the Delta Upsilon "Nazi Room" incident may be shocking, but social and political apathy can be prevalent among American college students.[150] The Colgate student body is no different. As explained in Chapter 2, Thomas Baker '69 felt that during his time on campus there was very little in the way of active religiosity, and news of events of global importance like the Six-Day War passed through Colgate with barely any recognition.[151] During my time at Colgate, the Israel/Palestine debate has been of little importance, which stands in sharp contrast with the emphasis the issue has on many contemporary college campuses. In addition, two days before I wrote this, an African American student carrying a glue gun he needed for an art project was misidentified as an "active shooter."[152] By the time the student realized what was going on, SWAT teams had been called onto campus. The racial overtones of the May 1, 2017, incident were hard to overlook. There was a large protest about the episode on campus the next day, but multiple protesters noted that many of their peers were completely unconcerned by the incident, going about their day as if nothing had happened.

With respect to the anti-Semitic and racist incidents of the 1980s, and noting the background of apathy at Colgate, the pattern of disinterest is worth considering. Although general student responses varied—the vandalism of 1982 was met with widespread condemnation, while Delta Upsilon's Nazi Room incident was seen as unproblematic—in both cases, the Jewish community and other marginalized groups clearly expressed their anger.

As all of this was going on, Colgate's Jews opted to increase their visibility on campus and take pride in their heritage. The Affiliation of Jewish Students (AJS), established on February 19, 1989, was part of this process.[153] Its specific mission was to fill what it saw as the "social gap" for Jews on campus.[154] Similar intentions were behind an article in the *Maroon* a few days before Purim in 1990. Noting that "many Jews feel uncomfortable celebrating such. . . religious events" as Purim, author Mark Freedman implored his classmates to "have fun, take care, and take pride" in their Jewishness.[155] In order to do so, however, Colgate's Jews needed a space of their own in which they could be Jewish.

Much like the creation of a Jewish academic space, the establishment of a Jewish social and cultural space was unwittingly sparked by Kwame Ture. As the discussion on campus after his talk included the need for a Jewish Studies program, so too did it include recognition of the need for a place for Judaism and Jewish culture at Colgate. As seen in Chapter 3, the consensus of the Jewish community after Ture's lecture was a deep desire for a location of its own: "we need a home. . . we need Jewish space."[156] At the time, the African American students had a space of their own and were planning a move to a new building, the ALANA Cultural Center. President Neil Grabois saw the opportunity to use the soon-to-be-vacated space to create a Jewish space at Colgate and to move one step closer to the establishment of a Jewish Studies program.[157]

Grabois enlisted the Jewish student community to help design a space that would best serve its needs.[158] Funding was more difficult, and fraught with memories of Colgate's past. When Grabois approached alumnus Michael Saperstein about financing the redesign of the building that would eventually bear his name, Saperstein was initially hesitant: his experiences as a student in the early 1960s made him wary of creating such a visible Jewish space.[159] In time, Saperstein's reluctance gave way to much different feelings. During the 1993 dedication ceremony, Saperstein was asked to carry the Torah into its new home and cried as he walked.[160] At that moment, a profound silence around Jewish identity at Colgate had been joyously broken.

A few incidents of anti-Semitism notwithstanding, the primary campus climate has been calm, sometimes bordering on apathetic. Adam Basciano '16, who revived the Colgate Israel Club in its most recent form in 2013, mentioned that most people "really don't care about many issues, and that there is a "dominating apathetic mindset toward social issues and anything outside of the Colgate bubble."[161] He remembered that when former Israeli President Shimon Peres came to campus to speak, there was a protest against the speaker, but it was very small.[162]

The lack of anti-Israel sentiment on campus makes Colgate unusual—there are quite a few college campuses where pervasive anti-Israel feelings are common.[163] Rabbi Bodian has credited a number of factors for Colgate's situation. First, since Bodian serves as counselor to Muslim students as well, many Muslim students know her quite well. Religious life at Colgate is also run by the university, not by outside organizations, and there is a very large interfaith community on campus, so all the religious groups know one another and work together often.[164] The Muslim Students Association and the Colgate Jewish Union have worked together to coordinate programming when the Muslim holiday of Eid and the Jewish holiday of Yom Kippur fall at around the same time on the calendar.[165] In addition, the Catholic and Jewish student organizations collaborate on interfaith events regularly, and the Middle Eastern and Islamic Studies and Jewish Studies programs often collaborate on curriculum.[166] In retrospect, it is not hard to see why a university where one is able to ask, "Can the rabbi's wife teach us to dance a Palestinian *debka*?" does not have pervasive anti-Israel or anti-Jewish feelings.[167]

In recent years, the administration has worked with the Jewish community to tear down anti-Semitism. One example occurred in January 2017. Though Delta Kappa Epsilon is no longer recognized by the university, the national fraternity still owns the small chapel adjacent to its former house. In January, President Brian Casey met with a member of the Blue Diamond Society, who brought to the President's attention the existence of a swastika on the brickwork on the side of the chapel.[168] After learning about the image's existence, President Casey, in his first year at the university, had the university contact the national fraternity and consult with an outside construction firm to remove the swastika.[169] Within four days of his lunch with the student, the swastika had been removed from the building.[170]

There have been many twists and turns in the history of Jews at Colgate University. At various times, the administration, fraternities, other students, and guest speakers have been anti-Semitic—sometimes wildly so. Much of the rest of the time, the campus has been simply apathetic. Even so, Colgate's Jews and allies have fought for their rights and over time, their successes have been remarkable. Today, Colgate's Jewish students have a cultural and religious space, an academic space, and a social space of their own—unimaginable not so long ago. And most importantly, Colgate's Jews are able to be themselves. For this, they must thank the resistance of their predecessors.

Endnotes

1. Adam Basciano (President of the Class of 2016, founder of Israel Club), interview by Emily Kahn, January 25, 2017, recording in possession of the author.

2. Cameron Pauly would like to thank his parents, editor Brett Pauly and anthropologist Stephanie Brommer, for the ideas and edits they provided to his chapter.

3. Bat-Ami Zucker, "Black Americans' Reaction to the Persecution of European Jews," *Simon Wiesenthal Center Annual*, no. 3 (1986): 177–197.

4. "Local Hillel Group Elects Bekoff Head," *Colgate Maroon*, December 1, 1948.

5. Gilbert Geis, Curriculum Vitae, *Centre for Tax System Integrity*, http://www.ctsi.org.au/people/Geis.CV.pdf; Gilbert Geis to Everett Needham Case, 3 November 1946, Box 47, Folder 2044, Office of the Provost and Dean of the Faculty 1928–2012, Colgate University Special Collections and University Archives, Colgate University Libraries.

6. Geis to Case; no documented response to these questions has been found.

7. Dick Carozza, "He Sought and Brought Out the Best in Everyone," *ACFE.com*, March/April 2013, https://www.acfe.com/article.aspx?id=4294977176.

8. Carozza, "He Sought and Brought Out the Best in Everyone."

9. Geis, Curriculum Vitae.

10. Philip Girard, *Bora Laskin: Bringing Law to Life*, University of Toronto Press, 2005, http://www.jstor.org/stable/10.3138/9781442671522, 155.

11. Maurice Hindus, *A Traveler in Two Worlds* (Garden City, NY: Doubleday, 1971), 136–139.

12. "Student Sit-in to Continue at Colgate," *Harvard Crimson*, April 13, 1968, http://www.thecrimson.com/article/1968/4/13/student-sit-in-to-continue-at-colgate/.

13. John Glynn (Alpha Tau Omega), interview by Cameron Pauly, May 11, 2017, recording in possession of the author.

14. Interestingly, the Blue Diamond Society is often referred to as BDS, making Colgate one of the few places where the acronym does not refer predominantly to the Boycott, Divestment, Sanctions movement against Israel, but rather to a Jewish organization.

15. Jerome Karabel, *The chosen: the hidden history of admission and exclusion at Harvard, Yale, and Princeton* (Boston: Houghton Mifflin, 2005), 23.

16. George Barton Cutten to Sydney Schoenberg, June 1, 1931, Box 56, Folder 30, President's Office 1851–2010, Colgate University Special Collections and University Archives, Colgate University Libraries; Everett Needham Case to Adam Clayton Powell, September 6, 1945, Box 56, Folder 5, Everett Needham Case Papers 1913–1982, Colgate University Special Collections and University Archives, Colgate University Libraries; Arnold M. Rose, "Anti-Semitism's Root in City Hatred," *Commentary* 6 (1948): 374–8.

17. Jason Petrulis, "George Cutten and Quotas at Colgate University: Some Findings Since the Last Report" (working paper, presented at November 7, 2016 Colgate University Faculty Meeting, October 2016).

18. Heywood Broun and George Britt, *Christians Only: A Study in Prejudice* (New York: Vanguard Press, 1931), 87–88; KWB to General Education Board, January 14, 1938, Series 1.4, Box 618, Folder 6530, General Education Board records (FA058), Rockefeller Archive Center.

19. Jason Petrulis, "Board of Trustees data" (unpublished raw data, presented at November 7, 2016 Colgate University Faculty Meeting, May 10, 2016).

20. Everett Needham Case to James Case, June 15, 1945, Box 15, Folder 32,

Everett Needham Case Papers 1913–1982, Colgate University Special Collections and University Archives, Colgate University Libraries

21. Deborah Dash Moore, "When Jews Were GIs: How World War II Changed a Generation and Remade American Jewry," in *American Jewish Identity Politics*, ed. Deborah Dash Moore (Ann Arbor: University of Michigan Press, 2008), http://www.jstor.org/stable/10.3998/mpub.273452.5, 29.

22. Moore, "When Jews Were GIs," 24.

23. Moore, "When Jews Were GIs," 30–31.

24. Moore, "When Jews Were GIs," 31.

25. "Local Hillel Group Elects Bekoff Head."

26. "Hillel Sponsors First Friday Eve' Services at Colgate, April 6," *Colgate Maroon*, March 7, 1951; "Mathews to Speak at Hillel Meeting," *Colgate Maroon*, May 21, 1952; "Rabbi to Discuss 'Cultural Pluralism,'" *Colgate Maroon*, February 28, 1951.

27. "Rabbi to Discuss 'Cultural Pluralism.'"

28. Marvin Forland (former editor of the *Colgate Maroon* and president of Colgate Hillel Foundation, ex-member of Alpha Tau Omega), interview by Emily Kahn, April 11, 2017, recording in possession of the author.

29. Forland, interview; Jerome Balmuth, interview by Alice Nakhimovsky and Richard April, December 2009, recording in possession of the author.

30. J.D.D., "Religious Lectures Valuable," *Colgate Maroon*, March 18, 1959.

31. Esther Bless, "C.J.U. Strives Toward Greater Participation, Sees Awakening of Jewish Consciousness," *Colgate Maroon*, November 2, 1971.

32. B.H.B., "Core of a Community," *Colgate Maroon*, March 10, 1954.

33. B.H.B., "Core of a Community."

34. "New Chapel House Bronze Bas Relief Designs on Display," *Colgate Maroon*, March 17, 1965; "Chapel House Vision Statement," *Colgate University*, last modified April 27, 2015, http://www.colgate.edu/about/facilities-at-colgate/chapel-house/about-chapel-house/vision-statement.

35. "Fraternities State Rushing Policies on Discrimination," *Colgate Maroon*, March 7, 1951.

36. "Fraternities State Rushing Policies on Discrimination."

37. Leonard Rogoff, "Is the Jew White?: The Racial Place of the Southern Jew," *American Jewish History* 85, no. 3 (1997): 217, 222, http://www.jstor.org/stable/23885563.

38. Emma Green, "Are Jews White?," *The Atlantic*, December 5, 2016, https://www.theatlantic.com/politics/archive/2016/12/are-jews-white/509453/.

39. Forland, interview; "Mathews to Speak at Hillel Meeting," *Colgate Maroon*, May 21, 1952.

40. Forland, interview.

41. Forland, interview.

42. Forland, interview.

43. Forland, interview.

44. Forland, interview.

45. President Case's secretary would almost always respond to questions regarding admissions statistics for Jewish and Black applicants and other discrimination queries by saying Case was "off campus" for some matter or another. This was a frequent occurrence, and often there was no followup from the President's office. It was surmised that this was more of a diversionary tactic than anything else.

46. Forland, interview.

47. Marc Rosenbaum, "Senate Votes to Suspend Phi Delt," *Colgate Maroon*, March 14, 1968.

48. "Fraternities Given Deadline to Decide," *Colgate Maroon*, May 4, 1960.

49. Glynn, interview.

50. John G. Stewart, letter to the editor, *Colgate Maroon*, March 18, 1959; Glynn, interview.

51. Glynn, interview.

52. Glynn, interview.

53. Glynn, interview.

54. Rosenbaum, "Senate Votes to Suspend Phi Delt."

55. "Phi Delt National Votes to End Restrictions," *Colgate Maroon*, September 22, 1966.

56. "Phi Delt National Votes to End Restrictions."

57. Rosenbaum, "Senate Votes to Suspend Phi Delt."

58. Rosenbaum, "Senate Votes to Suspend Phi Delt."

59. Rosenbaum, "Senate Votes to Suspend Phi Delt."

60. Rosenbaum, "Senate Votes to Suspend Phi Delt."

61. "Student Sit-in to Continue at Colgate."

62. Thomas Baker, interview by Emily Kahn, January 30, 2017, recording in possession of the author; Marc Rosenbaum, "Protestors [*sic*] Seize Ad Building," *Colgate Maroon*, April 18, 1968.

63. Hasia Diner, "Multiple Outsiderness: Religious, Ethnic, and Racial Diversity in America," *Contemporary Jewry* 24, no. 1 (2003): 45–46, http://www.jstor.org/stable/23455243.

64. Diner, "Multiple Outsiderness," 29–50.

65. Rosenbaum, "Protestors [*sic*] Seize Ad Building."

66. Baker, interview.

67. Many thanks to Professor Lesleigh Cushing for coming up with this title.

68. Lesleigh Cushing (Director, Jewish Studies Program, Colgate University), in discussion with the author, April 5, 2017.

69. "Colgate's Origins," *Colgate University*, accessed May 9, 2017, http://www.colgate.edu/about/colgates-origins.

70. Cushing, in discussion with the author.

71. Howard D. Williams, *A History of Colgate University: 1819–1969* (New York: Van Nostrand Reinhold, 1969), 74.

72. Peter Ochs, interview by Alice Nakhimovsky, January 4, 2017, recording in possession of the author.

73. "Colgate's Origins"; Williams, *A History of Colgate University*, 74–75, 80.

74. Julie A. Reuben, "The Reconstruction of Religion," in *The Making of the Modern University:Iintellectual Transformation and the Marginalization of Morality* (Chicago: University of Chicago Press, 1996), 88–132.

75. Williams, *A History of Colgate University*, 290.

76. Cushing, in discussion with the author.

77. Cushing, in discussion with the author.

78. Reuben, "The Reconstruction of Religion," 100–101.

79. Cushing, in discussion with the author.

80. Sally Sachar, "Holocaust Class Provokes Hatred, Hope," *Colgate Maroon*, April 17, 1979.

81. Sachar, "Holocaust Class Provokes Hatred, Hope"; Johanna Hunter, "Thinking About the Holocaust," *Colgate Maroon*, March 2, 1982.

82. Sachar, "Holocaust Class Provokes Hatred, Hope."

83. Sachar, "Holocaust Class Provokes Hatred, Hope."

84. Sachar, "Holocaust Class Provokes Hatred, Hope"; Hunter, "Thinking About the Holocaust"; Jim Hubbard, "Holocaust Class has Impact for Des Pres' English Students," *Colgate Maroon*, February 27, 1979.

85. Cyndi Skripak, "Faces of the Sage: A Celebration of Words," *Colgate Maroon*, April 20, 1982; Joe Piacquad, "Publications Fill Diverse Needs," *Colgate Maroon*, April 7, 1983.

86. Nina S. Sugar, letter to the editor, *Colgate Maroon*, April 22, 1980; "Holocaust Memorial Week," *Colgate Maroon*, April 28, 1981; John Bramson, "Lecture Ends Holocaust Remembrance," *Colgate Maroon*, April 27, 1982.

87. Sugar, letter to the editor; "Holocaust Memorial Week."

88. Adam Shyaviz, "Better Ways Needed to Remember the Holocaust," *Colgate Maroon*, May 5, 1987.

89. Shyaviz, "Better Ways Needed to Remember the Holocaust."

90. Steven Kepnes (Director of Chapel House and Director of the Fund for the Study of the Great Religions), personal communication, May 11, 2017; "Course Offerings," *Colgate University*, accessed May 9, 2017, http://www.colgate.edu/academics/departments-and-programs/religion/academic-program#courses.

91. "Judaic Lecture," *Colgate Maroon*, July 16, 1980; "On Cultures. . . ," *Colgate Maroon*, March 16, 1982; "Current U.S. Policy and the Mid-East: Lebanon and Israel," February 28, 1984, Advertisement, *Colgate Maroon*; "Two Events Next Week Will Focus on the Holocaust," *Colgate Maroon*, April 9, 1985.

92. "Holocaust Expert Will Speak," *Colgate Maroon*, April 24, 1984.

93. Jordie Slutsky Kattan, interview by Alice Nakhimovsky, January 13, 2017, recording in possession of the author.

94. Noah Wintroub, "Colgate Welcomes Renowned Jewish Scholar," *Colgate Maroon News*, March 6, 1998.

95. Colgate Jewish Union, "What is the C.J.U.?," September 15, 1981, Advertisement, *Colgate Maroon*.

96. Kepnes, personal communication.

97. Steven Kepnes, private collection.

98. Kepnes, private collection; Kepnes, personal communication.

99. Kwame Ture, public lecture, Colgate University, February 5, 1991, DVD, 147 min., http://library.colgate.edu/record=b5196884~S5.

100. Ture, lecture.

101. Robert Wistrich, "Anti-Zionism and Anti-Semitism," *Jewish Political Studies Review* 16, no. 3/4 (2004): 27–31, http://www.jstor.org/stable/25834602; Josh Kaplan, "Contesting Anti-Semitism: Human Rights, Israel Bashing, and the Making of a Non-Problem," *Anthropological Quarterly* 83, no. 2 (2010): 429–448, http://www.jstor.org/stable/40863658.

102. Anthony Weiss and Rebecca Spence, "Israel Seeks to Raise Profile of African Aid," *Forward*, September 9, 2006, http://forward.com/news/4785/israel-seeks-to-raise-profile-of-african-aid/; Ture, lecture.

103. Ture, lecture.

104. Ture, lecture.

105. Ture, lecture.

106. Ture, lecture.

107. Ture, lecture.

108. Ture, lecture.

109. Ture, lecture.

110. Ture, lecture.

111. Ture, lecture.

112. Ture, lecture.

113. Anti-Defamation League, *Countering Anti-Semitism, Racism and Extremist Propaganda: A Campus Kit* (New York: B'nai B'rith, 1993).

114. Charles Pete Banner-Haley, Jerome Balmuth, Moshe Gresser, Rhonda Levine, and Charles Rice, "African Americans and Jewish Americans: An Uneasy Alliance" (roundtable discussion, Colgate University, April 1, 1991).

115. Neil Grabois (13th President and first Jewish president of Colgate University), interview by Alice Nakhimovsky, January 10, 2017, recording in possession of the author.

116. Grabois, interview.

117. Grabois, interview.

118. Grabois, interview.

119. Kepnes, private collection.

120. Kepnes, private collection.

121. Lesleigh Cushing (Director, Jewish Studies Program, Colgate University), interview by Marit Vangrow, March 21, 2017, recording in possession of the author; Cushing, in discussion with the author; "Jewish Studies Program," *Colgate University*, accessed May 9, 2017, http://www.colgate.edu/academics/departments-and-programs/jewish-studies.

122. Cushing, interview.

123. Dena Bodian (Associate University Chaplain and Director of Jewish Life, Colgate University), interview by Emily Kahn, May 6, 2017, recording in possession of the author.

124. Mark Freedman, "Purim: Have Fun, Take Care, and Take Pride," *Colgate Maroon*, March 6, 1990.

125. Balmuth, interview.

126. Balmuth, interview.

127. David Glanz, "An Interpretation of the Jewish Counterculture," *Jewish Social Studies* 39, no. 1/2 (1977): 117–28, http://www.jstor.org/stable/4466953; Marshall Sklare, "The Greening of Judaism," *Commentary* 58, no. 6 (1974): 51–57.

128. Baker, interview; Mark Krinsky (former leader of Colgate Hillel Foundation), interview by Emily Kahn, December 27, 2016, recording in possession of the author.

129. Bless, "C.J.U. Strives Toward Greater Participation."

130. Alan Touger, letter to the editor, *Colgate Maroon*, May 3, 1970.

131. Bless, "C.J.U. Strives Toward Greater Participation."

132. Bless, "C.J.U. Strives Toward Greater Participation."

133. Robert Kahn, "Hillel Replaced by Hebrew Union. Rabbi is Sought," *Colgate Maroon,* April 29, 1970; Bless, "C.J.U. Strives Toward Greater Participation"; Mark Friedman, Kerry Baker, Rick Litvak, Jon Rosenberg, Ken Goldsmith, Cary Goodman, Joe Silny, Lance Ehrenberg, Justus Weiner, Marc Berman, Bob Ackerman, Adam Garson, Cliff Kramer, and Robert Kahn, letter to the editor, *Colgate News,* April 30, 1970.

134. Rod French, "CJU Condemns Student Apathy Over Mid-East," *Colgate Maroon,* September 25, 1970; "CJU Discusses D.C. Protest, Future Program Schedule," *Colgate Maroon,* April 15, 1972.

135. Susan von Hoffman, "'Is God Dead?' Not at Colgate. Religious Organizations Active," *Colgate Maroon,* February 25, 1975.

136. Henry Rabin, letter to the editor, *Colgate Maroon,* April 10, 1979; Larry Messerman and Andy Richlin, letter to the editor, *Colgate Maroon,* April 17, 1979.

137. Messerman and Richlin, letter to the editor.

138. Valerie Baruch and Lee Anne Morse, letter to the editor, *Colgate Maroon,* April 1, 1986.

139. Claudia Zayfert, "Jewish Union Promotes Heritage," *Colgate Maroon,* March 10, 1981.

140. Zayfert, "Jewish Union Promotes Heritage."

141. Gwen Tutun and Jennifer Mayer, letter to the editor, *Colgate Maroon,* March 17, 1981.

142. Barbara Shulman, "Case Violated," *Colgate Maroon,* April 20, 1982.

143. Shulman, "Case Violated."

144. Shulman, "Case Violated."

145. Penelope Patsuris, "Safari Party Exposes Underlying Racism," *Colgate Maroon,* October 4, 1988; James Parsons, "DU Responds to Allegations," *Colgate Maroon,* April 26, 1988.

146. Parsons, "DU Responds to Allegations."

147. Parsons, "DU Responds to Allegations;" Charles M. Williams, "Pelton Releases Statement on 'Jungle' Party," *Colgate News,* October 7, 1988.

148. "Campus Comment: What Do You Think of the DU Pledge Incident?," *Colgate Maroon,* April 26, 1988.

149. "Campus Comment."

150. Paul Rogat Loeb, "Against Apathy: Role Models for Engagement," *Academe* 87, no. 4 (2001): 42–47, doi:10.2307/40252040.

151. Baker, inteview.

152. Brian W. Casey, "Statement to the Colgate Community from President Brian W. Casey," *Colgate University*, May 2, 2017, http://news.colgate.edu/2017/05/statement-to-the-colgate-community-from-president-brian-w-casey.html/.

153. Karen Weiss, "Jewish Students Found New Organization," *Colgate Maroon*, February 28, 1989.

154. Weiss, "Jewish Students Found New Organization."

155. Freedman, "Purim."

156. Rabbi Matt Berkowitz, interview by Anat Guez, January 9, 2017, recording in possession of the author.

157. Grabois, interview.

158. Grabois, interview.

159. Grabois, interview.

160. Grabois, interview.

161. Basciano, interview.

162. Basciano, interview.

163. Leonard Saxe, Graham Wright, Shahar Hecht, Michelle Shain, Theodore Sasson, and Fern Chertok, "Hotspots of Antisemitism and Anti-Israel Hostility on US Campuses," *Brandeis University*, October 2016, https://www.brandeis.edu/ssri/noteworthy/antisemitism.html; Eric Alterman, "The B.D.S. Movement and Anti-Semitism on Campus," *New York Times*, March 29, 2016, https://www.nytimes.com/2016/03/29/opinion/the-bds-movement-and-anti-semitism-on-campus.html.

164. Bodian, interview.

165. Bodian, interview.

166. Bodian, interview.

167. Bodian, interview.

168. Brian W. Casey (President, Colgate University), personal communication, May 10, 2017.

169. Casey, personal communication.

170. Casey, personal communication.

6

Colgate Jews on the Global Stage

Amy Balmuth

One Degree of Separation from Stalin: Colgate Jews & the Russian Revolution

Maurice Hindus, Class of 1915, was among the foremost Western journalists to explain what happened when the USSR engaged in the unprecedented step of seizing all privately owned farmland in the early 1930s. His work, a series of books that are equal parts travel-writing, journalism, and cultural critique, is significant for its transnational perspective. Through his writing on Colgate and Soviet Russia, Hindus unpacks his own—extremely nuanced—view of religion and government.

Collectivization, as it was called, occurred without regard for the individuals who had tended to and depended on the land for millennia. It turned these peasants into laborers on collective farms in an attempt to mimic the industrial organization of city factories. This restructuring would create a kind of outdoor proletariat. The proletariat––according to Marx, "the really revolutionary class"––stood echelons above the peasantry in importance and would, along with other unnecessary classes, "decay and finally disappear in the face of Modern Industry."[1] The Stalinist government adhered to the Marxist view of the peasantry, making the confiscation of peasant land and destruction of their way of life an ideological non-issue. Confined to factory work and potentially ripe for rebellion, urban dwellers were hungry. The

Soviet government badly needed the grain to support its industrial drive, but was not keen on bargaining for it. Collectivization sent grain produced in rural regions to places that were industrializing. There was no concern for those left starving.

Collectivization was implemented in two steps: first, the elimination of the "kulaks," a comparatively wealthy group of peasants that owned land or machinery, and second, the confiscation of everyone's land and livestock.[2] Over 320,000 kulak farmers forcibly underwent dekulakization from the end of 1929 to the middle of 1930.[3] Dekulakization, as sterile as it sounds, was anything but that. Kulak families—along with poorer peasants, included in order to meet quotas—were shipped to isolated, inhabitable land in the Urals, Siberia, and Kazakhstan.[4] If they didn't die in the unheated boxcars that transported them, they often died later, in the harsh forests, mountains, and steppes where they were deposited with no resources.[5]

The threat of dekulakization caused mass passive resistance, often in the form of destroying livestock.[6] This resistance, combined with the disorganization of the collective farms, transformed relatively productive agricultural lands into the site of two major famines. While the exact statistics are unattainable—the Soviet government did not publish population data after 1932—the historian Robert Conquest has estimated 5 million deaths as a result of starvation and related disease.[7] This takes into consideration, in part, estimates by foreign journalists who despite their tendency to praise Stalinist policies claimed approximated 5–7 million deaths by famine.[8] Regardless of this statistical lacuna, the two famines reaped an immense—and newsworthy—human toll.

Hindus's texts are suspended between his understanding of the Russian peasant—the countryside was where his life began, after all—and his susceptibility to Marxist-Leninist propaganda. Ideology wasn't the only factor: American journalists were wooed with luxuries and threatened with visa denial. Hindus's judgments were likely impacted by worries that he would not be able to get a visa—a problem for

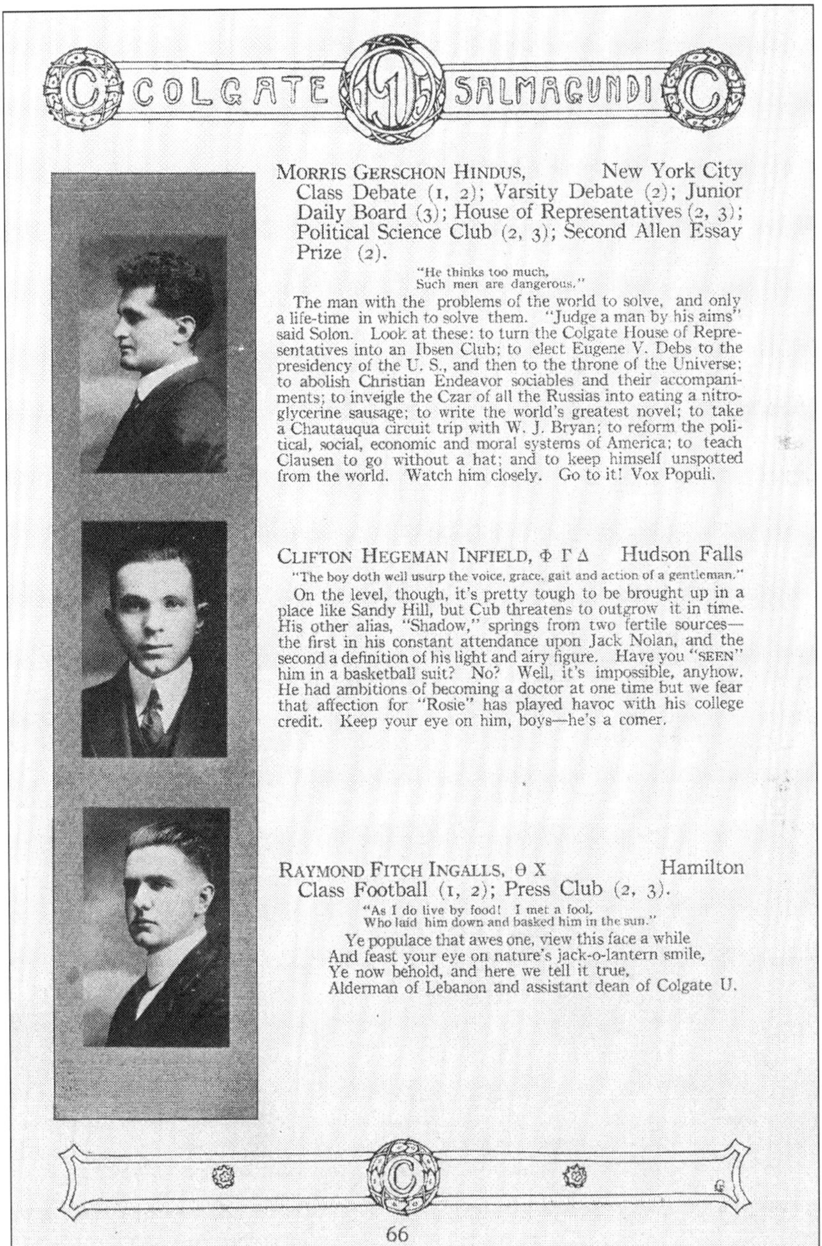

COLGATE 1915 SALMAGUNDI

MORRIS GERSCHON HINDUS, New York City
Class Debate (1, 2); Varsity Debate (2); Junior Daily Board (3); House of Representatives (2, 3); Political Science Club (2, 3); Second Allen Essay Prize (2).

"He thinks too much,
Such men are dangerous."

The man with the problems of the world to solve, and only a life-time in which to solve them. "Judge a man by his aims" said Solon. Look at these: to turn the Colgate House of Representatives into an Ibsen Club; to elect Eugene V. Debs to the presidency of the U. S., and then to the throne of the Universe; to abolish Christian Endeavor sociables and their accompaniments; to inveigle the Czar of all the Russias into eating a nitroglycerine sausage; to write the world's greatest novel; to take a Chautauqua circuit trip with W. J. Bryan; to reform the political, social, economic and moral systems of America; to teach Clausen to go without a hat; and to keep himself unspotted from the world. Watch him closely. Go to it! Vox Populi.

CLIFTON HEGEMAN INFIELD, Φ Γ Δ Hudson Falls

"The boy doth well usurp the voice, grace, gait and action of a gentleman."

On the level, though, it's pretty tough to be brought up in a place like Sandy Hill, but Cub threatens to outgrow it in time. His other alias, "Shadow," springs from two fertile sources—the first in his constant attendance upon Jack Nolan, and the second a definition of his light and airy figure. Have you "SEEN" him in a basketball suit? No? Well, it's impossible, anyhow. He had ambitions of becoming a doctor at one time but we fear that affection for "Rosie" has played havoc with his college credit. Keep your eye on him, boys—he's a comer.

RAYMOND FITCH INGALLS, Θ X Hamilton
Class Football (1, 2); Press Club (2, 3).

"As I do live by food! I met a fool,
Who laid him down and basked him in the sun."

Ye populace that awes one, view this face a while
And feast your eye on nature's jack-o-lantern smile,
Ye now behold, and here we tell it true,
Alderman of Lebanon and assistant dean of Colgate U.

66

Morris Gerschon Hindus in the 1915 Colgate yearbook.

someone who made his living writing books about Russia. He was also a product of his time, part of a liberal western intelligentsia inclined to believe Soviet propaganda.

But before he helped to shape western understanding of what was happening in the USSR, exposing the realities of collectivization and show trials with the perspective of a "traveler in two worlds," Maurice Gerschon Hindus milked cows in Madison County.

His rural Russian childhood instilled in Hindus a critical eye for the process of farming, as well as deep appreciation for the way American farmers went about it. Yet at Colgate, where he saw himself as a Russian intellectual, he abandoned agriculture for literature. This proved to be a fruitful move. His journalism career included multiple books on Russian civilization and propelled him to significance.

As Stalin transformed the Soviet state, accurate information about what was happening there became a precious commodity. A coterie of American journalists, including Maurice Hindus, took on the task of informing the public about the state of Soviet affairs. The transnational upbringing that had influenced Hindus's Colgate experience now gave him a perspective on the Soviet situation that his fellow journalists could not match. His native Russian allowed him to circumvent translators and speak directly to the peasants. Hindus describes his approach: "to be in the country, wander around, observe and listen, ask questions and digest answers to obtain some comprehension of the sweep and meaning of these events."[9] It was this approach, combined with Hindus's intimate knowledge of Russian peasantry and agrarian life, that makes his journalism and scholarly writing exceptional, admirable—and sometimes disappointing.

Hindus's account of collectivization, *Red Bread: Collectivization in a Russian Village,* weaves together his transnational identity with the brutal realities of collectivization and agrarian Soviet life. Much of what he sees is understood in contrast to his boyhood in Bol'she Bykovo. Hearing screams of children down the street, Hindus observes peasant boys and girls at play. The children were "armed with sticks" and divided into two armies: the bourgeoisie and the proletariat.[10] Hindus notes the "change in the form and spirit of children's play in the village."[11] The birch sticks that were now guns had in his time been horses; instead of drawing from ancestral traditions, the peasant children's play was inspired by socio-political conflict.[12]

On the same visit, Hindus comes across a farmer named Sergey, who had experienced the wrath of dekulakization. Hindus's description is sympathetic: Sergey is a man with "eyes . . . widened abnormally, as those of a man afflicted with illness and tribulation."[13] Collectivization had brought "the worst day in his life . . . —trouble, trouble, trouble, and no way of escape."[14] The interaction causes Hindus to reflect on the ruthlessness of the Soviet policy, on how Sergey's potential for plenty has been dashed by tax policy and the fact that soon even his land would be stripped from him.[15] While Hindus admires Soviet ideology, he has deep sympathy for its human victims. Sergey, he wrote, is "an insect . . . to be stepped upon and crushed."[16] Notably, Hindus does not take this moment to gleefully admire human progress. Instead, the interaction highlights the insignificance of the Soviet individual. In circumstances that trample on human rights, collectivization as one example, journalism like Hindus's stresses the importance of understanding the human experience.

Hindus's religious inclinations are difficult to sort out. In Hamilton, he was an avid Baptist church-goer. His Jewish background seems to have been a non-factor in his assessment of the Soviet experience; it's an aspect of his identity he constantly fails to acknowledge in his books. His religious views don't conform to those of his subjects or presumed readers—a detail that makes his commentary on religion burdensome to dissect.

When, in *Red Bread,* Hindus visits a run-down local church—the officiating priest now deceased—his personal ideas about Christianity are kept under wraps. In fact, the Russians he comes into contact with presume him to be an atheist. Upon leaving the church, he is met with harassment from local youth.[17] The young people ask Hindus why he visited the church if "surely [he] was an unbeliever like themselves? Weren't all men of culture unbelievers? Were Americans different?" From the viewpoint of the Soviet youth, Hindus's adopted American nationality is synonymous with support of scientific discovery—what the youth call "modern miracles"—which, to these young Soviets, seems incompatible to the exercise of religion.[18] In response, Hindus writes "I never do argue with Russian revolutionaries when the fundamental dogmas of their creed are in question. It is of no use."[19] Confronted with an ideologue, Hindus turns away from this "bombardment." His reaction echoes the American practice of establishing a distance between journalism and subject; Hindus' Colgate education had informed his journalistic approach.[20]

Despite his childhood in Russia and fluency in the language—two factors that might predispose Hindus to ask the right questions and write incisively about what he saw—at points in his work, he comes across as just another apologist. Cold War historians have excoriated western correspondents for whitewashing Stalin's brutality. S.J. Taylor's scathing book *Stalin's Apologist* tells the story of Walter Duranty, correspondent for the *New York Times*, who "fancied himself a Citizen of the World, a man of knowledge and influence, culture, and wit."[21] An addendum to Duranty's accolades might include the fact that the world citizen was completely comfortable with inaccuracy. Duranty perpetuated a lie about his own birthplace just because "it sounded good and enhanced his image."[22] By repeating the Russian communist adage "you can't make an omelet without breaking eggs," Duranty failed to expose the sufferings of Stalin's victims and is remembered by many historians as a criminal disappointment.[23]

Taylor applies a similar, though less scathing, critique to Maurice Hindus. "His evaluation of the Stalinist regime remained essentially favorable," Taylor writes.[24] Notably, Taylor refers to Hindus as a "western enthusiast" and "sympathizer to the cause."[25] According to Taylor, Hindus's tendency to overlook the damage done by the USSR, while brightening the silver linings, colored his judgments. While perhaps not as reprehensible as Duranty—a result, in part, of the smaller audience reading his works—Hindus's role in misshaping American ideas of Soviet collectivization should not be understated.

While his sympathy for Sergey, and recoil from the youthful idealogues he met at the church shows muted skepticism, Hindus's praise of the Stalinist Revolution is indeed evident in other places. While interviewing an engineer, Hindus asks him "and would you like to be rich?" only to be surprised by the man's response: "It is foolish to be rich. . . . Rich people exploit the poor."[26] It is Hindus's subsequent musing that backs up Taylor's claim: "If [the spirit of contempt for personal riches that characterized this boy and his generation would stay with them as they grew up], then the Russian Revolution, in spite of its barbarities, will put to shame all the other movements, including religion, that have been striving for ages to draw out of man his lust for individual accumulation."[27] By discounting the suffering inflicted by the Stalinist regime, Hindus justifies the means for an end that he still seems to have faith in.

Hindus, Jewish only by birth, pursued a career shaped by his Russian upbringing. His identity, even the parts he chose to suppress, emerged in his intellectual pursuits. It was a pattern followed by many Russian Jews who escaped the Soviet era. Dr. Albert Parry was the first professor of Russian and first professor from Russia at Colgate. Few people, and certainly nobody at Colgate, had his breadth of experience with the Bolsheviks, the Whites—and also, the OSS, CIA, and MI6. When Parry came to Colgate in 1947 as a Professor of Russian Language and Literature; he presented himself, as Hindus had, as a Russian. While he did not announce himself as Jewish to the University—or even to his own sons—the other circumstances of his life were enough to make him an exotic standout in an otherwise homogenous faculty.

Parry had come of age in the Soviet Civil War. His unpublished autobiography "Ask That Your Way Be Long," begins as the Whites thrust a rifle into his hands. He deserts, and then in order to survive, goes to work for the Reds, an interlude that comes to an abrupt halt when the Whites return. He and his friends flee, but not fast enough. "By morning, we were trapped. All at once battle crashed upon the village . . . Resistance was useless, for soon we knew we were surrounded by Whites on all sides."[28] The Whites put him in front of a firing squad. He turns to his brother and says "it's a pity the family won't even know where we are buried."[29]

The firing squad did not quite materialize (in the chaos, the would-be victims escaped), but Parry's life continued to be marked by war, even once he settled in the United States. From 1939 to 1941, he worked for the MI6 Committee to Help America by Aiding the Allies, a secret program aimed at getting the United States involved in the war.[30] Then, in the wake of Pearl Harbor, he sought a position in intelligence and eventually signed up as a civilian staffer at the Office of Strategic Services (OSS), the precursor of today's CIA.[31] At the OSS, he became an "information officer on Eastern Europe," a setup that allowed him to conduct intelligence work throughout the war in his "civvies."[32] As part of the OSS, Parry remained in Chicago surveilling the German-American community in the Upper Midwest, running a lecture circuit that doubled as a means of monitoring pro-Nazi behavior.[33]

Parry was brought to Colgate by President Everett Case, as part of an attempt to "[gather] a bold new group for the faculty at Colgate," in the words of Parry's friend Stevenson.[34] While his PhD from the University of Chicago was in American history, Case sought his Russian expertise. Once on campus, Parry established the Russian Studies program. The growing power of the USSR spurred many universities to establish Russian studies programs, few of which were at a liberal arts institution like Colgate.[35] For many years, Parry taught it all himself: language, politics, literature, and history.[36]

Parry was a frequent speaker on Russian foreign policy and the threat of nuclear war (he also wrote a number of articles for the *New York Times*). Still, he remained in Hamilton commenting—extremely accurately—on the cratering world around him. On October 16, 1957,

Noah Wintroub '98, greets Mikhail Gorbachev, the last General Secretary of the Communist Party of the USSR, during his May 1997 visit to Colgate. President Neil Grabois, seated, and Professor of Russian Anthony Olcott look on. Raisa Gorbachev is in the lower left. Courtesy of Colgate University Special Collections and University Archives.

The Colgate Maroon ran the headline: "Parry Predicted Firing of Artificial Satellite 'Sputnik.'"[37] The article claims "Parry, Chairman of the Department of Russian Studies, was among the first American experts to call attention to Soviet efforts in the rocket and missile field."[38]

In 1953, Dr. Parry addressed the Colgate Hillel Foundation on the topic "What's Behind the Kremlin's Latest Anti-Semitism?"[39] Parry's lecture was likely in reference to the Doctor's Plot—Stalin's anti-Semitic campaign that sought to eliminate parts of society that might compete for his power.[40] From Hamilton, New York, Albert Parry was watching. His talk offered opinions on "the current purges of Jewish officials and severance of diplomatic relations with Israel."[41] The war's end caused a swell of anti-Semitism in the Soviet Union, culminating in the secret trial of the Jewish Anti-Fascist Committee (JAC) in 1952.[42] The Jewish Anti-Fascist Committee, founded in the winter of 1941–42, was established to drum up Western support for the teetering alliance between Stalin and Western democracies.[43]

Under the veneer of legality, a number of prominent Jews—actors, writers, government officials, and a scientist—were found guilty of espionage and "nationalist moods."[44] But Parry wasn't the only member of the Colgate faculty with close ties to prominent Jews in Russia. Years later, the JAC trial would reverberate through Professor Shimon Markish.

The great Yiddish poet Peretz Markish was a member of the JAC and a target of the secret trial. In the wake of the trial, his widow Esther and sons David and Shimon sought escape from the Soviet Union, and were eventually able to emigrate 20 years after Peretz's execution.[45] Peretz Markish had passed on to his sons a passion and proficiency for words—David became a prose writer, and Shimon a literary and cultural historian.[46]

When Shimon Markish accepted the position of visiting professor of Russian and Jewish studies, he brought with him an intimate knowledge of the Jewish experience in the Soviet Union. In a 1983 Humanities Colloquium, Markish discussed the works of Vasily Grossman, a JAC member alongside Markish's father and the first Russian-language writer to frankly address the whole range of experiences in the Russian twentieth century: World War II (including mistakes made by the leadership), the Holocaust, collectivization, and mass arrests.[47] Grossman's novel *Life and Fate*, compares Stalin to Hitler as part of a classic examination of totalitarianism. The book, still read at Colgate today, was confiscated by the Soviet authorities while still in manuscript. Without Shimon Markish, who shepherded the book through its first printing in Lausanne, it might never have seen the light of day.

Dr. Gates Defends Nazis, Again: Nazism at Colgate

"It is rumored that a new dictatorship is well on its way in Europe," a 1933 edition of *The Colgate Maroon* commented in a section titled "Outstanding Current Events."[48] Despite the physical distance between Germany and Colgate, Nazism was a subject of debate for faculty and students drawn to politics.

Among them was Dr. Clifford Elwood Gates, Professor of German Language and Literature—a Nazi sympathizer who used his platform at Colgate to promulgate his views. Dr. Gates, a Colgate alumnus himself, had been on campus at the same time as Hindus. Considerably older than his peers, Hindus had been a keen observer of students who didn't fit the "Colgate man" mold. The two outsiders, a future Nazi and a secret Jew, bonded over their "unconventional views" of Colgate football.[49] In *A Traveler In Two Worlds,* Hindus describes Gates as "light-haired and blue-eyed," someone who looked so slight and young and shy that I thought knee-pants would have been more fitting for him than trousers."[50] Were it not for Gates's slight frame and "quiet-voiced, so unassuming, so withdrawn" attitude, he might have come across as textbook Nazi.[51] Most peculiarly, Hindus's description of Gates as academically strong but physically unassuming parallels then-common stereotypes of Jewish masculinity. Gates's position as head of the German department during the lead-up to World War II imbued him with a significant authority on all things Germany. By the time he returned to Colgate as a professor, Gates transformed from a withdrawn student to a vocal and commanding Nazi apologist.

The "tremendous drama going on in Europe" drew so much campus attention that in 1934 Dr. Gates spoke to the entire student body in a chapel address.[52] His speech, according to *The Colgate Maroon,* "retold the meteoric rise of the German Nazi Leader from a common laborer to dictator of a nation in one year."[53] At the end of his speech, continues the reporter, Gates reassured students that Hitler was " no longer the persecutor of the Jews."[54] Hitler was, in fact, someone the Jews could count on: "the greatest danger the Hebrew race faces today is the possibility of Hitler's losing office and giving place to the 'bloodhound' Goerring."[55] However, Gates's continued defense of the Nazi state reveals, at best, a lack of understanding of the severity of the situation in Germany and, at worst, confident anti-Semitism. His reassurance was aberrant within the United States: most American journalists continually warned about the situation in Germany.

One year later, in another address to the student body, Gates asserted Germany's renewed economic efficacy, justified its remilitarization, and claimed that "any violence against the Jews is severely punished."[56] Gates's concession of Germany's misdoings was amplified by his presumption of authority. *The Colgate Maroon*'s subheading "Authority on Germany Praises Work Done Under New Rule," reveals the status he had on campus as someone who really knew what was going on.[57]

Dr. Gates's opinions on Nazi Germany were supported on campus. A letter to the editor, written by Dexter H. Teed and featured in *The Colgate Maroon,* defended Dr. Gates against an article "freely criticizing" the professor based on what Teed termed "faulty facts."[58] The *Banter* article was part of the anonymous, collaboratively written "Sour Scrapes" column (unfortunately no longer available).[59] Teed found Dr. Gates "expressed honest opinions—-which is his privilege" and warned that "if student writers wish to criticize him—which is their privilege—let them get the facts."[60] While support for Dr. Gates's speech was fueled by the principle of free speech, his defenders neglected—or perhaps, willfully ignored—the fact that he relayed a message oozing with hate and misinformation.

Dr. Gates was not the only Colgate-affiliated individual downplaying the persecution of Jews in Germany. John Reiners, the first Colgate exchange student to study in Germany, wrote in October 1937, "I can't believe that there is any persecution to the extent that the American press pictures it to be."[61] Reiners was not uncritical: his observations, published sequentially, found that the Nazi regime was failing to meet its own standard and that the gap between classes "seems to be growing wider rather than narrowing down."[62] He also noted that in German universities "no Jews are allowed to matriculate, the number of women students is practically negligible, and only the richer boys are able to attend."[63] A homogenous student body, however, was nothing new to Reiners. Colgate would have been only marginally more diverse, so it's difficult to discern whether Reiners saw the homogeneity of the German university as a negative.

Reiners's observations are backed by facts; in 1934 the Nazi regime placed restrictions on college entrance that allowed only 10% of the student body to be female.[64] An article in *The Colgate Maroon* assured readers that "the program is not so radical as some make it out to be. Similar tendencies toward limitation of college entrants are to be found in many American institutions of higher learning."[65] More stringent entrance restrictions were also being suggested for American higher education, which critics of entrance policies argued had become "cluttered with an excess of human driftwood."[66] With "human driftwood"—also known as those of different ethnicity, race, class, or gender from the typical white, male, upper-class college student—proliferating in higher education, homogeneity became a standard of excellence. German and American universities, Colgate included, embraced racially discriminatory practices that would save the world's democracies from the ruin of diversity.

Gates and, to a lesser degree, Reiners, were not Colgate's only links to the Nazi regime—on occasion, actual Nazis came to Hamilton to share their views on "the Jewish question." In 1933, a German visitor named Dr. Karl H. Schmitt spoke in the chapel as a representative of the German Olympic Committee.[67] Dr. Schmitt had, he said, taken a break from surveying American college athletics to speak on "the Jewish question," echoing Dr. Gates by claiming "American newspapers tell but one side of the Nazi situation."[68] In a speech about German politics—in which he, of course, brought up the Jews—Dr. Schmitt, who had "been a Nazi for two years and in that time [had] grown to know Hitler quite intimately," declared Hitler to be an "outspoken enemy of armed conflict" who would improve the lives of the German people.[69] The lecture praised Germany's sociopolitical transformation and legitimized anti-Semitic sentiments on campus by emphasizing the phantom power-hungry aspirations of the world Jewry. Dr. Schmitt broadcast falsehoods about Jews to a wealthy, white, male, Christian audience who either couldn't, or didn't feel the need to, dispute his claims.

Not only were Nazi sentiments acknowledged in the academic sphere, Nazism itself was hardly a social burden. Colgate welcomed German exchange student Ottmar Eugene Lahr from the University of Berlin.[70] A member of the Nazi party, Lahr boarded at various fraternity houses, and won an intramural cross-country skiing medal.[71] Lahr's acceptance could be attributed to many things—perhaps the novelty of a foreigner in Hamilton or his cross-country skiing prowess. It did necessitate, however, a willing ignorance on behalf of Colgate students.

European tensions escalated, but in many ways the precarious political situation in Germany seemed worlds away as life plodded on in Hamilton, New York. It took a war for Americans, at Colgate and elsewhere, to realize the severity of Nazi crimes. Ten years after Professor Gates claimed "Hitler protects Jews" and Dr. Schmitt assured students and faculty that Germany just wanted peace, Arne Sorenson, the leader of the Danish resistance against Nazis took the very same stage.[72] Sorenson discussed the disconnect between Russia and the West in postwar peace talks, foreshadowing the foreign policy discussion that would grip Colgate's campus during the Cold War.

Anti-Semitism tiptoed out of the lecture hall, and refashioned itself as discrimination in the social sphere. Decades later, World War II and the Holocaust reappeared in peculiar ways at Colgate.

On the 50th anniversary of World War II, the work of Soviet photographer Yevgeny Khaldei was displayed in the Picker Art Gallery. It was the first American exhibition of the famous photographer, whose significance had been temporarily buried by the Soviet state's mistrust of his "cosmopolitanism." In other words, he was Jewish. But in 1995, Khaldei's Russian-Jewish intersection proved an advantage; Professor Alexander Nakhimovsky knew the only way to reach Khaldei was by tapping the Russian-Jewish network, where word of mouth would disperse information like dominoes.[73] The system worked; Khaldei came to Colgate October 25, 1995.[74] The visit recognized the eminence of a photographer with an essential perspective on World War II.

Nazi Germany and the Holocaust were woven into the fabric of Colgate academic life with little cause for contention—that is, until an anti-Semitic advertisement made the pages of *The Colgate Maroon-News* in an instance of dangerous carelessness. The advertisement, paid for by the Committee for Open Debate on the Holocaust (CODOH), offered $50,000 to whoever could arrange airtime on national network television for a film denying the Holocaust.[75] In between "Intramural News," "Colgate Hockey Takes OT Thriller," and an advertisement for a visiting alumna of the Harvard Business School, the CODOH ad importunes: "Is it not fair that those of us who do not believe the 'gas chamber' stories should be allowed 90 minutes—*only 90 minutes!*—to report the other side of the issue?"[76]

In the following *Maroon-News* issue, the Colgate community answered: yes, it is fair. Professors, students, community members crowded the newspaper's pages with op-eds condemning the advertisement, the publicizing of anti-Semitic revisionist history and the discretion of *The Colgate Maroon-News* editorial board. Chair of the Jewish Studies Department Dr. Steven Kepnes wrote "[the CODOH's] pamphlets re-hash old, outrageously fallacious arguments that the Holocaust is a hoax perpetrated by a Zionist conspiracy to gain world sympathy for the Jews."[77] For some students, the offensive content of the CODOH advertisement was compounded by the "carelessness" of the *Maroon-News* staff.[78] The error prompted a turbulent debate that went beyond furor about Holocaust denial, to discussion of the First Amendment and the role of the press.

Laurent Wiesel, president of the Colgate Jewish Union, hoped the ad would serve as a wake-up call to the reality of Holocaust denial; a catalyst for his fellow students to "go out and explore the subject themselves in order to defend the memory of the world's darkest hour."[79] His wish was partially granted—the Wednesday following the Holocaust denying ad, over 200 students showed up to Holocaust survivor Helen Sperling's lecture "Surviving the Holocaust: My Story."[80] The guest speaker was part of the 25 person CORE course "Modern Genocide and the Holocaust: History, Witness and Denial." Many students attended as an act of solidarity in wake of the *Maroon-News*'s oversight of anti-Semitism—then senior Noah Wintroub saw the 200 attendees as the "Colgate community saying that it won't stand for intolerance and hatred."[81]

The advertisement bore parallels to Professor Gates's protection of Nazis and calls for understanding both sides. But 50 years later, Colgate students had dismissed the "Jewish question" of Gates and Schmitt and found the answer of solidarity for the Jewish community.

New Cultures, Old Conflicts

The first time Bob Emmett participated in the Colgate Israel study group, he was a student. Bob Emmett recalls regional tensions as a participant in the 1972 Colgate Israel study group when, in the wake of the massacre of 11 Israeli athletes at the Munich Olympics, "within a half hour the sky was black with jets going to hit the PLO camps. . . . Old ladies in the Kibbutz [were] shaking their fists at the sky. So you kind of knew you weren't in Hamilton." The second time, he was an unexpected witness to the Yom Kippur War. The fighting began October 6, 1973 with a surprise, simultaneous attack from the Egyptians and Syrians.[82] Israeli forces were underprepared and overconfident as tanks barged through their defenses, shells rained down, and soldiers scrambled to defend their homeland.[83]

A 1972 graduate, Emmett himself led Colgate's 1973 group. Despite the war and myriad requests that they come home, Emmett and the 19 student participants stayed in Israel.[84] The group was sponsored by Professor of Economics Lester Blum, to whom Emmett was an administrative assistant.[85] Backed by requests from anxious parents, President Bartlett called for the group's return. The war caused a sporadic correspondence between Professor Blum, President Bartlett, and Emmett. The three eventually concluded evacuation could prove more dangerous than staying, after all "no international airlines were coming in the first few weeks. There was a bizarrely bad air war going on, over an area the size of New Jersey."[86] In any case, decisions regarding the study group's evacuation were under the jurisdiction of the U.S. embassy in Israel, which decided that the war posed little immediate danger to Americans.[87] Director of University Studies Robert Freedman conceded that "in a war zone, the university has no power," and that was that.[88] At a travel impasse, the study group resolved to stay. And for Emmett and the 19 students, that was more than okay.

Emmett and the students had been working on a kibbutz near Haifa, a safe distance from combat, an experience Emmett found "a good adventure that resonated on multi levels: intellectually, physical workout, sense of adventure, wanderlust, and all that."[89] Work days started at 5 a.m. and ended with book discussions on the study group's prerequisite reading.[90] Students attended classes at the University of Haifa until the Israeli students were sent to war.[91] After the university closed, professors came to lead evening discussions at the kibbutz.[92] Despite these noble scholarly efforts, students remember the experience as more "group" than "study." Nancy Grossman described the semester as "a whole lot less academic and a whole lot more experience."[93] Still, students returned home in one piece—and with the necessary academic credits.

The students, along with Emmett, felt a close connection to the kibbutz and Israel in general. As one of them said, "there was no fighting near Haifa, and they did not want to leave Israel."[94] But just because the fighting was not always visible did not mean the Colgate Israel study group was not both physically and emotionally impacted by the Yom Kippur War; the students did not exist in a vacuum. It was experiential learning to the extreme. "[The students] watched people kiss their families goodbye. Watched them putting on their uniforms, loading their Uzis, chucking them on jeeps."[95] Sirens blared, conscripts departed, and Colgate students remained. Area men left in hoards to serve their country, and soon the only men, other than those under 17 and too old to fight, were the Colgate students. Emmett assigned these "Colgate guys" to different homes in the kibbutz as stand-ins for the men who had left for war.

The war strengthened bonds between the Colgate students and the kibbutz community. Even when return became possible, appeals to go back to the United States fell upon deaf ears; loyalty to the kibbutz became paramount. Susan Stone found her purpose by bringing in crops during wartime; while she loved being at Colgate, the Israel study group was her best semester by far. For the students, it was more than a storybook adventure. Through their relationships with the kibbutz community, they experienced loss and fear remarkably foreign to their previous three years in Madison County. Emmett recalls that the kibbutz lost six young soldiers out of a community of 600 people.[96]

Alongside these feelings of affinity and loss was the sharp sense of the unfamiliar, not unlike Dorothy's suspicion, "Toto, I've got a feeling we're not in Kansas anymore." Emmett was assigned to patrol the garden, and was prepared to "kill a tree, basically" with an Uzi.[97] It was far from the typical off-campus experience.

While their experience wasn't firsthand, the Yom Kippur War caused shock and distress to many Jewish students back in Hamilton. The CJU spearheaded a fund drive that would go toward medical supplies in Israel. While she'd hoped to reach $1,000, Jeryl Lederman, the drive supervisor, was satisfied with the funds "knowing the apathy at Colgate."[98] The outbreak of war particularly galvanized students involved in CJU. In addition to canvassing for donations, members held prayer sessions, sent a telegram to President Nixon, and one member, Howard Liebman, echoed the experience of study group students in his longing to work on a kibbutz in order to free Israelis for the war.[99] While this campus sentiment was localized, it was fervent.

The Yom Kippur War defined the study abroad experience for Bob Emmett, Susan Stone, Nancy Grossman, and their fellow students, but it did not hamper the Colgate study abroad programs in Israel ad infinitum. Professor Peter Ochs led a group entitled "Judaism and Christianity in Jerusalem" in January 1986. Similar programs, like Professor Steven Kepnes's extended study, a semester-long course that culminates in off-campus study, "The Land of Israel" took Colgate students to experience Israel's cultural and religious history in January 2013. Most recently, in January 2016, a group of students participating in the Sophomore Residential Seminar "Jerusalem: City of the Gods" traveled to the Holy City with Professor Lesleigh Cushing.

Recent Colgate history indicates an impressive calendar of lectures, panels and discussions either on Israel, or presented by Israeli professors. This, along with the absence of a Boycott, Divestment and Sanctions (BDS) movement, has made the topic of Israel relatively uncontroversial in Colgate's academic discourse. Another neutralizing force on the contentious topic is the fact that academic events discussing Israel have consistently been presented with an interdisciplinary slant. For example, while he was a visiting lecturer, Professor Moshe Ma'oz spoke on "Negotiations for Arab-Israeli Peace: Obstacles and Strategies"—an event hosted by Jewish Studies, Political Science and International Relations.[100]

Israeli Professor of Islamic and Middle Eastern Studies Moshe Ma'oz was a visiting professor at Colgate in the 1990s and 2000s, a frequent guest lecturer and commanding presence on the university's squash courts. Ma'oz was an authority on Middle Eastern conflict, particularly regarding the Israel/Palestine question, long before the Middle Eastern and Islamic Studies Department was founded in 2004.[101]

Professor Emeritus at the Hebrew University of Jerusalem, he was also an advisor to the Israeli government and the director of the Jerusalem-based Truman Institute for the Advancement of Peace.[102] Ma'oz's connection to the Colgate community ran deep. His teaching was particularly transformative for Matt Berkowitz, who registered for every class Dr. Ma'oz offered at Colgate.[103] Moshe Ma'oz's popularity, at least among Jewish students, was reciprocated; he was wooed, despite the weather, by the "small, interested, and friendly atmosphere and interested students."[104]

While at Colgate, Ma'oz taught in the Political Science Department. But in an interview with *The Colgate Maroon,* he clarified that his classes "[did] not focus on one particular discipline but [examined] a wide array of social, ideological, emotional, economical, and political issues which comprise the Middle Eastern situation."[105] A similar interdisciplinary approach has been the touchstone of Jewish studies and Israeli academics at Colgate.

Today, the departments of Jewish Studies and Middle Eastern and Islamic Studies echo Ma'oz's interdisciplinary approach. Hebrew satisfies the language requirement of the Middle Eastern and Islamic studies major, and the departments are currently cooperating to hire a medieval historian—a look back on a time when the two cultures lived nearby and in incomplete but still enviable harmony.

Bursting the Colgate Bubble: Jewish Emissaries

Despite growing up in a predominately Jewish suburb (Pikesville, Maryland), when she came to Colgate, Katie David was deeply interested in the historical narrative of the Jews—particularly in Eastern Europe. After all, as she put it, "sometimes it's good to learn about your 'own history' in a place that's not filled with people like you."[106] Colgate University, in all its J. Crew catalogue glory, was the place where David began to explore the Jewish history of Russia and Ukraine.

Seeking to debunk the "Fiddler on the Roof" imagery that pigeonholed Jewish life into the quaint and the kooky, David listened to the firsthand trials and triumphs of the modern Eastern European Jew. The Jewish narrative became more than the pages of her "Jewish Fiction After the Holocaust" course materials. It wasn't stories; it was people. As a junior, David studied abroad in St. Petersburg, researching Jews who chose not to emigrate and the forces that fueled their decision to stay.[107] Her study continued into the summer and provided a welcome respite from the Colgate routine. It taught the independence—and critical skills like visa renewal—that prepared David for study the following year in Odessa, Ukraine on a Fulbright Scholarship.[108]

In Odessa, Katie David found a peculiar Jewish narrative: after the fall of the Soviet Union, Odessa was a place where it was advantageous and cool to be Jewish.[109] It was not a story David could have learned on campus. Like the emissaries who came before her, David used her "outsider" perspective—as an American in Ukraine, a Jew at Colgate—to understand the world anew. Amid the challenges, namely Ukraine's inefficiency and "customer is always wrong" culture, David thrived among individuals different from herself.

David was one of a coterie of students who, under the mentorship of Professor Alice Nakhimovsky, spent time abroad researching the Jewish experience. Marc Frankel's senior thesis in Russian Studies was his crowning academic achievement. An analysis at the nexus of Jewish and Russian studies, it was the product of two (January) weeks in the "speck of land in Siberia where people speak Yiddish," Birobidzhan.[110] Despite growing up in a predominantly Jewish town, Frankel experienced Judaism remarkably differently in Birobidzhan.[111] His experiences inspired his 2006 Watson Fellowship, which he used to continue studying small Jewish communities around the world.

For Frankel, Colgate provided harmony between the social and the academic. This harmony marked a significant departure from the perceptions of Jews past, who felt weighted by a social stigma and saw few opportunities to explore their identity in the classroom. Through his senior thesis and Blue Diamond Society membership, Frankel became involved in Jewish life on campus. Thus for both David and Frankel, Jewish life took on new forms. It did not require rote visits to the

"We're learning Russian in case the White House needs bagels and lox." Sign at Shelsky's of Brooklyn on Court Street, 2017. Courtesy of John A. Stone.

Saperstein Center, or surrounding oneself with Jewish peers. Institutional changes—to the curriculum, faculty, learning space—as well as social ones, created multiple ways to be Jewish, both at Colgate, and beyond.

Not all emissaries, however, took their Colgate experience worldwide. Some can be found not too far from Hamilton, in New York City. Manhattanite Peter Shelsky '01 is a Jew because of the food.[112] For the food, and also "because they tried to kill us, and we survived."[113] A testament to the open-endedness of the liberal arts, Shelsky owns an appetizing and delicatessen store that he started with a friend from across the hall freshman year. Shelsky's of Brooklyn is famed for bagels, lox, rugelach, and political activism—the deli's sidewalk has boasted signs such as "Lox Trumps Hate" or, after the 2016 election—in somebody's perfect Russian—"We are studying Russian in the event that the White House needs bagels and lox." Shelsky sees the signs as a small but meaningful way to spread awareness in the political climate of 2017.

While it wasn't necessarily a conscious decision, Peter Shelsky welcomed Colgate as a departure from the Jewish routine of the Upper East Side. College meant the freedom to not attend synagogue and meet a diverse crowd of people—which is exactly what Shelsky did. His restaurant career began at Sushi Blues, a since gone but not forgotten sushi restaurant on Broad Street. The owners, two "loud and obnoxious—in a good way—New York City Jews" were like second parents for him.

Unlike Hindus, Parry, and the other Jewish emissaries that preceded them, David, Frankel, and Shelsky were motivated in some way—whether academically or gustatorily—by the Jewish experience. Theirs was an experience not of mandatory otherness (though through their travels, David and Frankel elected to take up outsider status), but rather one of a self-selected community: the "cool Jews" of Odessa, Yiddish-speakers of Birobidzhan, bagel-lovers of Brooklyn. These communities didn't hatch overnight, as mysterious repayment for the hardship faced by the Jews that came before them. Rather, they were built, found, analyzed into the dynamic circles that they remain today.

Endnotes

1. Karl Marx and Friedrich Engels, *The Communist Manifesto,* ed. Jeffrey C. Isaac (New Haven: Yale University Press, 2012), 82.

2. Mikhail Heller and Aleksandr M. Nekrich, *Utopia in Power: The History of the Soviet Union from 1917 to the Present*, trans. Phyllis B. Carlos (New York: Simon and Schuster, 1986).

3. Heller and Nekrich, *Utopia in Power,* 233.

4. Heller and Nekrich, *Utopia in Power,* 235.

5. Heller and Nekrich, *Utopia in Power,* 235.

6. Heller and Nekrich, *Utopia in Power,* 238.

7. Robert Conquest, *The Great Terror: A Reassessment* (New York and Oxford: Oxford University Press, 1990), 46.

8. Heller and Nekrich, *Utopia in Power,* 242.

9. Maurice Gerschon Hindus, *A Traveler in Two Worlds* (Garden City, NY: Doubleday, 1971), 311.

10. Maurice Hindus, *Red Bread: Collectivization in a Russian Village* (Bloomington and Indianapolis: Indiana University Press, 1988), 38.

11. Hindus, *Red Bread,* 39.

12. Hindus, *Red Bread,* 39.

13. Hindus, *Red Bread,* 17.

14. Hindus, *Red Bread,* 17.

15. Hindus, *Red Bread,* 18.

16. Hindus, *Red Bread,* 19.

17. Hindus, *Red Bread,* 43

18. Hindus, *Red Bread,* 44.

19. Hindus, *Red Bread,* 44.

20. Hindus, *Red Bread,* 43.

21. S.J. Taylor, *Stalin's Apologist* (New York and Oxford: Oxford University Press, 1990), 9.

22. S.J. Taylor, *Stalin's Apologist*, 9.

23. S.J. Taylor, *Stalin's Apologist,* book sleeve.

24. S.J. Taylor, 165.

25. S.J. Taylor, 165.

26. Hindus, *Red Bread,* 136.

27. Hindus, *Red Bread*, 137.

28. Albert Parry, "Ask That Your Way Be Long" (unpublished manuscript, n.d.), PDF, 7.

29. Parry, "Ask That Your Way Be Long," 6.

30. Tom Parry and Jim Parry, interview by Alice Nakhimovsky, January 2017.

31. Parry, "Ask That Your Way Be Long," 526.

32. Parry, "Ask That Your Way Be Long," 526.

33. Tom Parry and Jim Parry, interview.

34. Parry, "Ask That Your Way Be Long," 563.

35. Tom Parry and Jim Parry, interview.

36. Tom Parry and Jim Parry, interview.

37. "Parry Predicted Firing of Artificial Satellite 'Sputnik'," *The Colgate Maroon News,* October 16, 1957.

38. "Parry Predicted Firing of Artificial Satellite 'Sputnik'."

39. "Hillel to Hear Parry on Red Semitic Purges," *The Maroon*, Februrary 18, 1953.

40. Jonathan Brent, "Doctors' Plot," *YIVO Encyclopedia of Jews in Eastern Europe*, 2010, http://yivoencyclopedia.org/article.aspx/Doctors_Plot (accessed May 10, 2017).

41. "Hillel to Hear Parry on Red Semitic Purges."

42. Alice Nakhimovsky, "Assessing Life in the Face of Death: Moral Drama at the Trial of Jewish Fascist Committee, 1952," *East European Jewish Affairs*, forthcoming.

43. Joshua Rubenstein, "Jewish Anti-Fascist Committee," *YIVO Encyclopedia of Jews in Eastern Europe*, 2008, http://yivoencyclopedia.org/article.aspx/Jewish_Anti-Fascist_Committee (accessed May 10, 2017).

44. Alice Nakhimovsky, "Assessing Life in the Face of Death"

45. Jerusalem, Post Reporter. "Markish Family Freed by Soviets, Arrive at Lod." *The Jerusalem Post (1950–1988)*, November 9, 1972, https://search.proquest.com/docview/925842997?accountid=10207 (accessed March 25, 2017).

46. Zsuzsa Hetényi and Alice Nakhimovsky, "Markish, Shimon," *YIVO Encyclopedia of Jews in Eastern Europe*, 2011, http://www.yivoencyclopedia.org/article.aspx/Markish_Shimon (accessed May 9, 2017).

47. Karen Kazlau, "Jewish Russians Topic of Lecture," *The Colgate News*, November 4, 1983.

48. "Outstanding Current Events," *The Colgate Maroon*, March 3, 1933.

49. "Outstanding Current Events."

50. Hindus, *Traveler in Two Worlds*, 149.

51. Hindus, *Traveler in Two Worlds*, 149.

52. "Giant Nazi State Under Self Dream of Adolph Hitler," *The Colgate Maroon*, February 27, 1934.

53. "Giant Nazi State Under Self Dream of Adolph Hitler."

54. "Giant Nazi State Under Self Dream of Adolph Hitler."

55. "Giant Nazi State Under Self Dream of Adolph Hitler."

56. "Dr. Gates Flails False Criticisms of Hitler Regime," *The Colgate Maroon*, October 29, 1935.

57. "Dr. Gates Flails False Criticisms of Hitler Regime."

58. Dexter H. Teed, letter to the editor, *The Colgate Maroon*, March 6 1936.

59. Teed, letter to the editor.

60. Teed, letter to the editor.

61. John Reiners, "Germany's Jews as Welcome as Roaches, Student Finds," *The Colgate Maroon*, October 29, 1937.

62. Reiners, "Germany's Jews as Welcome as Roaches, Student Finds."

63. Reiners, "Germany's Jews as Welcome as Roaches, Student Finds."

64. "Hitler's Limitation of College Entrants," *The Colgate Maroon,* January 9, 1934.

65. "Hitler's Limitation of College Entrants."

66. "Hitler's Limitation of College Entrants."

67. "Dr. Schmitt Speaks on Jewish Question," *The Colgate Maroon,* November 7, 1933.

68. "Dr. Schmitt Speaks on Jewish Question."

69. "Dr. Schmitt Speaks on Jewish Question."

70. "Exchange Students are Here from Germany, Puerto Rico," *The Colgate Maroon,* September 20, 1935.

71. "Dekes are Winners of Intramural Ski Trophy for 1935–36," *The Colgate Maroon,* March 6, 1936.

72. "Arne Sorenson, European Educator, will Speak in Chapel Next Monday," *The Colgate Maroon,* October 6, 1948.

73. Alice Nakhimovsky, "Moscow, Berlin, Hamilton: Yevgeny Khaldei at Colgate," *Converging Perspectives* (Hamilton, NY: Picker Art Gallery), 34–37.

74. Alice Nakhimovsky, "Moscow, Berlin, Hamilton."

75. Committee for Open Debate on the Holocaust (CODOH), "$50,000 to the One Individual…," *The Colgate Maroon-News,* October 31, 2017.

76. Committee for Open Debate on the Holocaust (CODOH), "$50,000 to the One Individual…"

77. Steven Kepnes, "Holocaust is Historical Fact, not a Matter of Scholarly Debate," *The Colgate Maroon-News,* November 7, 1997.

78. Lauren Braun and Rebecca Epstein, "*Maroon-News* Editors Should have Used Better Discretion," *The Colgate Maroon-News,* November 7, 1997.

79. Laurent Weisel, "There is no Debate About Whether the Holocaust is Real," *The Colgate Maroon-News,* November 7, 1997.

80. Anne Balfour, "Holocaust Survivor Shares Memories," *The Colgate Maroon-News,* November 7, 1997.

81. Balfour, "Holocaust Survivor Shares Memories."

82. Conor Cruise O'Brien, *The Siege: The Saga of Israel and Zionism* (New York: Simon and Schuster, 1986), 521.

83. O'Brien, *The Siege*, 521.

84. Bob Emmett, "Colgate Asks 19 Students to Come Back From Israel," *New York Times,* October 10, 1973.

85. Faythe Kunker, "Future of Israel Study Group Uncertain, Air Battles Prevent Evacuation," *The Colgate Maroon,* October 16, 1973.

86. Bob Emmett, interview by Emily Kahn, January 9, 2017.

87. Kunker, "Future of Israel Study Group Uncertain, Air Battles Prevent Evacuation."

88. Kunker, "Future of Israel Study Group Uncertain, Air Battles Prevent Evacuation."

89. Emmett, interview by Emily Kahn.

90. Susan Stone, interview by Emily Kahn, January 26, 2017.

91. Stone, interview by Emily Kahn.

92. Stone, interview by Emily Kahn.

93. Nancy Grossman, interview by Emily Kahn, January 3 2017.

94. Emmett, "Colgate Asks 19 Students to Come Back From Israel."

95. Emmett, interview by Emily Kahn.

96. Emmett, interview by Emily Kahn.

97. Emmett, interview by Emily Kahn.

98. D.H. Stonehill, "Israeli War Spurs Response," *The Colgate Maroon,* October 16, 1973.

99. Stonehill, "Israeli War Spurs Response."

100. "Jewish Studies at Colgate in cooperation with Political Science and International Relations Present Moshe Ma'oz," *The Colgate Maroon,* April 10, 1990.

101. Noor Khan, email message to Amy Balmuth, May 10, 2017.

102. Michael Wyner, "Ma'oz Brings Middle Eastern Experience to Colgate," *The Colgate Maroon,* November 15, 1996.

103. Matt Berkowitz, interview by Anat Guez, January 9, 2017.

104. Michael Wyner, "Ma'oz Brings Middle Eastern Experience to Colgate," *The Colgate Maroon,* November 15, 1996.

105. Wyner, "Ma'oz Brings Middle Eastern Experience to Colgate."

106. Kathryn David, interview by Amy Balmuth, March 20, 2017.

107. David, interview by Amy Balmuth.

108. David, interview by Amy Balmuth.

109. Kathryn David, "Cool Jews: Youth Culture in Odessa's Jewish Community," *Studies in Slavic Cultures,* forthcoming.

110. Marc Frankel, interview by Cameron Pauly, March 8, 2017.

111. Frankel, interview by Cameron Pauly.

112. Peter Shelsky, interview by Marit Vangrow, March 8, 2017.

113. Shelsky, interview by Marit Vangrow.

Afterword

Dominic Wilkins: As we sit here reflecting on this process, one of perhaps the most troubling aspects of this entire story are the parallels that can be drawn between the discrimination and the ignorance directed toward Jews at Colgate and what is happening in the United States today. Many of the themes and ideas we have touched on in this book are relevant here, most prominently the belief that there is a "right way" to be an American, and that this is to some extent dependent upon racial or religious characteristics.

The most striking parallel is the continued relevance of Jerry Balmuth's term "non-Semitism," the idea that dominant culture ignores the existence of other cultural forms. As opposed to active, overt, and intentional discrimination, this ignorance and dismissal is incredibly prevalent in the world today, as well as to some extent at Colgate. We often pay no attention to why we do certain things, or why these things are structured the way that they are. What those of us coming from a position of privilege consider to be "normal" or "standard" is heavily informed by its (often white, Western, Christian) history. Yet when we fail to recognize this, when we assume that what we do is how things "obviously should be done," we are forgetting that our perspectives from the privileged point of view are shaped by our subjective past. The ignorance of the ways in which Christianity has shaped life in the United States, whether the way in which we construct buildings, conduct ceremonies, or even how our weeks are structured to privilege Christian religious celebration over that of other religions, continues to create a situation unwelcoming for non-Christians in the United States

The authors at Albert Parry's grave, 2017. From left: Alice Nakhimovsky, Emily Kahn, Kim Ravold, Dominic Wilkins, Marit Vangrow, Cameron Pauly, and Amy Balmuth. The inscription reads "я пережил сволочей: I outlived the bastards." Photograph courtesy of Kim Ravold.

today—just as it did for Jewish members of the Colgate community. Ignorance of the default Western perspective that has become the norm within our discourse has meant that we as collective society have foolishly forgotten the contributions and alternative perspectives made to understanding our collective humanity that have come from outside the West just as Jewish faculty saw their ability to teach Jewish understandings of the Hebrew Bible hampered by Christian faculty who believed that those books could only be taught through their relationship with the New Testament. Far too many times the same language of erasure and suppression is used today for the same purpose as it was against Jewish students and Jewish faculty throughout Colgate's history.

Amy Balmuth: It was a semester of discovery. As a class, we heard anecdotes and scoured archival material that served as reminders for Colgate's sordid past. Discrimination and prejudice are woven into the fabric of higher education. Ignoring such a fact is not only dangerous, but inconsiderate to today's minority students as they navigate an institution historically determined to keep them out. Our text is not exhaustive, but I hope it highlights how history is living. Our past directly impacts our present. Jews at Colgate might not be asked to reveal their horns, and they are no longer barred from social life because of their religion, but we as an institution are far from the inclusivity that will make us better.

Emily Kahn: Over the past year, we collected oral histories from eighty-six individuals and received written testimonies from an additional seven. Some graduated sixty years ago and some graduated just last year. All had vastly different Jewish experiences at Colgate. This book has tried to be multi-vocal. It has tried to include as many perspectives as possible. Yet the nature of history is that some voices get projected and others silenced. Even with unlimited time, we would never be able to hear them all. Many of the Jews who may have wanted to share their stories have passed on. Unlike Albert Parry, most did not leave behind unpublished autobiographies or tombstone remarks. Other Jews were unreachable given limitations of technology, geography, or time. However, many Jews just did not want to be interviewed and, as was expected, not everyone responded to our inquiries. Maybe they did not care, maybe they did not have time. Or maybe, especially for older alumni, speaking about their Jewish experiences would have forced them to relive traumatic memories. We also recognize that our archive of oral histories, written testimonies, and overall focus of the book is male-dominated. That, unfortunately, is the nature of writing about an institution that has admitted women for less than fifty of its two-hundred year existence. By being cognizant of our methodological limitations, we can recognize that our history is incomplete. All history is. The truth is these ninety-two voices, accompanied by archival materials and newspaper articles, will represent the thousands of Jews who struggled and thrived at Colgate. In front of you lies *a* history rather than *the* history of Jews at Colgate. Hopefully in the future, more oral histories will be collected and preserved for the subsequent generations of Colgate Jews. Then additional histories of Jews at Colgate can be told.

Marit Vangrow: From reading relevant novels, archival sources, a general history of Colgate, and various newspaper clipping and journal articles, as well as listening to and conducting alumni interviews, our class gained a comprehensive, yet in some ways incomplete, understanding of the Jewish experience at Colgate. Emily's point that this is *a* history of Jews at Colgate rather than *the* history of Jews at Colgate is a crucial distinction to make. Our book is an attempt to understand how Jewish life has developed and changed over the course of Colgate's history. We must acknowledge that memory is not infallible, nor is it static; it morphs and changes over the years. This is not to say that the information provided by countless alumni is not valuable; it truly enriched our understanding of Jewish life at Colgate. However, we must be aware of the failures of memory and refer to archival sources such as the *Colgate Maroon* and *Maroon-News*, as well as records from the university to confirm the narrative set forth by those we interviewed.

As Dominic mentions, white, Christian men constructed the various traditions and practices that we as Americans consider to be normal or right. However, this book demonstrates how we must be aware of the systemic factors and conditions, such as racism, sexism, and xenophobia, that have shaped our history as a community, not only at Colgate but also on a larger scale. My section on Case is eerily relevant today as immigration again threatens the conception of America as a white, Protestant nation. Although Colgate no longer places quotas against specific groups of people, we must be aware of the greater patterns of discrimination in our country. The rise of Trump and his administration threatens the existence of specific groups of people who do not fit into the mold of white, heterosexual Christians. As members of Colgate's community, we must understand how bigotry and prejudice shaped our past so that we can fight such injustice today.

Kim Ravold: One important lesson to take away from this book is that change doesn't happen unless we make it happen, whether that means standing up for oneself, or using one's position of power to stand against injustices that plague institutions across time and space. Colgate is a more welcoming space today than it was 60 years ago, and while part of this change is due to a shift toward acceptance in American culture, Colgate would not be what it is today if not for the actions of individuals like Jerry Balmuth or Neil Grabois. Change begins at the individual level. Change happens when we recognize institutional barriers instead of ignoring them, when we listen to the voices of the oppressed instead of talking over them. We can't wait for other people to do the work for us. We can't leave the work undone. It's a constant, conscious process, one that must continue today for a better Colgate, and a better world.

Cameron Pauly: Taking part in the writing of this book has been one of the most challenging, and at the same time immensely rewarding, experiences of my life, and I am sure many of my co-authors would agree with me. Over the course of five months, the six of us, guided by the wonderful Alice Nakhimovsky, took a critical look at our own university. It may be uncomfortable to challenge idyllic visions of Colgate, but doing so is a vital part of a Colgate education which many others have also embraced, and an action that is necessary for the improvement of the university, American higher education, and ourselves. As a part of this process, I attempted to highlight the history of resistance to discrimination at Colgate through an anthropological lens. When writing a history such as this book, it is important to highlight the brave actions of the oppressed against their oppressors in order to inspire the same spirit in others. Through the stories presented here, I hope that our book can make an impact by raising awareness of an overlooked part of Colgate's history and by presenting models of resistance that are still very relevant today.

Index